Digital Culture Industry

Digital Culture Industry

A History of Digital Distribution

James Allen-Robertson

James Allen-Robertson © 2013

First published 2013 by
PALGRAVE MACMILLAN

Palgrave Macmillan in the UK is an imprint of Macmillan Publishers Limited, registered in England, company number 785998, of Houndmills, Basingstoke, Hampshire RG21 6XS.

Palgrave Macmillan in the US is a division of St Martin's Press LLC, 175 Fifth Avenue, New York, NY 10010.

Palgrave Macmillan is the global academic imprint of the above companies and has companies and representatives throughout the world.

Palgrave® and Macmillan® are registered trademarks in the United States, the United Kingdom, Europe and other countries.

ISBN 978–1–137–03346–8

This book is printed on paper suitable for recycling and made from fully managed and sustained forest sources. Logging, pulping and manufacturing processes are expected to conform to the environmental regulations of the country of origin.

A catalogue record for this book is available from the British Library.

A catalog record for this book is available from the Library of Congress.

10   9   8   7   6   5   4   3   2   1
22   21   20   19   18   17   16   15   14   13

Transferred to Digital Printing in 2013

Contents

Figures

Acknowledgements

As the hacker ethic would have us believe, no work can be attributed to a single individual. It is certainly true in this case; though I am the only named author, this book was a community effort. I would like to thank Kate, my patient and supportive wife, whose handiwork can be seen in the figures throughout. I would like to thank Neil Renton for putting me on this path, as well as Professor Roger Burrows, Dr David Beer, Brian Loader and Dr Martin Dodge for their guidance and comments throughout. I thank Professor Samuelson at Berkley Law for answering my questions on the esoteric US copyright law. Finally, I thank the infinite population of bloggers, tweeters, commenters and archivers that produced and curated the huge archive of documents that made this work possible.

This work was supported by the Economic and Social Research Council (grant number ES/F03587X/1).

Glossary of Terms

AHRA	Audio Home Recording Act of 1992
AntiPiratbyrån	Swedish anti-piracy organisation
ARG	Alternate Reality Game
ASCAP	American Society of Composers, Authors and Publishers
BBS	Bulletin Board System
BDE	Brilliant Digital Entertainment
BEN	BitTorrent Entertainment Network
BMG	Bertelsmann Music Group
Bootstrap	The self-sufficient process of connecting a new node to an existing network
MPEG	Motion Picture Expert Group – a specialist group within the International Standards Organisation
RIAA	Recording Industry Association of America
MPAA	Motion Picture Association of America
DAB	Digital Audio Broadcasting – a digital radio broadcasting standard, primarily used in Europe
DAT	Digital Audio Tape – a recordable medium similar to tape that utilised binary signal
DHT	Distributed Hash Table – a decentralised indexing service, useful for co-ordinating peer-to-peer networks (see also PEX)
DMCA	Digital Millennium Copyright Act of 1998
DRM	Digital Rights Management
EMI	Electric and Musical Industries Ltd
EULA	End User Licence Agreement – a form of private contract typically used in software between the rights holder and end user
F/OSS	Free (and/or) Open Source Software
IP	Intellectual Property
ISO	International Standards Organisation
JXTA	An open-source peer-to-peer protocol produced by Gene Kan
P2P	Peer-to-Peer

PEX	Peer-Exchange – a decentralised system of indexing service useful for co-ordinating P2P networks (see also DHT)
Piratbyrån	The Pirate Bureau – a Swedish campaign group that sought IP reform
PS3	Sony PlayStation 3 console
RAM	Random Access Memory – a form of computer memory analogous to short-term memory in humans
SCMS	Serial Copy Management System – a copy-protection scheme intended to ensure that DAT tapes could be impeded from being replicated
SDMI	Secure Digital Music Initiative – a group of more than 200 companies that sought to develop an industry standard of digital rights management
UCC2B	Article 2B of the US Uniform Commercial Code – a provision of the code that sought to enforce the validity of private EULA contracts
UCITA	Uniform Computer Information Transactions Act – a continuation of the UCC2B campaign after the American Law Society withdrew its support
VU	Vivendi Universal
Warez	Copyrighted works traded without legal authorisation
XCP	Extended Copyright Protection – a scheme of DRM launched by Sony integrated into a selection of its CD catalogue
YIPL	Youth International Party Line – a zine circulated by the anarchic Youth International Party, which published proprietary Telco network data

1
Introduction

The trial of the pirate kings

On 16 February 2009, four men stood accused of the promotion and facilitation of copyright infringement. The four defendants, Hans Fredrik Neij, Gottfrid Svartholm Warg, Peter Sunde and Carl Lundström were identified by the prosecution as the key agents that ran the Pirate Bay, an internationally infamous hub of media piracy. The plaintiffs, Warner Bros, MGM, EMI, Colombia Pictures, 20th Century Fox, Sony BMG and Universal, were demanding two years in jail for each defendant, as well as up to $180,000 in fines.

The trial lasted for little over three weeks; however, for that short period the Stockholm criminal court became a representational microcosm of the larger changes occurring in industrialised, informational societies. As events unfolded in the courtroom, a group of journalists live-blogged and Twittered from an adjacent room, whilst others inside and outside the court translated the courtroom's live audio feed from Swedish into a multitude of other languages. Automated Twitterbots collected all tweets related to the trial – marked by the posters with the tag '#spectrial' – and distributed them as a central feed for anyone who wished to follow the debate in real time.

The debates within the courtroom revealed a disjuncture of perspectives between the prosecution and the defence. The prosecution's argument was that the defendants actively engaged in the provision and distribution of copyrighted material through the Pirate Bay. Their aim was to bring down the four men who they perceived to

1

be the ringleaders of global digital piracy. This would set a precedent they could use to quell the rampant unauthorised distribution of their content that had been taking place for almost a decade. The defence's argument was twofold: they as individuals had no part in the illicit distribution of copyrighted material, and file-sharing was much, much larger than they were. Their testimonies throughout the trial repeatedly iterated that no copyrighted material ever touched their servers. They insisted that the actual content of the site was user produced and that it was the users that decided what to make available on the Pirate Bay. Even ownership and responsibility for the site was uncertain. When the prosecution demanded the identity of the individual ultimately responsible for the site, they became visibly frustrated with the anarchic structure that consisted of an extended decentralised network of individuals with server privileges (Swartz, 2009b). As far as the defence was concerned, no-one owned the Pirate Bay; it belonged to everyone.

The confusion didn't end there because the decentralised structure of the site's communication system sabotaged the prosecution's technical evidence. When Magnus Mårtensson, lawyer for the prosecution, presented his evidence, he wasn't prepared for the reaction he received. Mårtensson had acted as a user at the site, downloading music albums with the same software as any other user would whilst documenting the process via screen shots. Though the process seemed solid it was quickly challenged by defendant Gottfrid Svartholm. Svartholm knew the tech, and he knew there was no proof that the Pirate Bay's hardware had been used during the transfer of copyrighted material. Throughout Mårtensson's documentation process the software he was using had autonomously been making its own decisions, and Mårtensson had no evidence of what those decisions were. The software had been running systems called 'DHT' and 'peer-exchange', systems that meant groups of computers could cluster together to distribute information, without anything (such as the Pirate Bay) co-ordinating them. As Mårtensson had no other documentation detailing the actions of these algorithmic agents, he was forced to admit that he had no evidence of the Pirate Bay's involvement with the process of data distribution. Though the Pirate Bay had opened the door to a network of unauthorised digital distribution, any number of other systems run by other people in other countries may have been responsible for the network's co-ordination; or, thanks to the autonomy of the software, none at all.

The site under scrutiny was not the only system of its kind, nor was it the largest. It was one of the more famous ones, meaning it had garnered more attention from the media industry than others did, but there were hundreds more. Some of them had sites to visit where users could find their way to media content. Others were fairly anonymous systems, co-ordinating in the background for users who'd never even heard their name. The reprimand of the four individuals standing in court was not a panacea to the problem of media piracy. However, the copyright industries were becoming desperate. It had been eight years since they had won the fight against Napster and since then piracy just seemed to be getting more prevalent, more disparate and more difficult to pin down. The studios fighting the Pirate Bay were focusing their efforts on four individuals with the aim of quelling a social change far beyond the remit of four individuals. They looked for a hierarchy but were presented with networks – organisational and technological. Throughout the trial the defendants never placed themselves as leaders of a media revolution, but instead foregrounded an assemblage of communication technologies, changing social norms and the political ideology of the pirate.

This book

This book is about that assemblage of technological innovation, changing social norms and ideological drive. It is about the synergising of the copyright industries with information technology and its disruption of, and its absorption into, contemporary capitalism. More specifically it is about the interrelations between key actors, events, organisations and computer code, and how they drove and directed the development of our contemporary digital mediascape. To get to the point, it is about how illegal digital piracy made legitimate digital media distribution what it is today. It is about the history of digital media distribution.

The 'copyright industries' (Potts et al., 2008) are often identified as the music industry, the film industry, the television networks and the publishing industry, and we can also add advertising and the relatively young software industry to what is becoming a key economic group in the Western economy. The role that these industries have in

Western capitalism has been discussed greatly by a variety of theorists such as Miège (1989), Bagdikian (1983, 2004), Hesmondhalgh (2007) and McChesney (1993, 1999, 2004). Often these discussions take a political economy approach, where there is a clear concern that the concentration of power in these various media industries is damaging to our society. As Hesmondhalgh (2007) points out, concentration, mergers and takeovers are inherent in capitalism and are in no way unique to the culture industries. However, for many that take a liberal, critical stance on the monopolisation of cultural production, it is that these industries are monopolising our culture which is the key issue; a perspective more presently found in the work of law scholars Lawrence Lessig (2005, 2008) and James Boyle (2009), fiction author, columnist and activist Cory Doctorow (2008), and to a lesser extent ex-director of MIT's Comparative Media Studies Programme, Henry Jenkins (2008). This concern with cultural monopolisation expressed in these texts alongside a broad vox populi critique is derivative of the core arguments from the work of Theodor Adorno and Max Horkheimer in their seminal essay, 'The Culture Industry' (Adorno and Horkheimer, 1997). This essay, though both rejected and developed by theorists such as Miège (1989), still retains its status as the first significant critique of mass culture.

More recent work has attempted to revitalise the critical theorists' conceptualisation of the culture industries. Lash and Lury's 'Global Culture Industry' (2007) looked to update Adorno and Horkheimer through a focus on the brand. In their view the brand had become the dominant output of the culture industries in contemporary developed societies. In the introduction to their work they lay out their perspective on how the culture industries have changed with the influx of the brand and the devaluing of the commodity. They make an argument for the end of the top-down mechanised power of centralised cultural control. Instead they argue that cultural domination has taken the form of dynamic symbolic brands. Through their re-appropriation by consumers into their everyday lives, brands afford power to the culture industries through this covert infiltration into their everyday thoughts and interactions with others. However, though 'Global Culture Industry' positions itself as a development of the culture industry idea, updated for our symbol-saturated times, its research focus is chronologically situated before the mass digital distribution of culture where 'Digital Culture Industry' begins. This work conceptually and substantively addresses a different development of the copyright industries, one that I would argue to be closer to the original commodity-focused theories of the critical theorists than the diversion into branding taken by the more recent iteration. This work is not a continuation of the work by Lash and Lury, but an entirely separate diversion. Though I should be standing on the shoulders of giants, I don't necessarily have to keep to a chronological order. This work draws from Adorno and Horkheimer's culture industry without the contemporary mediation offered by Lash and Lury.

However, that is not to say that this work is a close follower of Adorno and Horkheimer either. As my research began it became apparent that the original culture industry concept is weakened by its abstracted and simple portrayal of the sphere of cultural production. It is a simplification that has held much weight in political economy conceptualisations of the copyright industries. Much of contemporary popular critique of mass culture draws from the tenets of their essay: that mass culture is debased; profit-centric; and used to subjugate the population. Yet Adorno and Horkheimer's argument seeks to simplify the narrative of cultural industrialisation, making often convoluted, complex stories of multiple interacting actors and influences deceivingly simplistic. This book appropriates the term 'culture industry' for good reason. It too is concerned with how the mechanisms of culture's circulation and engagement actively impact upon society. It shares the belief that there is power in the control of media's circulation. However, where it diverges greatly is the core of this book. Far from being a top-down domination of culture by corporate forces, the digital culture industry is a story of conflict, creative disruption and the intertwining of 'corporate' and countercultural social spheres. Perhaps more importantly, unlike the abstract macro narrative painted by the critical theorists, the narrative of the digital culture industry is far from simple.

A far from simple narrative

A story that has been told many times over is the tale of how a disruptive young upstart brought media in digital form to the masses, and through illicit file-sharing technology, forced the copyright industries to change their worn-out ways. The Napster story has become the creation myth for our current world of digital media, but many times the detail is overlooked and the story is often portrayed as a battle of opposing sides – the recording industry versus the people, the innately good and the innately evil, the roles of course being swapped depending on personal perspective. However, there is much more to the digital culture story than Napster, which this book hopes to address.

The history begins in Chapter 3, which looks at the early years of digital media distribution. The chapter covers the development of the MP3 format, designed with portability and ease of access in mind, but with no intention for it to reach the mass market. The history then moves on to the creation of the famous MP3-enthusiast site, MP3.com. A key influence in the early days of digital distribution, MP3.com pre-empted many of today's innovations and services in digital media. The chapter covers its rise, court cases, and eventual dismantling and appropriation into the first industry-approved digital download services. Of course there is the Napster story, not a story of sudden genius and unerring rebellion, but one of collaborative programming communities, venture capital and a network design cultivated not for information freedom but for information dominance. Napster's development, transformation into a business and eventual court cases are covered in parallel with the MP3.com story.

Napster allowed the movement of music; however, today people are using these networks to distribute films, television programmes, software, images, text and entire archives of data. The technical leap from Napster to now cannot be overlooked, not simply because it is a sloppy narrative, but because it was what happened after Napster that had the real impact. The politically driven network GNUtella introduced a liberal information ethic to the fray of peer-to-peer (P2P) piracy and provided the technical foundations for the tsunami of P2P networks that followed in Napster's wake. Chapter 4 provides a detailed account of the development and implementation of the first truly decentralised and community-driven P2P network – GNUtella. The history follows the technology through its development by anarchic programmer Justin Frankel, and beyond to its wider adoption by communities of free-software programmers. The first half of the chapter, 'Nullsoft', lays out Frankel's career as an independent programmer, his ideological belief of 'sustainable software' and the eventual buyout of his company by AOL. The second half,

'GNUtella' describes Frankel's time under AOL and his surreptitious development of the GNUtella software. The section goes on to follow the ad hoc communities that took over its development and its wide dissemination into various legitimate ventures. The chapter ends with 'Politically decentralised', a conceptual examination of how the ways in which GNUtella differed from Napster provided the tools for a robust decentralised file-sharing community.

Chapter 5 explores the story of the FastTrack protocol, the technology behind the most prominent and influential P2P file-sharing software of the mid-2000s. The chapter begins by following entrepreneurs Niklas Zennström and Janus Friis whose controversial software company developed and licensed P2P software for other companies to run their own file-sharing platforms. The chapter begins with 'Zennström & Friis', a look at the development of the software and company, as well as the conflicts and issues they experienced in their attempts to operate a legitimate company with an illicit product. 'Sharman takes over' follows the sale of the company and the file-sharing software 'Kazaa' to Sharman Networks and the ways in which Zennström & Friis managed the licensing of their FastTrack protocol. 'Grokster v. MGM' follows the landmark case in the US that rewrote intellectual property (IP) law to deal with the encroaching threat of digital piracy made possible by the prevalence of FastTrack. 'Incorporating the competition' looks at how the FastTrack code and the illicit actors in the narrative became integrated into various legitimate business ventures. Finally, the chapter ends with 'The business of piracy', a look at how Frankel's network design was subverted into a highly controlled, exploitable system of illicit piracy, and the unintended consequences that came from the fusion of Frankel's design with business logic.

Chapter 6 examines BitTorrent, the most recent development in P2P file-sharing. The narrative begins with Bram Cohen, and his very personal drive to produce the most efficient data transfer system in the world. The chapter begins with 'Perfect', a look at Cohen's development of the BitTorrent software and how his design reversed the rules of network communication. The chapter continues with 'The legitimate BitTorrent', a look at Cohen's uneasy foray into turning BitTorrent into a business venture, the softening reactions of the incumbent movie industry to P2P, and his venture's eventual failure due to industry licensing demands. The final part of the chapter, and of the illicit histories, is the story of the Pirate Bay, an infamous piracy site that utilised BitTorrent to allow its users to share copyrighted material across the internet. The section charts the website's history, from its roots in the Swedish political art group Piratbyrån, through to its role in the development of the first 'Pirate Party', a political party that campaigns for IP reform. The section also follows the site's legal conflicts, its nomadic life moving from one country to another and the problems faced by the courts in dealing with an international, decentralised network. The chapter ends with 'A piratical ideology', arguing that the primary impact of the site was not as a facilitator of copyright infringement, but as a disseminator of piratical ideology.

Having provided the background to digital distribution's illicit past, the book continues by focusing on the values and ideology that drove it, the industry that resisted it and the changes this conflict has made to the copyright industries and our engagement with their products. Chapter 7, 'Hacking the market', presents the two perspectives at play in the conflict of digital distribution: the perspective of the incumbent media industries, and the values and drive of programming communities and software developers. The chapter begins with 'Keeping it in the family', a look at the value the compact disc (CD) had brought to the music industry and its reluctance to enter into the digital market. The section presents an argument for the actions of the copyright industries but also demonstrates how their reluctance left them vulnerable to the capacities of the digital medium, and the communities that were skilled in its manipulation. These communities are addressed in 'A hacker's market', where the ideology of the 'hacker ethic', demonstrated throughout the Napster, GNUtella and BitTorrent histories is laid out. The section demonstrates how the hacker ethic placed those most interested in digital distribution in the perfect position to implement it, causing great disruption for the incumbent media industries. The incumbent industries, through their reluctance, were not only forced to compete with illicit digital distribution in price, but also with the definition and expectations of digital media.

Chapter 8 looks at the ways in which contemporary legitimate digital media vendors, borne on the back of digital distribution's illicit past, operate. The chapter begins with 'Bring in the technologists!', the story of Apple's iTunes Store and how the first successful legal download store was founded. The story illustrates the ways in which expectations of digital media grounded in piracy led to the shift of power away from the world's biggest recording labels, to the sphere of information technology. The chapter continues with 'Codes of control', an examination of the ways in which digital distribution has afforded new regulatory powers for the copyright industries and their new digital partners. The section begins with a short story about Sony Entertainment's attempts to implement security into its CDs. The story illustrates the tension between the models of selling media as a product, and selling media as a licence. The section goes on to discuss the digital media product, and how its instantiation as data allows these unprecedented levels of regulation by media vendors. The section 'Competing with free' looks at the ways in which the digital medium allows vendors to deliver media in a form that competes with the open pirate market and mimics the standards set by the hacker ideology. It examines the terms of service of some of the most successful digital retailers, and demonstrates how these terms allow them to provide new ways of engaging with media, as well as new forms of long-term relationship between vendors and customers. The chapter ends with a summary argument that our contemporary digital retailers, to balance the demands of the pirate market and the necessities of retailing IP, have significantly altered the way we engage with and understand media.

The concluding chapter begins with 'A history of digital distribution', where the focus moves away from the small historical details, and broadens to examine the history as a whole. The section uses this perspective to consider the history of digital distribution as an all-encompassing narrative to enable us to understand the roots of digital distribution and its societal impact better. The second half of the chapter, 'Change', looks at how the story of digital distribution can demonstrate mechanisms of social change and technological innovation. It also makes an argument for a micro approach to sociological history, one that focuses on building grand narratives of change based on micro empirical details.

The rationale for this perspective of social change, and the new digital documentary methods that support it, is where the book begins in Chapter 2. The following chapter provides my rationale for the approach taken to sociological history and explains how I produced social histories from digital documents. The chapter begins with a section on 'The event biography', a conceptual tool developed to ensure the histories did not focus only on technological or human drivers of change, but on the intertwining of both, within societal structure. In 'Trawling the archive of archives' I outline my method of digital documentary analysis and the affordances it provides in writing a history concerned with small interactions and agency. Before moving on to the histories, the chapter ends with 'Digital documents and their discontents', an examination of digital documents, and the challenges they pose to sociological historiography. When researching the history of digital distribution I swiftly found that the task presented challenges that could not be answered by existing standards and methods of research. This is largely why this chapter is here, to explain how I produced a history of digital distribution, and why I did what I did. Some might consider it to be the place where I provide disclosure, reveal the skeletons in the closet (all good sociologists should embrace their closet skeleton). It is partly that, but more broadly it is also an argument for seeing the internet as a depository of everyday life – a fantastic recording of every extraordinary and mundane moment of history as it happens. If you are reading this book because you have a great interest in the history of piracy and digital media, but aren't too fussed about the backstage goings on, feel free to skip ahead to Chapter 3. However, if you are curious about how these histories were produced, and about the affordances and issues that digital documents can present, read on.

2
Writing a Digital History with Digital Documents

The event biography

The popular image of technology and social change is one where the development of our society is persistently driven by new technological discoveries. In this relationship humans have come to accept that our society will frequently become rewritten by great technological progress. As such, taking a historical approach to social change is often drawn upon in the sociological study of science, technology and innovation. We look back across the changes in our history to understand the role technology and innovation had in getting us to where we are today. Such technological determinism believes that our technological revolutions have made us and our modern condition (Williams, 2003). Writers such as Toffler (1981) and Poster (1995) posit grand societal changes as being driven by technological innovations, and point to the inherent capacities of a technology as the elements that define those transformations.

However, those writers that study the history of science and technology have often demonstrated how social influences interweave with technological development (Bijker et al., 1987; Friedman, 1997). Rather than an unstoppable inhuman force, writers such as Grint and Woolgar (1997) question the assumption of technology driving social change. Instead they ask whether technology determines the social, or whether it is the social that determines technology. They argue that, rather than a technology having inherent capacities and so predefined social impact, technology is written and read by humans. Our writing of technology imbues it with unexamined

11

cultural assumptions and ideology, derived from economic and social factors (Feenberg, 1999). As users read the technology, they interpret it and define its use, and how it will be integrated into pre-existing social structures. This recursively will further influence how it is subsequently designed or written. Examples abound: the telephone was originally designed to broadcast concert music, and its conception as a two-way device was not considered. Frissen (1995) argued that (once it had developed into a two-way device) the telephone was redefined again by women, from its intended use as a masculine office tool, into a feminised domestic social device. Pinch and Bijker's (1984) study of the bicycle illustrated how social convention, norms and values evolved the bicycle across numerous branches and iterations. Gitelman and Pingree's (2004) book *New Media: 1740–1915* presents a whole collection of 'dead media'; media technologies that briefly became a part of our social reality, but were swiftly discarded as the technologies failed to achieve mundanity and integrate with us. All examples illustrate the ways in which technologies not only define us (Kittler, 1999), but are also defined by us.

During my research into the history of digital distribution networks, as the narratives unfolded, it became apparent that each history was a story of both algorithmic and human agency. Throughout these chapters you will see a degree of focus on the software and the technical details of how they operated. This is not an effort to make a determinist stance, but an attempt to draw attention to the role of the code in the narratives. As you read the following chapters it is hoped that you will see that the design of the code plays a strong role in other elements of the history. This 'Software Studies' (Fuller, 2008; Kitchin and Dodge, 2011) approach to the technical agents within the histories allows a richer understanding of how technical design and human agency interrelates. It is hoped that the following chapters will demonstrate the ways in which technological design played a strong role in the digital distribution story, and that broadly there is great value in analysing algorithmic, as well as human, agency.

With this focus on both the human and the algorithmic, it is safe to say that this book takes a middle ground between technological determinism and social constructionist views. Hutchby (2001) provides us with a means of understanding the interrelation of technology's material realities and their subsequent redefinition through human use. He argues that, though technologies can be defined and redefined through their reading, the options for that redefinition are not infinite. A telephone may be redefined through its use, as Frissen demonstrated, but the material realities of its construction mean it will never be a slot machine. Technologies are not blank slates ready for definition through human agency. Their material basis and capacities restrict their possible interpretations. Hutchby argues that technologies have 'affordances', a spectrum of possible uses and definitions that may be discovered or developed by its users, made feasible by its underlying material capacities. It is an argument that allows us to understand technological innovation and social change as an interplay between solid technological capacities, and the social situation of their development and use. This framing of technological innovation is the foundation for the 'event biography' approach; an intertwining of social and technological factors.

The term came from a consideration of how much the histories centred on the agency of individuals within each event. As I researched each piracy network, the stories that arose would usually focus on two or more key people responsible for driving the changes that were occurring. This led to the view that perhaps what was being produced was a series of biographies of influential actors who were able to significantly alter contemporary society with relatively little action through the 'secondary agency' (Mackenzie, 2006) of code and technology. However, it swiftly became clear that this framing was inadequate; it discounted the myriad factors that had had an impact on their agency and the unintended consequences of their action – it was in a way too agent determinist. Instead, what seemed to be the primary unit of analysis was the event, a particular 'assemblage' (Latour, 2005) of actors and structures, consequences and connections that the actors were but one aspect of. As such, it seemed the real unit worthy of a biography was the assemblage itself, and thus the term 'event biography': an attempt to recount the various constitutive aspects of a particular event.

It is not a failing to admit that the idea of an 'event' is difficult conceptual terrain. Though an event may be any type of happening or occurrence, typically from a historical perspective the term is reserved for happenings that have a degree of significance, such as a public ceremony or something that is recognised as a happening that will significantly alter the course of history. For Sewell, events are 'sequences of occurrences that result in transformations of structures' (Sewell, 1996: 843). Giddens' structuration theory, from which Sewell derives his conception of social change, posits that social formations are made up of an articulated network of 'structures'. The definition of 'structure' largely relies on the context in which it is used. Within this work structures refer to both the economic and the cultural. Economic structures are things such as the distribution of wealth and access to resources. Cultural structures are things such as the assemblage of social norms, morals and values. Structuration theory attempts to account for both the role of human agency, and the society that that agency has to work with and within. It recognises that agency works and reworks the society we occupy as that society works and reworks us, what Giddens refers to as the 'duality of structure' (Giddens, 1981, cited in Sewell, 1992).

These structures, which human agency simultaneously produces and is constrained by, are composed of 'cultural schemas', 'distributions of resources' and 'modes of power'. Cultural schemas are akin to the norms and values of a social formation. The distribution of resources provides the means for and stakes of action within the social formation; often social change is driven by the use of these resources and/or the desire to alter their distribution. The modes of power specify which cultural schemas are permissible and which are not. In terms of social change it is generally considered that normally the social practices, distributions of resources and modes of power remain constant. There are, however, ruptures in this continuity, but they are often suppressed by these three mechanisms of the social formation. However, there are sometimes ruptures which escalate and cannot be contained, at which point social change occurs, the formation adapts and continuity begins anew. It is an attempt to balance both, rather than singularly prioritise, agency and structure, and accounts for the passage of time, instability and durability in social formation. For Sewell, an event is one of these successful ruptures, which has a ramified sequence of occurrences and results in a durable transformation in norms and values, modes of power and the distribution of resources (Sewell, 1996). Through social history we can document and examine how agents' thoughts, motives and intentions are constituted by the structures that surround them. We can also see how these agents, in certain circumstances, come to use these characteristics to significantly reconfigure the structures, to cause events, and so bring about social change. Using structuration terms, an event biography is an attempt to document in great detail both the structures and agents involved in a particular event, the interplay of those structures and agents, what disruptions that interplay produced and what continuities have remained. It is a holistic approach to historical documentation, where emphasis is placed on small details, with an awareness that intended and unintended consequences can, due to the interplay of agency and structure, arise from what appear initially to be the smallest, most insignificant moment.

The structure of this book reflects my utilisation of the event biography tool. The wider narrative of digital distribution has been written as a series of individual pieces. Each piece combines historical narrative with a topical focus to not only inform the reader of the processes that brought about digital distribution, but also to direct their gaze to the implications of those developments. My aim was not to simply reveal the actual events and actions that developed digital distribution, but to contextualise those developments into wider social life and to tease out the underlying theme of the event. The chapters are snapshots of the history, and though presented in chronological order, often overlap. This overlapping is derived from co-linearity of the different narratives, some beginning earlier and some ending later, but all of them overlapping with other parts of the wider narrative at some point. The history could have been presented as a single thread within which all snapshots are covered, adhering strictly to the chronological ordering of events. However, in doing so the intertwining of these snapshots may have been lost in the false pretence that a history can be explained as a single linear tale.

A linear style of presentation would insinuate that the narrative could be conceived as a cohesive whole, rather than as a collection of disparate, yet sometimes interacting events and influences. By avoiding the singular narrative, I hope to demonstrate that the history was not a simple procession of 'progress'. This structuring into individual biographies also means I am able to retain the detail of exactly when events occurred, the chronology being key to understanding the interrelation of the narratives. The multi-narrative style also illuminates the interrelationships and unintended impacts between different areas of the wider narrative, demonstrating the power and role of small details to reach outside their own immediate sphere. The re-referencing of events within different chapters and the multiple appearances of the same actors demonstrate the unintended crossover between the different event biographies. It is my hope that the structure of this book will not only assist the reader in gaining a thorough insight into these histories, but also prove enjoyable as connections are noticed and relations between the different event biographies become apparent.

Trawling the archive of archives

The internet, although primarily characterised by its facilities for communication, is also a multilayered space of data aggregation. Utilising a mass of human and non-human contributors and organisers, the contents of the internet is as much a space of archival process as it is a space of communication. When Tim Berners-Lee began tinkering on his personal project, 'Enquire', which eventually led to the HTML protocol that comprises what we know as the web, it was based on a desire to organise and track large masses of data; an intelligent way to handle the tasks of data archive and retrieval (Johnson, 2010: 88). However, the internet is not a single archive but, instead, can be conceived of as a type of meta-archive or an archive of archives. A variety of media applications (social network sites, specialist news sites, media-sharing sites, piracy networks) alongside the digitisation of analogue archives (Lexis/Nexis, business registrations, court documentation) means that the internet is instead a composite of multiple archives. These are contributed to and maintained by a multitude of human and algorithmic actors, constantly adding to the various masses of information about our world (Beer, 2009; Gane and Beer, 2008). As more agents participate in the archival process, the scope of its information grows in both breadth and depth. The daily, hourly, moment-by-moment documentation of individual lives, actions, events and agency immensely alters the possibilities for highly detailed event tracing, and further deepens the opportunities afforded to Foucault's 'archive reason' – the constant striving to focus on the particularity and singularity of the event (Featherstone, 2000: 169). The internet is becoming (and arguably will always be in a state of becoming) what Gane and Beer refer to as the 'archive of the everyday' (2008: 77).

The most prominent feature of the meta-archive is its facility to connect multiple archives. This connectivity allows for cross-context searching, which greatly improves the chances of finding pertinent but unexpected documents. With a search engine as the access point to the meta-archive, it is possible to receive query results from multiple types of archival source at once. Google illustrates this well with its ability to condense various types of archival data into one set of search results, providing websites, news articles, Twitter-feed posts, images, videos and maps in one query reply. This connectivity also facilitates contributors' propensity to situate their 'documents' (a term which will be addressed later in this chapter) within a larger context, tagging and linking to other documents elsewhere in the myriad archives. For many contemporary publishing platforms, an automated system known as 'trackback' displays links to other documents that have linked to a document, meaning the reader can see what the current document is referring to, as well as what has referred to the current document. Featherstone, drawing on Levinson (1997), remarks that the embedding of links within online documents not only directs the readers' gaze further (perhaps by supplying the specific evidence that will support their claim, whilst overlooking the evidence that denounces it), but also allows them to move past the document and find their own path through the narrative (Featherstone, 2000: 176).

The structures that facilitate this connectivity have some disadvantages, however. To get physical documents into a digital format they need to be processed, either manually by an individual, reading and re-entering the text or automatically via a scanner. Both are fallible systems because the individual may misread the text and the text-recognition systems on scanners may also make errors. In his speech to the University of Chicago, Andrew Abbott recalls a moment when a student's document search was unnecessarily drawn out by a text-recognition system's inability to understand Federal Government documents after it had changed its standard font; the system was trying to interpret the newer documents via the rules of the previous font, turning the letter 'c' into the letter 'o' (Abbott, 2009). As many of the documents for this work were not translated to digital but were instead directly inscribed into it, the potential for these problems was reduced; however, it is still possible that typos meant that documents were overlooked due to their being disregarded by finicky search systems.

It should also be remembered that these spaces are often privately owned, and as such vary in their platform, permissions and motives. They are more often than not operating with an underlying profit motive, meaning that, if access is freely available, other restrictions on either the consumer or producers may be in effect in view of generating revenue. Databases such as Lexis/Nexis require subscription for access, as do some leading newspaper websites. Other spaces such as specialist news sites have their own commercial considerations, which may impact the information they supply. The right to archive or distribute documents is also a consideration as seen in piracy networks and Wikileaks, where IP rights assert exclusivity of access and distribution, denying the prospects of third-party archiving and so denying the researcher access. Lastly, recent revelations regarding the development of search engine technology have introduced us to the issue of search personalisation. Pariser (2011) highlighted the issue of internet 'bubbling', the idea that we each experience the internet differently through the manipulation of search results to better match who the search engine thinks we are. Google's own development process also works off of what is referred to as the 'A/B' method, where different variants of the Google site are delivered to different groups of users live (see Christian, 2012). User behaviour is then monitored to determine which Google variant is the most successful. Rather than simply a method of occasional testing, it is likely that the Google site never stays the same for long, nor produces the same results for any two people. Introna and Nissenbaum (2000) warn of the politics of search engines, and how search engines operate to promote and censor content in their own interest. As such, the gateways of the meta-archives can surreptitiously manipulate what we find within.

However, with these caveats in mind we can be confident that, due to the mechanics and design of the web, the majority of the documents are well organised, searchable, replicable and malleable to a greater extent than physical documents, making it a highly viable system for archival research. As the focus of the research – the production of digital distribution systems – was a highly internet-located phenomenon, searching for its documents online was a valid approach. The reporting, technology releases, discussion and community work surrounding it often took place on the internet and were greatly overlooked by offline coverage. Furthermore, through social networking systems and blogs the activities of various individuals and events could be followed in close to real time during the periods where the history being documented was occurring at the time of research. As such, the benefits of utilising the internet as a meta-archive far outweighed the caveats in the case of this topic.

The practical research process was simple and on the whole unstructured, but it fulfilled many of the necessities for tracing the various event biographies that made up the history of digital distribution. Alongside the typical books and journal articles found in all academic research, the work utilised a variety of data sources and documents that could be classified as traces of human action, left on the net for a particular purpose. The form that a document took differed depending on its reason for production, the technological platform that supported it and its intended audience. Though reviewed for validity (which will be addressed later), no document was excluded from consideration as the priority was to trace a history, rather than to adhere to a predefined framework of what constituted valid evidence. Information was gathered from a variety of internet-hosted sources, including, but not limited to, print news databases, specialist topic blogs, personal 'diary-style' blogs, specialist news sites, podcasts, social networking feeds (primarily Twitter), court document archives, business registrars, domain name registrars, amateur videos, amateur music, amateur documentaries, images, software release note files, internet archives (literal archives of the internet that host defunct non-operational websites) and corporate press releases. What source was chosen at what point of the research was entirely subject to what was necessary to accurately trace the event biography under question, and relied little on a structured framework of methodological 'protocol', finding such restrictions to artificially limit the flexibility of the meta-archive approach.

Instead, the process and goal was one of refinement – beginning with a broad, sweeping but unsophisticated understanding of the topic of digital distribution, which was then refined to a narrower selection of individual event biographies. Those biographies were then addressed separately and fleshed out with a detailed investigation continuing until no more information could be found, either due to the focus of the event ending (i.e. company liquidation), or because of the biography reaching the present day. Having already done a broad but shallow precursory review of what the key events and actors were in the field of digital distribution, refinement of those individual biographies could begin. Though the ultimate goal of each biography was to produce an account that incorporated as much pertinent detail as possible, it was necessary to understand that biography as a whole before the detail could be addressed. Thankfully, it was usually possible to find a large summary of the key events and actors within that specific biography through a variety of ways. Sources such as enthusiast-made histories, autobiographical histories, Wikipedia entries and specialist news articles were used to ascertain this broad, sweeping understanding of the event biography. Even entire news sites could be used to generate a summary. By finding a specialist news site and entering a few relevant search terms it was possible to order the results by date, which would generate a quick timeline of the subject in question. These summaries would provide a quick and easy means of garnering a snapshot of that particular topic and additionally provided a starting point to understand the context behind the headlines. Wikipedia may also be considered an unusual choice, often contested as a 'legitimate' source of information. However, this too can be reasonably used as a springboard to further research if used simply to garner a broad perspective of the biography. It should be noted that after completing one particular event biography it became clear that the initial Wikipedia entry that provided the research springboard was significantly misinformed, and would not have been an appropriate source to draw directly from (though this did not invalidate its role as a research 'launch pad').

Having established the key moments, issues and actors of the event biography, the process of sifting through the net would begin. This required large amounts of time, utilising different search engines, archives, news sites and other aforementioned sources to collect any piece of information about the event that could be found. Often these sources would provide a snowballing effect, leading from one document to the next either directly through article suggestions or links, or indirectly by assuming knowledge of a certain event that the researcher was unaware of, providing a new avenue of inquiry. This would lead to the targeting of certain pieces of information when unanswered questions arose: 'when was company "x" incorporated', 'website "y" registered' or 'software "z" released' (sometimes even when a certain functionality became active within some software). This often required searching in more unusual places, such as court document archives, domain name registrar records or software release notes. The goal was to pinpoint these events to the exact day (even then the very hour would have been preferable), as often it was the detailed day-to-day occurrences which mattered the most in shaping the larger monthly and yearly events that had been identified in the broader biography summaries. The key piece of information from each document was a date which, due to the automated time-stamping of blog and social network posts, the functionality of archives and the formalities of 'official' documents, was often forthcoming. For some dates a small degree of extra work was required, such as when an article referred to an event in the past by day (i.e. 'the events of Thursday') required quick consultation of a calendar to ascertain what day of the week the dated article had been published, and then what was the exact date of that referenced day.

As far as possible (in some cases technical restrictions disallowed it) these documents were copied into a research database which would automatically make the documents searchable and had the option of adding tags to the articles, aiding categorisation and later recall. After the research for the history section had concluded, the database contained approximately 1,400 relevant documents, including text, audio, video and images. Every document found would be read and information would be drawn from it. What is meant by that is twofold – the document could provide a sense of what was occurring at the time, a recounting of conflicts, a sense of the jostling of ideologies, an individual's opinion of a conflict, information that would provide context and sensitised the researcher to the story of the event. However, more concrete information could also be drawn from these documents, such as when certain events occurred, who was involved, whether one actor or group interacted with another actor or group and the role of any structural social restrictions. This was the hard data that were eventually used to produce visualisations of the event biographies.

The most significant of the visualisations were a variety of specialist and one final master timeline. These timelines were produced initially out of necessity for the research process but eventually came to play various significant roles. Initially I had produced the timelines to aid in grasping the ordering of events. This ordering was key to understanding each document because placing it in its causal context was necessary to better understand the information it provided.

Without an understanding of chronological ordering, little in the way of pattern or causal development could be ascertained. Often a document would be reviewed upon initial discovery and then later re-reviewed after further information about prior events had been gathered. In the light of newly discovered prior events, what was deemed pertinent information in a document would change, requiring a constant review of all documents held.

Although it was sometimes possible to find or automatically produce an event summary, there were other instances where such an overview was unavailable. In such cases this facility to slowly build up a chronology of events allowed me, armed with simply the name of the data transfer protocol, application or an individual's name, to construct the entire history piece by piece by asking new questions highlighted by each new document found. Here the timeline became invaluable in chronologically ordering the details discovered, slowly producing an overview, and visually illustrating where gaps in the history required filling. These lacunae provided further guidance if investigatory leads began to dry up; if there was a two- or three-month gap where nothing pertinent to the event history had been found, that particular period would be targeted in various news databases to ascertain if anything notable had occurred.

Another usage of the timeline was to verify the validity of the information discovered. For example, if documents mentioned an event that had already been mapped, the date would be cross-referenced with the timeline to check accuracy. If an incongruity was found then the event would be re-examined and additional sources would be searched for until as accurate a date could be found, whilst also determining why there had been incongruity in the dates in the first place. Though not an often occurrence, these difficulties that documents had in providing correct dates could lead to a further interesting avenue of enquiry as questions over whether events were purposefully obfuscated arose.

Prior to these smaller more focused timelines I produced a broader master timeline. During an initial review of the field of digital distribution, basic dates and statistics, not directly related to the event biographies in this book, were acquired. This master timeline eventually became useful not only as a wider perspective on the field of digital distribution, but also aided in contextualising the event biographies, providing a background to further understand the world that the biographies were developing within. This information would eventually feed into the biography narratives when appropriate.

Digital documents and their discontents

The question of what constitutes a document has become increasingly blurred, especially as our documentation of everyday life increasingly begins to take place online. Throughout this chapter I've discussed the use of 'digital documents' – items of information that exist online in internet archives. The use of documents for historical enquiry is well ingrained in both historiography and sociology (Chirot, 1984; Langlois and Seignobos, 1908; Plummer, 2001; Scott, 1990; Skocpol, 1984) and there has been much discussion of what constitutes a 'document'. Enquiries dealing primarily with the lives, actions or events of the past rely on the traces left behind, which means dealing with documents. However, what counts as a document in documentary analysis can be rather vague. In common understanding, historical documents are usually considered to be text on paper that comes with a degree of status provided through its authorship by an individual, group or institution of recognised importance. Under a traditional model, documents are texts and it is their purpose of production that indicates their value. Royal correspondence, parliamentary reports or any other form of 'official' record are held in high esteem. The classification of documents with this focus on the purpose of production led to the separation of texts into 'documents' and 'contemporary literature'. Documents were the official texts of office, whilst everything else was contemporary literature. This influential view from Sidney and Beatrice Webb (cited in Scott, 1990) considered documents to be texts of action, to have purpose in themselves, such as how correspondence from the king would have purpose in directing his ministers. Contemporary literature is everything else that is contemporary to the time, produced as residual traces, which are secondary to the superior status of documents which directed and made history. Contemporary literature was useful to give background information, but the document retained a higher status in recounting the events of the time. This definition is restrictive, especially when researching underground, or ad hoc communities where there is little in the way of official directive documentation. Documentary analysis of much internet-based phenomena would fall at the first hurdle if it were necessary to follow this criteria.

Rather than be recognised and documented by any traditional authority, the majority of phenomena that takes place on the internet has been algorithmically documented by the medium of communication. Langlois and Seignobos, writing on the traditional historical method, consider documents to be the 'traces which have been left by the thoughts and actions of men (sic) of former times' (Langlois and Seignobos, 1908: 46). Traces implies much more than a piece of paper – instead it opens the classification of 'document' out to anything that remains from human action.

Buckland (1997) discusses the concept of the 'document' by drawing on the work of Paul Otlet, founder of European Documentation, and Suzanne Briet, the woman known as 'Madame Documentation' for her treatise *Qu'est-ce que la documentation?* (*What is Documentation?*). Both Otlet and Briet argued for the expansion of the category of 'document' beyond text. Otlet (1934) considered any object to be valid as a document, arguing that objects could be documents if it was possible to be informed by the observation of them. Briet (1951) saw a document as 'evidence in support of a fact'. She shifted the perception from things being documents in and of themselves, to a view that something was a document if treated as such. Briet argued that a stone in the wild was not a document, but that a stone in a museum was, precisely because it was considered necessary to document the stone. She even went so far as to posit that an antelope can be a document, if it is treated as such. Anything written about the antelope would then be a secondary document; the primary document being the antelope. Buckland argues that the work of Otlet and Briet indicates a trend towards 'defining a document in terms of function rather than physical format' (Buckland, 1998). Rather than focusing on the purpose of the document's production, Otlet and Briet were arguing for a greater focus on its function to the observer. Document became a title bestowed upon something that was 'information-as-thing' (Buckland, 1991), rather than an inherent quality of an object.

Prior's (2003) more recent work in documentary analysis builds on Briet and Otlet, and argues that any item can be classified as a document if it is suitable to the researcher's field of action. By field of action Prior means the conceptual boundaries laid by the author in determining a space or event under study, for example 'the Wall Street Crash', 'the Industrial Revolution' or 'the production of BitTorrent'. Within these fields of action a document can both be a receptacle of information, but also an agent in its own right, utilised by actors but also working on actors as well. For example, one might draw on a news article that documents the events surrounding a particular court case, yet it should be recognised that that article may have, at the time, caused changes in the field of action. In Levy's (1999) opinion, documents are actors that speak for us; by fixing our speech into a repeatable form they allow many others to hear what we have to say. Not only does this definition of documents allow for the flexibility of classifying anything as a document through its function, but it also calls for the recognition that what the researcher is drawing from was not simply produced for their benefit, but had its own place within the history they are documenting.

A flexible understanding of what constitutes a 'document' aids greatly in the tracing of a contemporary history with a significant online presence. The flexibility of the definition allows for the employment of a huge variety of sources, allowing a tracing of greater detail and depth. Under more traditional production-focused definitions the project would have been limited to relying on court documents and business registrations, domain registrars and perhaps a small amount of print news articles (though these would be considered to be lesser more contemporary literature than document). Instead the history could be truly 'traced' from whatever sources were able to inform this observer, allowing for a richer more detailed recounting. However, this flexibility of what can be considered a document does not absolve anyone of the necessity to be selective and critical. In any method of research it is vital to ensure that what is drawn upon to generate data is properly evaluated. It is not necessarily with the case that such evaluation would seek to exclude documents, but it would ensure their proper use. After working out just what a document is, this is the task that preoccupies documentary analysts and historians alike; how to move from the source to the fact (Langlois and Seignobos cited in Scott, 1990).

The issues surrounding the use of documents as evidence are similar to the issues arising from other methods of ascertaining empirically founded truth. Although as Jennifer Platt points out, there is little in the way of a formalised method for using documents, the key to their use is understanding how to use them (Platt, 1981). For Burgess (1984) the major consideration is a document's authenticity, for Platt (1981) it is authenticity, availability, sampling procedure and the consideration of what inferences can be drawn from them, whilst John Scott (1990) focuses on authenticity, credibility, representativeness and meaning, though he indicates that he is heavily influenced by the work of Platt. These are not entirely suitable for direct application to internet-based documentation. More contemporary writers such as Bolter (1991), Levy (1994, 1999, 2000a) Hampshire and Johnson (2009), Dougherty and Schneider (2011) and Sternfeld (2010) have considered the ways in which the digital document differs from the artefacts and texts that have long dominated the definition of 'document'. Although similar considerations and problems of relying on documents remain, digital documents also have their own unique difficulties, many of which were encountered during the research for this book.

Mediated information

The language of Platt, Burgess and Scott is based around the assumption that documents are produced by direct observers or actors in a particular field of action. Though the researchers are mediate to the event, distant from it in either time or space, it is assumed that the document authors were proximate, present either at the time of production or close enough to it. The documents allow those proximate to an event, to speak to us through the infinite repetition of their speech via the document (Levy, 1999). Although this work did utilise some documents that could be considered to be primary sources, the majority of documents were news reports with much of the information within them produced by individuals that were themselves mediate from the events they were reporting on. These reports were produced from other documents that we may or may not be privy to, which were summarised into the documents (the news reports) which we were privy to. Scott (1990: 23) argues that the traditional historian's preference of primary sources over secondary ones is unfounded. The many variables that could affect a primary observer and their reporting of an event means that the distinction of considering primary sources as being accurate, whilst secondary are inaccurate, lacks sophistication in approach. Much of the secondary source documents utilised for this research were articles found online that reported on various events or themes. Those articles were produced from a mix of primary and secondary sources, combining newswire reports with interviews, enquiries and information gathered from mediated primary sources, such as Twitter and company blogs. This combining of various sources was of course mediated by the writer of the document, with them discerning what would and would not be included in a report, and the way in which that information was presented. This is of course problematic in all sources, as Scott has pointed out, not just secondary but in reports of primary observation also.

Langlois and Seignobos (1908, cited in Platt, 1981) identify a great deal of factors that may introduce distortion of 'truth' into a document. Amongst these factors are distortions that arise unintended by the author, but are derived from their own particular ideals, vanity or a desire to portray an event as dramatic and of significance. One particular source of documents in which these issues play out significantly is the Torrent Freak specialist news site. The site reports on stories from the field of P2P file-sharing, IP politics and media concentration. The site's contributors take a particularly oppositional position to the status quo of media distribution, championing the disruption from communication technologies and the ideology of IP reform. Torrent Freak discloses its ideological position through the way the site presents itself and although they may strive to present a balanced story, their primary focus, their known audience and the personal beliefs of the authors culminate to bias their reporting to a degree. Events are described in such a way that certain actors are portrayed in a good light, their actions being clearly positioned as dramatic, heroic and noble whilst others (usually representatives of the creative industry) are written as, at best, ignorant closed-minded industry lackeys, and at worst, evil money-grubbing corporate suits.

It is in no way the intention to portray Torrent Freak as a biased source, only to recognise that the personal politics, values and knowledge of a site's contributors and readership will influence their portrayal of events. This is no less true for other sources such as traditional news print which often portrayed Torrent Freak's heroic actors as underworld criminals worthy of jail, based on the author's conception of the politics of the situation. As such no source should be considered unbiased factual reporting, yet all are useful so long as the researcher is alert to the politics of the author. The task is to be able to discern the facts, names, dates and actions, from the fiction, dramatisation, caricaturing and overemphasising. A more difficult task is to account for the intentional and unintentional overlooking of information which may not further the particular angle of the story being written. To account for this during the research it was preferable to seek reports of the same event from multiple sources that were known to hold differing ideological positions. By looking to see where reports agreed, conflicted and presented unique information, I was able to come to a much clearer determination of the 'facts'. Information that was agreed upon by multiple sources was considered to be acceptably validated. Information where sources disagreed was followed up with further searches. It may be that only one source digressed from a line held by five others, in which case a further evaluation of the source (its ideological underpinnings, readership, affiliations, knowledge and understanding of the event, etc.) would often lead me to a conclusion regarding its validity.

Though I would like to present one, unfortunately there was no hard-and-fast rule to this process, which was ultimately down to my own discretion. Though this kind of problem arises with physical documents, digital ones are susceptible to distrust. The possible anonymity of the medium, coupled with the negative invocation of 'amateurism' (Keen, 2008) that can often be attributed to online content can evoke feelings of uncertainty when utilising such documents as evidence. Where little conclusion can be ascertained regarding conflicting reports, the most appropriate solution is to report the conflict and attempt to include the discrepancies of account within the narrative of events. When I presented this method of digital documentary analysis at the Oxford Internet Institute, one commentator likened it to the 'Wikipedia method' of dealing with conflict; a comparison that I quite like.

The process of dealing with the issues that arise from mediated information is ultimately one of trusting the information provided to you. For Langlois and Seignobos they advocated a position of methodological distrust, where the primary view of the researcher is that all documents are false unless they can be proven otherwise. John Craig, whom according to Platt was one of the first researchers who dealt systematically with the issues of trust and truth in documentary analysis, takes the opposite position, defaulting to one of trust. In Craig's words, 'All men have an equal right to be believed, unless the contrary has been established from elsewhere' (Craig quoted in Platt, 1981: 41). Although not in strict adherence to Craig's position, this research did prefer to approach a source as being at least honest in its intentions even if it could not be honest in its production.

Information scarcity

In part this position of defaulting to trust rather than scepticism was due to the lack of information available and the restricted amount of sources that reported on the topic of digital distribution. In the early years of digital distribution particularly, where much of the innovation work done was by individuals or small groups separate from the copyright industries, finding records of activities and events was difficult. For information regarding the build up to a distribution system's public release little, if anything, was documented until after the fact, usually via interviews with the primary developers. Even after public release, the various distribution systems were of incredibly niche interest in the early years, with broader reporting being provided by one or two reporters on technology news sites, with the detail being left to the amateur enthusiasts. This meant a great deal of information was either never recorded or was only recorded by only one source. There was of course a great deal of information that was never recorded by anyone or what little there was was lost when websites closed down, either due to a loss of interest, funds or time by their hobbyist administrators or through company liquidation.

This dissipation of digital documents is a source of much anxiety for those concerned with their value as record. The web in its most fundamental form is not set up for versioning and audit trails. Though some sites do provide these mechanisms, the majority of documents that make their way onto the web will dissipate shortly thereafter. Past information is not as prioritised as present information. As web technologies focus on achieving real-time data acquisition and presentation, the documents that we did have are being overwritten for the immediately new. As Dougherty and Schneider put it, '[t]he documents on which we base our history of the web disappear as we write it' (Dougherty and Schneider, 2011: 256). This has led to a rhetoric of digital documents as being fluid (see Bolter, 1991), as opposed to the 'fixed' pre-digital documents on which our rules and understanding of documentation are based. However, Levy (1994) argues that it is not that pre-digital documents are fixed, and digital documents are fluid, but that both can be fixed and fluid, alternating between the different states over time. Why we perceive pre-digital to occupy one state and digital to occupy another is a matter of speed and rhetoric. The speed with which digital documents can be altered and reproduced implies to us a fluidity as our perception of them becomes dominated by their periods of change, rather than their periods of fixity. Ultimately, Levy concludes that documents' fixity and fluidity is not the issue, but that the rhetoric of documentation values the permanence, immortality and monumentality of the fixed document. What we are seeing is a perception of digital documents as a challenge to that rhetoric of fixity through the speed of their circulation and alteration. If Levy's assertions are accurate then perhaps rather than bemoaning the fluidity of our rapidly dissipating documents we should bemoan our own inability to keep up with them as they experience the document life-course at rapid speed.

The lack or loss of information is not a problem unique to digital documents, nor documentary analysis in general. For Prior, a lack of information in documentary analysis is analogous to the issues surrounding 'perspective' in social research. During my research I often found that the amateur enthusiasts would produce documents that covered what major news outlets would not. The openness of their ideological stance made it easy enough to ensure an awareness of the possibility of bias but obviously did not reveal if any information had been strategically omitted from any reports written. As a result the information regarding earlier digital distribution methods is skewed towards the position of the only individuals writing about it – the digital distribution champions. There are also occasions where only one source is available that will provide the level of detail preferable to the work. For example, the coverage of Napster was heavily reliant on Joseph Menn's book 'All the Rave' (2003), a detailed look into the Napster story based on a mass of interviews that Menn conducted with the major actors in the Napster story. Menn was one of very few individuals able to gather such a comprehensive, detailed behind-the-scenes account of Napster, and his work is unparalleled. As an established journalist having written many articles for the *LA Times*, Menn's work provides a fantastic professional resource, but is still only a single perspective on the Napster tale and has been criticised for the alleged bias Menn held against one particular actor who was (whether for reasons of narrative or source material) portrayed in a less than favourable light. Similarly, certain periods of the history rely heavily on one or two journalists, being the only individuals covering the topic with a significant level of depth relative to the shallow reporting of the major news outlets.

Scott considers the impact of a lack of information to be primarily on the reliability and representativeness of the evidence gathered. Although Scott writes about representativeness of the data in relation to gathering collections of certain document types (death certificates, work logs, census data, etc.) as a sample (much like a sample of participants), the issue of representativeness still applies when using documentation to construct a narrative. With little in the way of corresponding or opposing evidence, the reliability of the small amount of information one does have cannot be evaluated as well as it could be with a much wider range of sources. As mentioned earlier, much of the evaluation was dependent on having many sources that document the same event to check for correspondence and conflict. With sometimes having only one or two sources this process was greatly undermined, leaving the narrative vulnerable. In these situations I sought to evaluate with a different approach by comparing new documents against what I already knew about that particular field. 'Are the actions of the actors described congruent with other accounts of their behaviour and personality?' 'Do the events described in the source "fit" with evidentially established events?' The timeline provided a useful tool for quickly establishing whether any dates provided fit chronologically, but it was often a case of utilising the smaller details ('Where was a particular individual at the time?' 'Had the company acquired funding by then?' 'Had software development progressed to that point?') to establish how probable the events described were.

Authority

Traditionally, it is the established news outlets that are considered to have credibility (in varying degrees) in their reporting. The outlets have professional journalists who adhere to a set of standards under which they risk their job if they flaunt them, and are answerable to an editor. Conversely writers and reporters working on enthusiast news sites are considered to be amateur, without standards, review and beholden only to themselves, often with little risk as they hide behind their pseudonym. Under these conditions research that utilises amateur reporting often more than professional work may justifiably be criticised as lacking in credibility, due to the lack of forethought for the sources they are using.

However, during the research what emerged was that the traditional preferential treatment of 'professional' journalism is unfounded in this field. In an area of niche technological knowledge and murky legality it is often the enthusiasts which provide the information more than the professionals. For the most part the problem was a lack of reporting from the major news outlets, which did not consider the ongoings of these particular groups and communities to be of great importance at the time. Though major events would be covered, such as the trial of the Pirate Bay, it would be merely a mention of its occurrence, rather than substantial coverage.

Some expert sources were highly useful. Specialist news sites such as CNET, Ars Technica and Wired provided strong coverage of some of the event biographies. The major difficulty was that it would often be the same author that covered digital distribution. This led me back to the aforementioned difficulties that came with a lack of information and a single perspective. In most other expert news organisations outside tech specialism, coverage was lacking in detail and understanding. These organisations were not significantly engaged with the topics they were writing about, leading to difficulties of clarity. In the case of some of the event biographies, the decentralised nature of the organisations and technologies under scrutiny and the confusion it generated would cause great difficulties of clarity for even the most ardent fan. Convoluted backstories, misinformation and unsubstantiated rumour made the terrain of illicit underground network difficult to fully grasp for anyone but the most engaged community member. Often it would be clear that the author had misunderstood a situation or how a technology operated and would attempt to apply an everyday understanding of organisation to often very disparate ad hoc groups. As a result the print news articles were usually inaccurate when checked against a collection of other independent reports on the same event or topic. This is not a slight on the sphere of professional journalism (the difficulties of following a field so new and alien cannot be overlooked); however, it is a challenge to the idea that credibility always comes with expertise in all spheres.

Andrew Keen's (2008) polemic against the culture of amateurism and user-generated content despairs for the erosion of authority and expertise in a Web 2.0 world. However, though it may have been preferable to have accredited, professional and highly knowledgeable individuals covering all aspects of digital distribution's development, I didn't. What I did have was an army of enthusiastic amateurs with first-hand experience of what they were reporting on and a thoroughly intricate understanding of the technologies being discussed. Their immersion into the debates, following of the technological developments and their personal use of the technology meant that these enthusiasts were in a much better position to understand the murky field of digital distribution in its infancy. Furthermore, the amateur authors would often have greater access to the underground communities and actors than the major news outlets. Torrent Freak often got first refusal on contact with the Pirate Bay administrators, having proven themselves both sympathetic and trustworthy in not distorting the facts as the administrators saw them, whilst major outlets were extended the minimum of contact. As such it was often the expert reporters that were furthest from a story, whilst the amateurs, being members of the illicit sphere of digital distribution, were (in network terms) just next door.

However, this integration with the community, and the developers with legally unstable positions, sometimes placed the writers in a difficult position. Alongside the aforementioned tendency to bias due to their integration with the community that they reported on, the writers often found it necessary to operate anonymously. The dubious legality of the digital distribution innovators, alongside the often valuable information handed on to reporters on their activities (where backup servers have been moved, the technicalities of a new privacy system) and the potential damage to their reputations for being 'piracy sympathisers' (and possibly pirates themselves) has meant that pseudonyms were often utilised when writing for the enthusiast news sites. This anonymity obviously introduces an opportunity for scepticism when evaluating the documents produced by an anonymous source. This anonymity is perhaps a weakness in relation to the more traditional news sources which often, though not always, provide an author's name.

There is, however, one interesting method used to control for the possibility of misreporting or error in the documents produced on amateur sites. Often a comments section was provided below the article, giving readers the opportunity to post their own comments on the article. This provided a degree of peer review as the commenters often corrected or questioned various elements of the article. Obviously, the great majority of those reading the article were sympathetic to the inherent biases that it contained; however, there were often dissenting voices amongst the crowd that provided a critique. This critique would sometimes lead to debate within the comments and then revisions by the article's author.

As such major news outlets and enthusiast sites are inherently different types of document source. However, they can both be of use by playing to their strengths and trying to account for their weaknesses. Though they lacked the understanding of the enthusiasts, major outlets were dependable when providing basic what, when, who, how and why information. However, the enthusiasts provided the intricacies, the detail and the depth of information missing from the professional stories. The most preferable situation was to have an account of an event from both expert and amateur sources. However, even when that was available it would sometimes transpire that it was the amateurs leading the experts. Despite the anonymity and bias, Torrent Freak's amateur insider knowledge was utilised by the experts when they were unable to acquire the information themselves. Professional news outlets such as the *Wall Street Journal* (Smith and McBride, 2008), the *New York Times* (Stelter and Stone, 2009), the BBC (BBC News, 2008), CNN (France, 2009), the *LA Times* (Healey, 2007) and the *Guardian* (Kiss, 2009) have all cited Torrent Freak, utilising not only its in depth knowledge, but also the statistics on piracy the site produces.

Authenticity in the face of information overload

The issues raised regarding the ability of the major news outlets to grasp the intricacies of what they were striving to report on are not limited just to them of course. As much as the web's affordances make it relatively easy to discover information, the wealth of data can also become a difficulty in itself beyond the already difficult task of evaluating sources. When faced with hundreds of results from a single enquiry, quite how to deal with that information is an immediately pressing issue. One of the most prominent issues that arose when following present history, that is history that was occurring as the research took place, was what could be described as 'internet echoes'. Often, when a story broke on one site, it was swiftly reported on other sites – many simply writing variations of the same information. However, some would build on that information, reporting the same, but also taking extra steps to secure interviews or further information beyond the initial report. This meant that during the research process if a particularly pertinent story about digital distribution broke, multiple sources would report on it, but all in slightly different ways.

It was important to ensure that this 'echoing' did not artificially inflate the status of such an event, but equally it was important to review all the different accounts of the event, to check for both variation and similarity. Variation meant the possibility of drawing new pertinent details, whilst similarities aided in determining what the agreed 'facts' were. This was, however, made difficult in that some articles were simply reporting that another source was reporting on the event, making the research process particularly time consuming. It also demonstrated that, though it contains a wealth of information and can be treated as an archive (of archives), much of the time the internet's primary function is to disseminate information through multiple channels. This common 'boom' of coverage would also lead to misinformation or inaccuracies as authors inferred details from what they had read elsewhere, or gave credence to speculation from commenters on other sites by taking their ideas and writing them into the more widely established facts. As such what would occur would be a replication of information across the web, but also a degree of mutation between documents as individual writing styles, perspectives and politics influenced the recounting of the events. Although documents would often link back to their own sources of information, determining the original source of the information boom was difficult, meaning that the search for the 'authentic' document would often be abandoned in favour of an approximation based on an amalgamation of its repetition.

With pre-digital documents, abandoning the original document in lieu of approximating from other sources that replicate it, is fairly poor practice. Platt (1981), Burgess (1984) and Scott (1990) consider the authenticity of the document to be a crucial element in evaluating its value. To them authenticity refers to a consideration of whether the document is what it claims to be or a replication or a forgery. Forgeries are made with the intent to deceive but also a replication may be deceptive through unintentional inaccuracy. Langlois and Seignobos (1908) consider a copy of an original to be of value so long as the text has not been corrupted and altered in transmission. Scott mentions that one should also not only consider if something is a copy, but also perhaps even a copy of a copy, thus leading to even greater chances for distortion from the original. When dealing with digital documents on the internet, in the true technical sense, everything is a copy of a copy. The very act of consuming a document means that you the viewer are consuming a copy. The process of transmitting the data from its source to your screen, is a process of copying, multiple times, across multiple spaces; multiple copies.

In daily practice this is a non-issue – we are confident that what has been copied is a perfect bit-by-bit replica of the original to the extent that we do not conceive of it as a process of copying, but a process of transmitting, of sending, where we the viewer are receiving the original information we have requested. However, it is also not necessarily the case that the original will remain unchanged. The simple act of altering the document's file format or hosting it in a different archival system can alter it significantly (Hampshire and Johnson, 2009). An original can be produced, copied and then edited leaving the copy as the original whilst what was the original becomes something different altogether. To speak of authenticity in terms of originals and copies becomes meaningless under these circumstances. Though Levy may argue against the dichotomy, there is a reason why the digital document is easily characterised as 'fluid'. Under such circumstances there is no guarantee that the digital document read now is the same document produced on the date that it claims. Corrections, alterations or complete rewrites without any notification are entirely plausible. Many of the documents employ, or authors will self-impose, systems where if additions or revisions are made to a document, they will be made explicit. Though there is the likelihood that if caught a document's audience may react badly to apparent covert alterations, there is no guarantee of this system and it varies from source to source. Thus the idea of an authentic document becomes undermined by the malleability of what has been produced.

Though I sought to copy every document that I found alongside noting its internet-based source and URL, if the internet version alters or vanishes does my copy still retain its status? It is quite easy to alter my copies and without a version that exists independent of my collection, there is little to use for verification. With a physical document, a researcher can possess it, secure it and fix it to ensure no alteration occurs. If they cannot privately own it they can at least direct their readers to the museum or archive where it lives. There its authenticity can be verified through various tests based on the document's physical properties. I can also direct people to this project's museum of documents. I can even provide them with their very own copy if they'd like one, a copy just as good as my own. Unfortunately, that in itself is, under our well-trodden logic of documentation, an indicator that the documents should perhaps not be trusted. I could perhaps count on the continuation of the document versions that are independent of me still living on the servers where I found them. However, the internet is the 'landscape of the present' (Dougherty and Schneider, 2011). This research demonstrated how many of those documents that are 'born digital' dissipated over time, overwritten, lost or inaccessible.

One of the key concerns of the digital archivist is not simply that the document may disappear, but that the means of interpreting it will also. In order for a digital document to speak reliably it needs a supporting environment of software. Equally, for that software to work it requires a supporting environment of hardware. Each level must have complete compatibility with the next in order for the document to be accessed. As a consequence the archiving of the digital document not only requires archiving the document, but also ensuring the archival of an environment in which the document can be accessed. Though it is possible that we may be able to develop initiatives where we use emulation to simulate the hardware necessary to run the software for these documents, the result may be an endless task of rewriting emulation software to integrate with the realities of archival hardware degradation and the necessity to replace parts with ever-changing slabs of silicon (the *Economist*, 2012; Levy, 2000a; Rothenberg, 2000). All of this of course relies on the proactive archival of those documents. Should they not be chosen as worthy of retention they will likely be lost and any concerns of emulating hardware or the correct storage format will be moot.

It is almost certain that, in the years to come, the sources that host the documents employed throughout this work will slowly dissipate as sites shut and archives are lost. At that point there will be little evidence that the book's assertions are supported beyond the (hopefully) well-preserved and -maintained archive that I have retained; an archive that alone is completely unverifiable. This is not an attempt to undermine my own work, but it is important to highlight this key issue of the performance of any type of research that uses internet-based sources. As more of our history begins to take place on the internet, the inherent malleable flux of it will bring serious difficulties to the long-held notions of what a document is, and how it can speak with authenticity and authority. However, equally, as more of our history begins to take place on the internet, we will be given little choice but to make the digital our field of enquiry as well. With born-digital documents comes the necessity to develop born-digital methods, ones that are dynamic, flexible and willing to challenge well-ingrained research practices (Dougherty and Schneider, 2011). Though I have focused on the difficulties of performing digital documentary analysis, it should not be forgotten that without the digital document, the following chapters would not exist, and a great deal of incredibly important history would have been forgotten. The digital document provides us with huge possibilities for insight into our social world. As the internet continues to aggregate increasing amounts of everyday minutia, we step closer and closer to building an archive of social reality. How we use that archive and the success of our attempts can only be judged by the quality of our results.

3
MP3.com and Napster: The Entrepreneurs of Risk

The MP3

The MP3's route to widespread user adoption was long and indirect. It began in the 1970s as an unproven concept of transmitting music over telephone lines. Professor Dieter Seitzer, working at the University of Erlangen-Nuremberg, was trying to optimise the transmission of speech over telephone lines as part of a wider project to expand the capacities and features of the telephone network. The idea of optimising music was a side-interest, but when he was denied a patent because of the examiner's verdict that the concept was 'impossible', he assigned one of his PhD students to prove them wrong. This kicked off a large collaborative process of research across the 1970s and 1980s to work out how to optimally compress audio whilst still retaining the music. Development was slow as often the researchers would be hindered by the limitations of contemporary technology. Researchers were only able to store a short sample of audio at a time due to relatively small storage capacities, and computer processing time was limited at the universities in which they were working. Eventually the researchers successfully compressed an entire song, 'Tom's Diner' by Suzanne Vega, in 1991. They took their work to the Fraunhofer Institute with the intention of rolling it out as a worldwide standard. Their proposal for the standard got submitted to the International Standards Organisation subdivision known as the Motion Picture Experts Group (MPEG). At the time, other groups working independently of each other at Phillips and Bell Labs also submitted similar inventions. MPEG merged a selection of these

14 technologies together to produce the ISO-MPEG-1 standard, a system of compression and decompression for both video and audio (Knopper, 2009). The designation 'MP3' comes from the construction of the standard itself. Comprised of five parts, the audio compression was only one of many aspects of the large project. Occupying the third part, the part of the standard that dealt with audio compression, were outlines for three generic codecs. The '3' in MP3 stands for the third codec of this third part (IIS Fraunhofer, 2009).

The goal for the MPEG was to develop a standard that would alleviate some of the difficulties that large media production companies had internally with storage and transmission during production work. As a variety of industry groups had worked to be at the forefront of digital media, standards were disparate, incompatible and proprietary. What was required was a single open standard that could alleviate these difficulties. The goal for the MPEG-1 was open, unrestricted access that could store media at a high quality whilst keeping size down. By standardising the data used by these media companies, it could be stored, used and transmitted over different platforms. Little interaction was needed between the sender and receiver because the standard meant the data would 'just work' rather than requiring engineers to liaise to ensure compatibility. The logic of the MPEG-1 standard was unrestricted rapid and simple mobility (Sterne, 2006).

The MPEG didn't see this openness as a problem. Media production was predominantly inside the remit of the groups seeking this open format, and few outsiders had the hardware to make use of it. However, in December 1991 a near-working version of the MPEG-1 standard began spreading across hobbyist forums, nearly two years before its official release in August 1993. Disseminated so far and wide across so many participating labs and research groups meant the standard couldn't be kept secret for long. Patel, Smith and Rowe were researchers working in the Computer Science Division at UC Berkley. They noticed that their work was often hindered because industry groups developing MP3 decoders were keeping much of their knowledge secret. Instead they used the MPEG committee draft of the standard to implement their own MPEG-1 decoder software which they swiftly released into the public domain, allowing others to use their decoder for their own innovations (Patel et al., 1993).

As experts simplified encoding and decoding MP3 files by building user-friendly tools and providing online guides, the standard spread across the internet and adoption increased throughout the 1990s. Rob Lord was a student at the University of California Santa-Cruz studying psychoacoustic audio compression; the same method by which the MP3 compression worked. Lord found the standard online and, with the help of his contacts at Sun Microsystems, encoded his band's music into MP2 (a lower quality but space-efficient element of the MPEG-1 standard), hosted it online and spread it via newsgroups. He found the reception from new fans worldwide so impressive he started up the 'Internet Underground Music Archive', a site that offered free MP2s of music by unknown bands (Knopper, 2009). Another programmer and musician, Justin Frankel, decided that the MP3 decoding software that already existed needed work and created WinAmp, a clean, accessible MP3 decoder which became the go-to application for playing and organising MP3s. As the music industry was enjoying the boom years of the CD in the 1990s, a whole new way of engaging with music was emerging across the internet just waiting for someone to capitalise on it.

MP3.com: a new type of music

It was late 1997 when Michael Robertson met Greg Flores. Flores had recently moved to San Diego and was interested in getting some work in the local computing industry. Having previously run his own computer consulting business Can Do Computing, Flores had seen Robertson's company, Filez, listed as one of the 'Top 25 Cool Companies of San Diego' in the *Tribune* and decided to give him a call. Filez was a search engine that provided a way of searching through the contents of thousands of file servers, allowing users to enter a query and find software, graphics, music and movies that were available on open and freely accessible file-servers around the internet. Today, this kind of functionality is built into popular search engines such as Google; however, at the time, specialisation was a must as most popular engines only provided access to websites. The two men found they could work well together, and Flores joined the company without pay. One of Flores' roles was to find new ways to drive traffic to the site. Although he took interest in watching what sites were climbing in popularity via site-ranking charts, he also took a closer look at their own site's search logs. Flores found that users were increasingly using their service to look for a file format called MP3. Having not really used them before, Flores downloaded one and was astonished by the sound quality that came from such a small file. After sharing his discovery with Robertson they decided to pursue the MP3 angle further. Their next step was to look into the availability of the domain name www.mp3.com. The domain had already been registered to Martin Paul, an employee of Network Solutions. Robertson and Flores contacted Paul and informed him they were interested in purchasing the rights to the domain. Paul was interested in why they would want the domain at all and when the men informed him that they wanted to start up an MP3 site he replied, 'What is MP3?' Paul had registered the domain name not because he was interested in MP3 files but because it was his handle that had been assigned to him by his employers at Network Solutions and he thought it might be nice to register it as a site. After a bit of haggling Robertson and Flores got the domain for $1,500 (Burke and Montgomery, 2002).

Having purchased the domain, Robertson and Flores turned their attention to the content. Still having little experience with MP3 files they decided to hire it in and acquired mp3shoppingmall.com, a small site that provided news and information about MP3. With the site they acquired the services of its Scandinavian owner who they paid a small monthly wage to run MP3.com. After transferring the content of mp3shoppingmall.com over to MP3.com they went live and got more than 10,000 unique hits. These numbers were particularly impressive because at the time the site had not been submitted to any search engines. These hits had come from users blindly surfing to MP3.com in the hope of finding something. Within 18 hours of the site going live, advertisers were to purchase ad space on the site. After selling $5,000 worth, Robertson had cleared the cost of the domain name and the content within the first day.

Robertson's vision for the site was as a space for connecting music with music fans efficiently. MP3.com would serve as a new distribution system for music consumption and as a means for artists to directly connect with their audience. Artists could upload their music as MP3 files and either sell them or give them to their fans for free. MP3.com hoped to be the first legitimate digital distribution system for music. To Robertson, this new way of selling music was much more efficient than the physical model of selling CDs and allowed for easy tracking of consumer purchasing and listening habits. The cost of distributing physical discs was high and promoting new music was difficult because the primary marketing tool, radio, had become increasingly difficult to penetrate due to the increasing degrees of centralisation and monopoly over the radio stations. For major labels, promotion and distribution was costly enough; for unsigned artists it was untouchable. To Robertson, the way forward seemed obvious; however, the labels disagreed. Uninterested in his site the major labels didn't buy into Robertson's idea, leaving him to do the groundwork searching for independent musicians to provide the content for his site (Burke and Montgomery, 2002).

As Robertson was unsuccessfully trying to sell the concept of digital distribution to the recording industry, another company, Diamond Multimedia, was also having problems convincing the recording industry of its vision. In late 1998 Diamond released the 'Rio PMP300', the device considered to be the first commercial MP3 player. Shortly thereafter California-based Diamond received an injunction from the Recording Industry Association of America (RIAA), which was looking to halt the spread of the new gadget. According to the RIAA, Diamond's Rio PMP300 violated the Audio Home Recording Act of 1992 (AHRA) because it did not have sufficient copy protection incorporated into it. The AHRA was initially brought in to protect the media industry from the proliferation of Digital Audio Tape recorders, which allowed home recording and copying of music without loss of sound quality. The Act required that all recording equipment implement a system of rights management called the 'Serial Copy Management System' (SCMS), which controlled whether a recording could be copied indefinitely, only once or at all. The system was meant to be a compromise between electronics manufacturers and the RIAA as it meant that indefinite copying could be controlled but consumers would be able to make a single copy of their digital content for back-up purposes (Gonzalez, 2000; Samuelson, 2003).

The US lower courts ruled against the RIAA which then went to appeal the decision. The RIAA claimed that as the act of moving an MP3 file from the computer to the device required copying the file, it encouraged replication of copyrighted material and would encourage online piracy. It was the gateway drug argument for copyright infringement. If a user was legally allowed to replicate copyrighted material in one setting, it may encourage more illicit infringement in other settings. The Ninth Circuit Court of Appeals disregarded the argument and upheld the lower courts' decision. The Court held that the device was not a digital recorder but a computer peripheral and therefore did not require SCMS. The device allowed for what the Court called 'space-shifting' the copying of a recording for the purpose of listening to it on other devices. The Court declared that copying recordings that had been legally acquired for the purpose of space-shifting was perfectly legal under the copyright law's definition of 'fair use'. As well as this ruling, which secured the rights of consumers to copy their legitimately acquired digital recordings, the ruling also placed computer hardware outside the remit of the AHRA (Kaplan, 1999).

Whilst this court case had been raging, Robertson's MP3.com had been booming. After realising that the major labels were not going to collaborate with him he had set his sights on unsigned artists instead. Artists were initially sceptical – many maintaining the prevailing opinion of the industry that a recording contract was key to success. Robertson and his team had to prove the worth of the service themselves. They provided the artists with web pages, converted their music to MP3 and scanned images of the band and their cover art. The process was very labour intensive so the company produced a series of user-friendly templates to empower the artists to create their own web page on MP3.com, an early example of user-generated content. This system spurred rapid growth and by July 1999 – just after the *RIAA v Diamond* case had been resolved – the site had 15,000 artists listed and a catalogue of nearly 100,000 songs to download (Burke and Montgomery, 2002).

Napster: building a network

When people tell the Napster story, the usual beginning is its release in June 1999 when Napster officially began operating. Another beginning could be in 1996 (prior to MP3.com's launch) when Shawn Fanning met Sean Parker and Jordan Ritter over an Internet Relay Chat (IRC) channel called w00w00. w00w00 was an online chat space for the discussion of net security, both how to build it up and how to knock it down. It was here that Shawn Fanning developed his interest for computer security and dabbled in both. Parker's entrepreneurial edge and love of computers also drew him to the IRC channels. Always on the look-out for the next big thing, w00w00 was Parker's connection to the newest ideas and developments in software. His current project was software that would sift through the web and return information based on a user's interests. Ritter was already an established member of the hacking community and being older than both Fanning and Parker had secured a job with a security company as a researcher; a hacker with pay. It was these connections with other programmers such as Parker and Ritter that formed the knowledge and support for Fanning's work on Napster: the inspiration came from the IRC medium itself.

The problem that Fanning set out to solve was expressed by his room-mate at Boston University; every time he looked for an MP3 the link turned out to be dead and the file had gone. Using systems similar to Robertson's original Filez.com, Fanning's room-mate often found that the search results were outdated and the file he was looking for had gone. Search engines and indexes lacked real-time presence awareness. They knew that a file had existed in a certain location when they did their scan, but they would not know if it was still there until it re-scanned those places again, often a few days too late. IRC worked differently as it was necessary to keep track of whether an individual was connected to the channel or not. If IRC worked like a site indexer you would probably attempt to talk to another user and find that they had logged off two days ago. To ensure real-time status it was necessary to somehow keep track of all of the unique connections and disconnection's occurring in the chat rooms. This persistence worked because the organisation of all connecting parties was managed by a central server. Everyone wishing to join the IRC channel would connect to the central server and the moment they disconnected the server would know and inform everybody else.

For Fanning to construct a file-sharing system, the basic principles from IRC could remain the same; all that was needed was a few extra layers of functionality. First, there had to be a persistent supply of files. With the Filez.com system of file-finding, most of the MP3s found were personal collections that had been left on freely accessible servers, some on purpose, some by accident. The actual files were out there, but they were hidden away in people's computers and although some had been left on servers, most MP3 collections were closed off in personal computers that did not function like servers. Second, the system most widely used for finding MP3 files was deeply

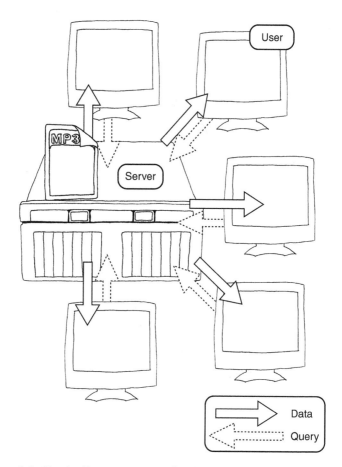

Figure 3.1 Simple client server network architecture

flawed in its lack of persistent presence awareness. Third, there had to be the capacity to transfer these files between computers easily (Figure 3.1).

The Napster software managed to overcome these problems elegantly. First, when setting up the software client the user would designate a folder that would be open to the public, usually the one that already had their MP3 collection in it. The Napster client would then act as an intermediary and make the folder open to other

Napster users with minimal technical knowledge on the part of the user. Then the Napster client would connect to the central Napster servers and send them information about the files contained in the designated folder. The client would maintain the connection so that, when the user logged off, the central servers knew those files had gone with them. To find files the user would type a query into the Napster client which would then ask the central server index and return a list of files with their locations. This gave the index of files the presence awareness that was so lacking from other search facilities and meant that all of the results had a file at the end of them. Finally, the user could select which file they wanted and prompt the software to download it. The software would initiate a direct connection between the two computers and transfer the file. This meant the transfer happened without the involvement of the central servers, leaving them to the task of co-ordinating and indexing. If all transfers went through the servers they would have overloaded in seconds, something that over Napster's history they were constantly threatening to do without the extra load of file transfers (Figure 3.2).

The software was developed with a large amount of help from the w00w00 community, with various builds of the software being distributed amongst them to help to fix bugs and improve code. They formed the core group who received the first working versions of the software and also ran the servers. Originally maintained by another w00w00 member, the servers were eventually turned over to Jordan Ritter. Ritter ran them free of charge and consistently improved them so that they could handle more and more users, often working for long stretches of time using Ritalin to keep himself sharp. Much of Fanning's coding happened at his uncle's office, finding that he was unable to work in his dorm room at Boston University. Eventually, he stopped going to university altogether and dedicated his time fully to the project. It was here his uncle (John) saw what Shawn was working on and saw it as a business opportunity. John Fanning already owned a business called Chess.net but had a history of failed ventures behind him that had left him in large amounts of debt. John suggested turning Napster into a business, offering to help Shawn out with the business end of the project. Up until then Napster had been nothing more than an interesting project to Shawn. However, pleased that his uncle believed in Napster, Shawn agreed

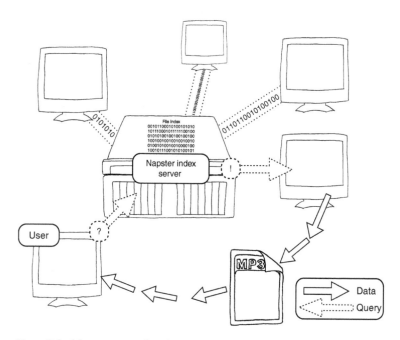

Figure 3.2   Napster network architecture

and John quickly drew up the papers. In May 1999, Napster Inc. was born.

Sean Parker, entrepreneurial as he was, shared this vision of Napster as a business venture and set to work contacting the many computer industry contacts he had made from networking around Northern Virginia. As John Fanning set up the Napster offices in a dilapidated former hotel on the Wharf, Parker contacted Ben Lilienthal whose server he had configured a year earlier. Lilienthal was a 26-year-old entrepreneur who had sold his email business to CMGI and had some money to spare. Interested in the possibilities Napster presented he contacted Jason Grosfeld, who had backed his business before. Grosfeld, a prior investment analyst for Black Rock Financial, had just started his own hedge fund and was looking to capitalise on the growth of broadband and computing power; Napster seemed perfect.

Grosfeld and Lilienthal weren't the only people to think so either. Both Parker and John Fanning continued to solicit the attentions of various technology investors and top-tier IT specialists. As the amount of users continued to grow from hundreds to thousands, Grosfeld conducted an investigation into the legality of the service. In the hopes of alleviating Grosfeld's worries, John Fanning contacted Andrew Bridges. Bridges was an IP lawyer who at the time was defending Diamond Multimedia in the suit brought by the RIAA over the Rio MP3 player. Bridges wasn't interested and forwarded him on to an associate who also passed until Fanning eventually captured the attention of Washington-based lawyer, Seth Greenstein. Greenstein wrote Napster a 27-page memo that outlined a variety of defences for Napster's obvious liabilities against the recording industry. This document would be invaluable to Napster's future leaders when the industry came calling. Lilienthal, having enlisted the interest of venture capital firm Draper Atlantic, was optimistic about the legal issues, but less so about John Fanning. Investing in Napster meant investing in John. When Fanning had drawn up the incorporation paper work in May 1999, he had assigned himself 70% of the company, leaving Shawn with only 30%. Only interested in Shawn they attempted to encourage him to leave his uncle's majority control and start up a new company with the same product, but Shawn refused. As negotiations broke down between the investors and John Fanning, who refused to give up his majority share, Grosfeld and Lilienthal bailed out.

Despite these setbacks John Fanning still managed to secure some funding from Draper Atlantic in exchange for future rights to 1 million shares (or 10% of the company) at 20 cents each, regardless of their price at the time. There were a multitude of meetings throughout June and July 1999, many of them unsuccessful. Investors loved the project and loved Shawn even more, but when the time came to negotiate terms the meetings often fell apart. It was at one of these failed meetings that Napster's second initial investor, Yosi Amram, came on board. Fanning was due to discuss an investment deal with Andy Evans, a San Francisco-based venture capitalist who managed money for Bill Gates, and Amram was invited to sit in. Amram and Fanning had met through their love of chess in Cambridge Massachusetts, playing games together in Harvard Square. Amram was a graduate of both MIT and Harvard Business School and made his money founding a small dot.com start-up called Individual Inc. which conducted automated net trawling to provide companies with email or fax reports about useful information it had found. Fanning had already asked if he would invest in Napster but Amram turned him down saying he would not invest if Fanning was the CEO. However, seeing Andy Evans' interest impressed Amram and he reconsidered. Although Evans eventually failed to invest, Amram agreed to on three conditions: Amram would name the CEO; Fanning, the new CEO and Amram would form the board meaning Amram could always outvote Fanning if needed; and the whole company would move to California where Amram could keep an eye on them. Fanning accepted.

When they arrived in California, Shawn, Parker and John Fanning met Amram's choices for Napster's new CEO, Eileen Richardson, and VP of business development, Bill Bales. For the first few months the four of them haphazardly attempted to work out what they would do next and Richardson worked on securing further investment. The infrastructure that had existed since the initial w00w00 releases of the software was straining under the weight of increasing amounts of users. The software had long since spread outside the w00w00 group through a combination of subtle grassroots word of mouth and comparatively blundering media coverage. With a new college term approaching it was likely that usage would increase to the point that the system would collapse. However, Napster's new team was making little progress in these fledgling months as the veneer of legitimate business wore thin. Parker described a state of perpetual chaos in the office where his presentations were cut short by Richardson and Bales who expressed irrational panic and irrational optimism respectively. The primary aim of the executives was that of growth; grow the user base to such a degree that the record companies would be forced to negotiate. Then they would worry about the business model (Menn, 2003).

MP3.com: selling digital

In July 1999, a month after Napster's official release, Michael Robertson of MP3.com floated his company on the stock market. It had been surviving almost exclusively on advertising; however, the growing popularity of the site had generated a lot of interest from investors. The site's profile had been steadily growing with music fans taking greater interest in the MP3 format. Larger artists such as Tom

Petty, Alanis Morissette and Tori Amos had also begun to use the site to give away free tracks as album promotions. MP3.com also got its first taste of litigation when it was dragged into a lawsuit filed against a small company called Nullsoft by PlayMedia. Nullsoft was the developer of a software MP3 player called WinAmp which was gaining in popularity thanks in part to its promotion and distribution on MP3.com, alongside many other MP3 software products. Nullsoft had been accused of infringing on PlayMedia's copyright by utilising its MP3 decoding algorithms in WinAmp. MP3.com got dragged in because of its role as a WinAmp distributor. However, a month later Nullsoft was acquired by AOL and one day after the case was settled. Nullsoft purchased a licence for PlayMedia's code (which it was no longer using anyway) and MP3.com walked away unscathed. Just under two months later MP3.com's IPO raised $344.4 million, selling 12.3 million shares at $28 each, $2 above the highest estimate. Nullsoft went on to develop even more innovative software that led to significant friction between Nullsoft's anarchic founder and his new corporate owners (Glasner, 1999; Lipton Krigel, 1999a, 1999b).

MP3.com was doing well and the investment from the IPO alongside its continuing advertising income gave the company the money it needed to innovate. The site's users, though enthusiastic about the possibilities of MP3s, were still not accustomed to the idea of purchasing them. MP3s were still thoroughly tethered to the home computer. They were an addition to the music collection rather than a replacement. The lack of compatibility with existing hardware outside of their computers combined with the relative low audio quality meant that MP3s were not seen as a legitimate alternative to CDs, especially not one that should be paid for. For many users, MP3.com was a sampler site to find new music which would then be bought from a CD retailer. Robertson capitalised on this by making a deal with Buy.com, a well-known online retailer, that allowed Buy.com to sell CDs and music merchandise directly from MP3.com, whilst Buy.com would open a speciality store to promote the MP3.com artists (Olsen, 1999).

The next step Robertson took was to launch My.MP3.com, an online media platform that provided two services. The first was to allow users to listen to a CD instantly after they had purchased it. If users purchased a CD online from a participating retailer they were able to enter a code into MP3.com and have that album added to their account. Whilst they waited for the physical product to be delivered they would have access to an online streamed version. Once the CD was delivered they would have the 'real' version of the music, and also retain access to a convenient streaming alternative. The second service was an extension of the 'instant listening' facility called 'Beam-it'. Beam-it allowed users to add previously purchased music to their account by using their CDs as proof of purchase. A user would simply put the CD into their computer and the site would verify its validity. If it was genuine the equivalent music would be made available on the user's account to stream at their leisure without having to upload the content themselves. MP3.com was providing one of the first media-focused online storage services where users could stream their music collection on any computer and leave their discs behind. Robertson's long-term plan was to roll out a series of complementary services that allowed streaming through mobile media devices, telephones and home audio hardware. An MP3.com customer's music collection would never be far away. Robertson had My.MP3.com all planned out. His only hurdle was the major recording industries, and the suit they filed nine days after it launched.

To make the My.MP3.com service work the company needed to host a large catalogue of music on its servers for users to stream. Part of the appeal to consumers was the instant access and lack of effort on their part. Users didn't have to upload the music, a process that would have been laborious and slow at a time when the average home user was using dial-up. Instead, the company uploaded music to its servers so that users only had to authenticate their access to it. However, to pre-empt the majority of music requests, MP3.com had to provide a large enough catalogue. This obviously meant that artists from all major record labels had to be accounted for, as well as more popular indie label acts. To get the content to host, MP3.com bought 45,000 CDs, encoded them into files and uploaded them to its servers. It was this act that brought the music industry's attention to MP3.com.

The plaintiffs – represented by the RIAA – complained that the single act of copying the CD was a violation of their copyright that warranted damages of $150,000 per CD. MP3.com held that it was a fair use of the content and that it was simply moving the music from one medium to another for the convenience of customers who had already purchased the music. Similar 'music locker' services were being employed by other companies at the time – the difference was that the users did the uploading and the companies were paying licensing and royalty fees. MP3.com didn't feel that licensing was legitimate, believing that both it and the users were operating within the law. The company and its users had paid for access to the content and, as it was legal for a user to perform the same action under fair use, why not with the company's assistance? In April 2000 the court disagreed and sided with the industry, and the company's market value plummeted by 40%. Damages were yet to be determined and the case would reconvene in August 2000 unless MP3.com could settle with all five of the plaintiffs beforehand (Borland, 2000a; Macavinta, 2000b).

In May 2000 the company removed all major-label content from its service, dropping its market value further, only to get a slight reprise when it made its first settlement with companies one and two, Time Warner and BMG, a month later. MP3.com paid an undisclosed settlement and licensing fee allowing it to restore those labels' content on its service (Hu, 2000a; Konrad, 2000). In July 2000 the company settled with the third label, EMI, on similar terms. Although things looked promising, Robertson was sceptical. Prior to the settlement Robertson had criticised the industry's visions for digital retail stating that people would not be willing to pay for digital content if it was wrapped in a system that controlled how it was used. EMI had announced that it would be looking to digital distribution as the next step in music retail; however, it was also working with other labels on a secure digital music initiative (SDMI) to regain control over their products. Similar to the SCMS, the SDMI would set an agreed standard so that only industry-approved MP3 files would work with industry-approved hardware and software. This system of 'data rights management' (DRM) would allow the regulation of not only the copying of media, but also how it was used, what devices it could be used on and how many times it could be played; not to mention who was allowed to produce the software and hardware to play the files. Compared with the open flexibility of the MP3s floating around Napster and Robertson's site, for users these 'official' MP3s were far from better (Macavinta, 2000a; Miles, 1999).

Napster: exciting disruption

Napster had existed relatively under the radar up until the lawsuit brought by the RIAA in December 1999. Searches for relevant news articles dated before the trial produced only five results: four of which resulted from online tech news sites Newsbytes.com and Salon.com. The RIAA, again representing the five major record companies, accused Napster of facilitating copyright infringement. This infringement, they argued, had cut into their CD sales and they demanded the service to be shut down immediately. This motion brought Napster's existence to the attention of the mainstream press and with it, the mainstream population. Between February and August 2000 Napster's user base climbed from 1.1 to 6.7 million and it would continue to climb to 50 million before its eventual closure (McCourt and Burkart, 2003; Naughton, 2001). What had been a grass-roots, bottom-up spread now had top-down international media coverage. *Newsweek* even ran a cover story on Shawn Fanning in March 2000. The article celebrated Napster's ability to provide access to a range of music and posited it as a technology of the young and the future, stating that 'only a 19-year-old mind could have invented it. Certainly no one who grew up in the analogue days...'. The article recognised the contention brought by the RIAA yet it positioned the music industry as an old dog that required a push into the inevitable future. For the internet service providers (ISPs) complaining about the amount of bandwidth being dedicated to Napster, *Newsweek* saw Napster as the reminder that the internet is a place for users to publish as well as to consume (Levy, 2000b). *Time Magazine* followed suit and published another cover story on Fanning the following October. The story portrayed him as the average college teen who had a genius spark of inspiration and changed the world. Writing of his decision to leave college to work on the Napster project, the article celebrated his decision as the act of a man who worked selflessly for a greater cause (Greenfeld et al., 2000).

These articles presented Fanning with a degree of fascination, showing him both as average suburban teen and revolutionary disruptor in one. What these articles did not present him as, however, was a criminal. Although there was coverage of the trial, the stimulus for the coverage in the first place, to the press Fanning was never a criminal. The danger he embodied was portrayed as exciting disruption rather than unwanted destruction. These articles had a strong role in the Napster mythology, fuelling the narrative of new versus old that dominated the debates long after. To the press Napster espoused an ideology of democratisation of access through creative destruction. Had the press known that a decade later their own industry would suffer digital disruption, they may have taken a different approach (Barnett, 2009; Kirwan, 2009; Thorpe, 2009). As *Time Magazine* appeared to celebrate the disruption of one content industry, co-chairman of Atlantic Records Group Val Azzoli rather prophetically said, 'It's not just music I'm worried about. It's all intellectual properties. If you can take music, you can take everything else too' (Greenfeld et al., 2000).

In the courtroom Napster's ultimate fate lay in its architecture. Both sides appeared to agree on how Napster worked technically; however, they came to radically differing definitions due to their interpretations of the system. Neither side argued about 'how' Napster worked; the fight was about what legal category that technology fit into. Napster Inc. classified itself as an ISP. Like an ISP it provided connections and routed data without hosting it. Under the Digital Millennium Copyright Act of 1998 (DMCA), ISPs were not liable for copyright infringement that their networks facilitated, if they acted to remove offenders from their service. Furthermore, Napster Inc. claimed that computers were 'home recording devices' and thus protected under the AHRA. The RIAA challenged this assertion citing a prior ruling that computer hard drives were not classifiable as home recording devices (Pemberton, 2000; Spitz and Hunter, 2005); this being the ruling that lost the RIAA its case against Diamond Multimedia a few months earlier. Instead, the RIAA wished to define Napster as a listing service, agreeing that it did not host the content, but it also did not act to transmit the content either. Napster's function was one of search, indexing and linking, something not protected under the DMCA or the AHRA.

The eventual court decision was made on 26 July 2000 by Judge Marilyn Hall Patel, who granted the record companies' injunction request. Patel stated that the industry had successfully demonstrated that Napster was facilitating the unauthorised transfer of copyrighted material, and that the defence's claim of fair use – that Napster could be used for space-shifting – was not strong enough. Although the system could be used for such purposes, the burden of proving this lay with Napster, which could not produce sufficient evidence to back its claim. In Napster's favour she stated that it was clear that the material being transferred was not then being used for commercial purposes, but simply by users for their own personal use. Napster was facilitating a newly emerging consumer demand for online access to media. However, Napster was not simply providing a digital version of an already-purchased physical product for space-shifting, but provided the capacity to distribute digital copies to people who had not proven ownership of the physical version. Patel noted that, though Napster facilitated this unwarranted access, she also believed the studies presented by the music industry to demonstrate that users were foregoing purchasing for downloading were flawed. Ultimately, however, her verdict was that Napster's operation would lead to a clear economic loss for the rights holders. The court ruled that until it was able to operate in a way that did not infringe upon the copyrights of others, Napster would cease immediately (*A&M Records v Napster*, 2000).

However, this immediate cease did not happen. Just under two months prior to this ruling, Napster Inc. had secured investment from Hummer Winblad Venture Partners. With the $13 million investment also came a change of leadership with Hank Barry being installed as interim CEO by Hummer Winblad. Barry was a graduate from Stanford Law School and had a background in technology and entertainment law, acting as advisor to clients such as Walt Disney and, coincidentally, A&M Records. One of his first actions as interim CEO was to file appeal to the court after the injunction was ordered, winning Napster the right to continue operating unfettered until the appeal was settled (Barnes, 2000; Hartley, 2009).

A few months later in October 2000, Bertelsmann Music Group (BMG), one of the plaintiffs in the ongoing case, broke ranks. It announced that it would also be investing $60 million in Napster Inc. to develop a legal service that preserved the Napster experience. In exchange for the loan, Bertelsmann would drop its support of the lawsuit and take a 58% interest in Napster once the service was developed. By delaying stake ownership until after Napster had re-launched as a legal product, BMG protected itself from being drawn into the trial that it continued to pursue with the other media companies. Between November 2000 and February 2001, Napster Inc.

worked on its legitimate system whilst the original infringing infras-tructure continued to buzz with increasing amounts of new users. Bertelsmann allowed the system to continue, concerned that Napster would lose its user base if the system was removed before an alterna-tive was available (BMG, 2000; Clark, 2000; Menn, 2003). In February 2001 the court announced its decision on Napster's appeal. The Ninth Circuit Court of Appeals upheld the original declaration that Napster did indeed infringe the copyrights of the record companies: Napster was liable for copyright infringement and had to cease operating immediately. The only change to the original documents was the scope of the injunction. The original injunction found Napster liable for any copyrighted files that moved through its network. The new one instead maintained that Napster had to be aware of specific files first, and then fail to take action to remove them before it would be liable (*A&M Records v Napster*, 2001). Napster was left with a debt of $40 million to the record companies and no legitimate business. If Napster was to survive it would have to fully revise its system to act legitimately. It would be impossible to control the open system as it was. The only solution was to completely rebuild Napster as a legitimate service. Napster shut down the infrastructure shortly after the ruling and the index servers went offline, dissolving the network.

The now defunct Napster Inc. had to move fast to regain its user base and avoid dissolution. In July 2001 Bertelsmann replaced Hank Barry with its own manager, Konrad Hilbers, who had pre-viously worked as senior management for Bantam Doubleday Dell, AOL Europe and before Napster, Bertelsmann BMG. Months went by with little progress on a legal service. The major labels had placed a $250 million price on content licensing making legitimate col-laboration incredibly difficult. Bertelsmann refused what it saw as a ridiculous fee and Napster was left with little content for its system. Living up to the breadth of content available on the original system would be hard enough. Without major-label artists the project was dead in the water.

As Napster's funds began to dwindle it returned to Bertelsmann for more money to continue work. However, instead of providing fund-ing, BMG suggested that it purchase Napster instead. With Napster's poor track record in achieving licensing deals with other labels, it was hoped BMG would have greater success negotiating licenses.

Napster's board of directors rallied against the terms of the purchase and refused to sell. CEO Hilbers resigned his post in protest along with several senior executives, including its founder Shawn Fanning (Borland, 2002b). Napster filed for bankruptcy in June 2002. This protected the company from the infringement lawsuits that were due the following year, but also meant Napster's assets would go to auction. With more than $100 million in liabilities to record companies, law firms and Bertelsmann, the only bid for the company came from Bertelsmann. The latter offered to wipe the slate clean of all debts and in exchange it would get Napster.

However, the transaction did not go smoothly because other record companies and publishers took issue with the sale. They claimed that the loan BMG initially made to Napster was not really a loan but equity in the company, and thus should be discounted as part of the deal. The loan had been made when other banks were unwilling to take the risk and had an interest rate much lower than average rate. Under such conditions the loan could arguably have been seen as a move to stake a claim on Napster's equity rather than as a financial transaction. With much of the investment from BMG just going towards the daily running of the company and Hilbers maintaining contact with his old BMG boss, the purchase seemed less than legitimate.

The question for the courts was whether BMG's investment was equity or a secured loan. If it was a loan the deal stood and BMG had a massive advantage over other potential buyers. If it was an equity investment then the funds had been used up in running the company and the debt to BMG should be discounted, making the purchase an equal bid and removing BMG's advantage. The court made its decision in September 2002 siding with the majority record industries and denying Bertelsmann the purchase. Hours later, Hilbers announced that Napster would be forced into liquidation and any hope of its creditors getting their money back was gone (Borland, 2002a; Menn, 2003). Just under three months later Roxio bought Napster's assets taking its technology, brand name and trademarks for $5.3 million whilst leaving the company's debts. These were left for Bertelsmann to fight alone. The legal battle began in 2003 and ended in 2006 with a $60 million settlement to Universal Music Group. The settlement resulted in the sale of BMG Publishing to Vivendi, concentrating the recording industry even further (Kane, 2002; the *New York Times*, 2002).

MP3.com: dismantling innovation

It was August 2000 and MP3.com had managed to settle with four of the five plaintiffs before the court date. Shortly after the EMI settlement MP3.com came to an agreement with Sony under similar terms as the other labels. However, the remaining company, Universal, chose not to follow the example of its peers and took MP3.com to court. Again, Robertson argued that the service was designed not to infringe on copyrights but in fact to promote the sale of industry content by requiring a CD to be purchased before access was given. The court disagreed and the company was found liable for a potential $118 million in damages to Universal, dropping its stock value to the lowest it had been in a year. Matters were not improved by the sudden filing of yet another lawsuit by independent label Zomba, which also claimed the My.MP3.com service had violated its copyrights (Luening, 2000).

However, at least with the major lawsuits out the way, MP3.com could resume work towards producing a cloud-based music service. The company announced its intentions to become a music infrastructure service and acquired more licenses to increase its catalogue size further. The company cleared its issues with Universal for $53.4 million, but also picked up another lawsuit filed by Unity Entertainment (Borland, 2000b; Hu, 2000b; Kary, 2001). In early 2001 the company announced that it would be providing software tools to give completely free access to its licensed music collection to developers. This meant that anyone could design complementary software or hardware that would depend on the MP3.com content database. This provided rival companies the opportunity to produce music services without having to pay licensing fees. It was a bold move that had the potential to cause an explosion in innovating new ways of accessing music beyond radio, discs and television. At a time when many were frustrated by the music industry's continued dedication to SDMI, MP3.com opened the door 'in the spirit of open-source' (Oien quoted in Hansen, 2001a). The industry initiative meant only a select few companies were being allowed to produce software and hardware to work with digital music. Outside innovators were desperate for access and MP3.com was offering a loophole. The company was adamant that it was not stepping on the toes of the SDMI group; however, many industry analysts were sceptical.

In March 2001 the company lost its case against indie label TVT Records and was set to pay out yet more damages; however, it also announced a new service called 'Transfer2Device'. The service allowed users to wirelessly transfer music from their MP3.com accounts to portable devices without first having to connect to a PC. Though MP3.com had said that it would limit its work with device developers until it had adopted the SDMI standards, it was still perhaps a bit too close for comfort (Hansen, 2001a; Mariano, 2001a). Throughout March and April 2001 the company began to promote big label bands but also received notification of another lawsuit from a group of well-known musicians, again in response to its original iteration of My.Mp3.com. In May 2001 it announced the launch of its NetCD service, a purely digital download service where customers could purchase an album in digital format with no physical equivalent. This was a landmark shift in digital distribution where the MP3 was positioned not as an aside to the CD, but as a product in itself. Two years before Apple's iTunes hit the market and brought digital music to the mass market, MP3.com had started the first digital music store. Eleven days later Vivendi Universal (VU) announced its intention to take over MP3.com (Borland and Hu, 2001; Mariano, 2001c).

The acquisition took just over three months, during which VU announced it intended to utilise the MP3.com technology infrastructure of NetCD to build its own digital distribution platform, PressPlay. Many were sceptical about the manner in which the deal had been dealt with and were concerned that the litigation MP3.com underwent was more than simply a disagreement over copyrights. Universal had been the only label from the original lawsuit that refused to settle and took MP3.com back to court to claim eventual damages of $53.4 million. At the time of MP3.com's IPO it had been valued at $28 a share with a market high. However, after the major-label's settlement, damages pay-outs and a ruling that opened the doors for further claims, that value had been reduced to $5 a share; the rate at which VU bought the company (Borland and Hu, 2001; Burke and Montgomery, 2002).

Shortly after the acquisition Robertson was removed from his position as CEO and replaced with the company's president Robin Richards. Robertson was given a job as advisor to VU CEO Jean-Marie Messier, though he also expressed a wish to move on to new projects

(Mariano, 2001b). A couple of months later under new ownership the company split into two, one remaining as MP3.com and providing music streaming, the other becoming MP3 Technologies, a separate company that would provide the technology for MP3.com as well as other VU projects. Primarily, MP3 Technologies would be involved in developing VU's PressPlay system as well as eventually providing the media group with consumer behaviour tracking and profiling systems that would form the basis of targeted marketing campaigns (Lettice, 2003; Mariano, 2001c). At the end of 2001 MP3.com made a deal with disc distributor CD Baby, which provided warehousing and sale of CDs for the independent artists on the site. This ensured a continued provision of physical media from the site even as it launched its risky PressPlay service. PressPlay offered consumers access to VU's catalogue at various subscription rates. Different rates determined the amount of song streams a user could access as well as the amount of downloads. The files offered were far removed from the open MP3 standard that, despite the death of Napster, was still being traded across unauthorised sharing networks. A far cry from Robertson's hopes of an always accessible music collection, PressPlay's files were locked down to prevent replication, could only play on computers and excluded mobile MP3 players (Hansen, 2001b).

The service operated fairly unsuccessfully across 2002 and was eventually sold in May 2003. The major labels had become increasingly disinterested in the digital market and had been closing services wholesale. Roxio purchased the service from VU for $12.5 million and eventually combined it with the Napster brand it had bought at auction six months earlier. The MP3.com brand was also sold a few months later to CNET, a prominent technology news group, which purchased the domain name but not the content and eventually relaunched it as an MP3 information and streaming site, much akin to the company's original incarnation. The MP3.com archive which consisted of all the artist-generated websites and millions of songs were an uncertainty. VU initially sent out emails informing artists that it would be destroyed as the company no longer had a use for it. Robertson pleaded with VU to allow the archive to be copied to Archive.org, a non-profit group dedicated to maintaining the remains of old non-profitable but culturally significant web content. Such a move would allow the MP3.com archive to remain as public domain content and allow the artists to regain their work. However, the company dismissed the idea as too dangerous and many believed the archive to be lost, which in a sense it was. A few months later it emerged that the archive had been sold to a VU spin-off company called Trusonic which provided muzak to hotels, restaurants and other businesses. The archive was incorporated into its catalogue and, although artists received royalties if their music was used, the rest of the catalogue remained VU's private property (Orlowski, 2004).

Myth

The public history of digital distribution to a great extent begins and ends with Napster. In its short time it seemingly appeared from nowhere, incited media revolution and was martyred by the incumbent media industries. However, within this history, the part played by Napster is not quite as selfless or grand. The development of Napster undermines the media's imagery of the inspired college revolutionary, and puts in its place a much more realistic arrangement of creativity and innovation; one based on imitation, iteration and communal development. His college room-mate, the w00w00 community and Jordan Ritter all assisted in the development of the Napster system. Pre-existing technologies such as IRC and the increasing prevalence of the MP3 format were contributory factors that made the environment ripe for Napster's development. It was not the case that Napster began the shift to digital distribution as a spark of inspiration and fervent activity. The key components of Napster's development had already been put into place – what Fanning did was to combine them.

Though Fanning's software got taken up as a symbol of the democratising of media distribution, a key feature of Napster's design was that it was centralised around one controllable access point. This controllable point was seen to be exploitable by John Fanning and Sean Parker, and was approached as such in their hunt for investment capital. The centralised architecture meant the venture capital firms and BMG could cultivate aspirations of turning the user activity of the Napster network into a profitable product. Had Napster been allowed to continue on its intended trajectory, it is unlikely that it would have remained a symbol of free-media revolution. Instead,

Napster would have become the first step in the development of a mediocre business facing digital media enterprise.

The true destabilising force in the tale was the MP3 format. The open standards of its use and design lacked any consideration of rights or ownership over the information it encoded. Had this been implemented from the beginning the Napster system and the developments at MP3.com would have been unable to happen. Instead, the MP3 had been allowed to disseminate within technically minded music-loving communities. It was these communities of individuals looking for MP3 files that sparked Robertson's interest. His innovations at MP3.com, though relatively forgotten in comparison with Napster, were more revolutionary in that they began to build up an infrastructure focused on the value of access to media rather than media objects. They capitalised on the faculties of the MP3 to provide the services to time- and space-shift media collections. Robertson's most radical move was to perceptually detach the music from the necessity of the CD. Direct retail of MP3 files demonstrated the concept of digital retail whilst My.MP3 encouraged the perception that the CD was simply one way of accessing purchased music. Robertson's eventual plans to roll out the My.MP3 system to integrate with media hardware manufacturers indicated a trajectory that would have bypassed the CD for day-to-day music engagement, leaving it simply as packaging for the initial purchase, or perhaps even bypassing it altogether.

The reaction to Napster and the innovations at MP3.com indicated that the incumbent media industries were not looking for such a disruption to their well-honed distribution system. Both disruptors were centralised – Napster in its architecture, and MP3.com in its organisation. Centralisation meant liability. By claiming control and ownership over these disruptive systems the innovators made themselves vulnerable. If the digital distribution of media were to continue, the network architecture would have to be decentralised and the individuals focused purely on the act of distribution.

4
GNUtella: Decentralising the Masses

It was 1999 and Justin Frankel was working in his cubicle at AOL when he came across Napster. As a programmer and music lover Frankel appreciated the ingenuity of the code but took issue with the profit motive that drove Napster Inc. Frankel approved of file-sharing as a way of empowering people via the free flow of information, but disagreed with someone making a profit from it. To Frankel, if you created a network like Napster, it shouldn't be about controlling the network, but doing everything possible to stop its control: that was good karma. Of course, the Napster that controlled the network also allowed it to form, it facilitated all of this sharing, but Frankel also saw that this centralisation made it vulnerable to control and disintegration. If a truly open and free file-sharing network were to succeed, it would have to operate differently; to Frankel it was an interesting problem.

Nullsoft

Frankel began his coding career before high school, teaching himself by playing around with his brother's Atari 8-bit computer. By the time he got to high school he was proficient enough to run the school network, wrote them an email program and developed a key logger to log what his teachers typed on their machines; the latter project more for his own amusement than for school productivity. After graduating in 1996 he went to Utah University to study computer science but dropped out after two semesters due to disagreements with his professors (Kushner, 2004). Like many technically savvy people of the time,

Frankel was picking up a lot of music from the internet, but finding that MP3 software to play it was in short supply. Being the tinkering type Frankel began a small coding project to make himself some MP3 software that had the functionality and efficiency he wanted. Shortly after finishing the first build Frankel formed the company Nullsoft – an anarchic nod to Microsoft – and began distributing his software which he dubbed WinAmp, short for Windows Amplifier, under a shareware licence. On his parent's advice Frankel reluctantly added a donation option to the software where users could voluntarily give him $10 for his work. In the first 18 months, 15 million people had downloaded WinAmp with a sizeable portion making the voluntary donation. With tens of thousands of dollars coming in every month and popularity rising, Nullsoft received more and more calls from companies looking to buy into Frankel's product. However, not being the type to go for a corporate lifestyle he remained cool to many of the offers he received, often prioritising his ideals over business. The software had always carried the tag line 'WinAmp whips the llama's ass', an homage to Chicago street singer Wesley Willis. When a large pharmaceutical company wanted WinAmp for corporate presentations, it offered him big money to purchase it without the tag line; Frankel refused (Kushner, 2004; Wisniowski, 2008).

Frankel had a different business ethic to the companies that came to solicit his software. His approach that he called 'sustainable software' placed the software and its users above business considerations. This ethic applied to Frankel's next project, SHOUTcast, an internet broadcasting program that allowed anyone to set up their own internet radio station which could easily be listened to via WinAmp. Released in December 1998, SHOUTcast brought some to speculate that the American Society for Composers, Authors, and Publishers (ASCAP) would take issue with the software due to its circumvention of the DMCA which had been passed two months prior. Under the DMCA, web-casters were required to pay a statutory licence fee to record companies in addition to the normal licensing fees that analogue radio paid. The fee, which curbed the proliferation of internet radio, had been set at 6.5% of the station's gross revenue (though the industry had been aiming for 41.5% and at the time was appealing the percentage). With SHOUTcast providing the opportunity for anyone to become a broadcaster, ASCAP was going to have a tough time enforcing the rules (Copyright.gov, 1998; Hu, 1998; Macavinta, 1998; Van Buskirk, 2006).

In March 1999 Nullsoft received a suit from PlayMedia accusing Nullsoft of infringing the copyright of its AMP MP3 playback software. PlayMedia claimed that the WinAMP code was significantly similar to its AMP code and wanted an injunction placed on Nullsoft to stop it distributing WinAmp. Nullsoft claimed that the accusations were unjustified but also made the move to use another open-source decoder instead. Shortly afterwards in May 1999 MP3.com was named in the suit as the largest distributor and promoter of WinAmp. However, a few weeks later Nullsoft was purchased by AOL for $100 million and days after that the dispute was settled out of court: Nullsoft paid for a licence it no longer needed, MP3.com walked away unscathed and Justin Frankel entered the corporate world of AOL (Jones, 1999; Lipton Krigel, 1999a, 1999b, 1999d).

Along with Nullsoft, AOL bought Spinner.com, a leading online music company specialising in web radio. AOL, despite being an ISP, was looking to move into media and it saw online music delivery as the next step. AOL moved Nullsoft from Sedona to San Francisco to an office it would share with the Spinner team, where it became clear to Frankel that this buyout may not have been the best move for him. The massive amounts of money flying around scared off his girlfriend, the hacking communities he had previously frequented began accusing him of being a corporate sellout and the office got turned into a cubicle jungle: 'Three months after we arrived, they built all these cubicles, and it sucked' (Frankel quoted in Kushner, 2004). Nullsoft continued to work on WinAmp and SHOUTcast, and, despite being in a corporate environment, still had an anarchic twist to it that AOL couldn't (or wouldn't due to the profitability of Nullsoft's creativity) suppress. Despite the 'Dilbertisation' of Nullsoft the team was still fairly autonomous as AOL focused on continuing its expansion into the media business.

On 10 January 2000 AOL announced its intention to purchase media behemoth Time Warner. At a purchase price of $165 billion it was the biggest merger in history but also was, as the *New York Times* put it, 'the best evidence yet that old and new media are converging' (Hansell, 2000). Time Warner needed a way into the net and AOL needed access to media that would encourage more subscriptions. AOL was also already working on a digital jukebox service, ready to be filled with content from the Time Warner catalogue and planned to bundle Time Warner cable TV with internet subscriptions. Napster, the only real danger to the media industry, had been quelled, the courts having ruled it to be operating unlawfully. Despite the impending appeal, BMG was moving in to monetise the internet upstart and by February 2000 Napster would be taken offline for good. With Napster out of the way the concept of the internet as a profitable, managed, media distribution platform was flourishing.

Napster also had another enemy, one who felt that sharing was good karma, but profiting from sharing was bad karma. Frankel, along with long-time Nullsoft programmer Tom Pepper, had spent their company time working on a Napster rival that would completely deflate the once poster child of internet file-sharing. Frankel and Pepper had made GNUtella[1] an open-source file-sharing system that allowed entire networks to be created without a central entity managing it. GNUtella could share not only MP3 files, but also video, software, pictures, documents; if it could be digitised, GNUtella could share it.

Rather than having a centralised server that mediated every user's connection, GNUtella operated to set up a fluid but robust network of individual computers. As the freely available public document 'GNUtella for Users' or GNUFU (written by a GNUtella user for the purpose of aiding other users) describes it:

> You can imagine the original model of the GNUtella network as friends phoning each other to get information. One asks five others, each of whom asks 5 others, and so on. After the first step the number of people reached is 5, after the second it is 25, after the 5th 3125, after the 7th 78,125 and after the 14th about 6.1 billion. That would be enough to reach every human being on this planet.
>
> (Babenhauserheide, 2004)

As every person in the network is contacted, their IP address is noted down in a log that is then also passed around between users automatically. This log acts as a dynamically updating 'phonebook' that the program consults when trying to reinitiate connections later on, saving the hassle of the network rediscovering users again. This distribution of addresses is called 'pong-caching'. The other way the program discovers other users on the network is whilst it is running its searches. Whereas Napster collated all the information about people's files on its central database so that people could search for specific files, GNUtella worked in more of a community-centric fashion. When the user typed the search query into the program, the program would prompt the few users it had connected to (we'll call them group 'A') if the query matched anything they had. If one of group 'A' did they would initiate a transfer and the file would be sent between the individual users, just like Napster. If they didn't have anything, the query would be passed on to the users that group 'A' knew of (group 'B'). If no-one in group 'B' had a matching file then the query would be passed on again and then again until a match was found, or the maximum number of groups had been queried, usually around seven. If a match was made then the hosting user's address was noted and prioritised for future use as it had provided content relevant to a search and could possibly be relevant in the future. As no single entity was required for the network to exist, users could drop in and out without affecting the reliability of the entire network (see Figure 4.1 for an illustration of the GNUtella network architecture).

Whereas with Napster it was possible to shut down the network by simply removing the central index servers, with GNUtella, as long as there were two computers each with a copy of the program, the network could reform. However, the program was really more a proof of concept than a polished piece of software and there were major usability flaws for the average computer user. For example, without a centralised static server to connect to, making the initial connection to the network was difficult and required the user finding another GNUtella user's address themselves through word of mouth. Later versions included a system to 'bootstrap' onto the network without knowledge of another GNUtella user. The software included a few addresses of servers that maintained directories of users' IP addresses. This list was constantly updated by the GNUtella software logging in and providing new logs of addresses it had collected. All a user needed from this directory was one IP address that was still active on the network. Once they had connected to them they would be provided with a list of other users that was constantly being updated and passed around by the software. After that point the software would always have a list to refer to when it needed to bootstrap onto the

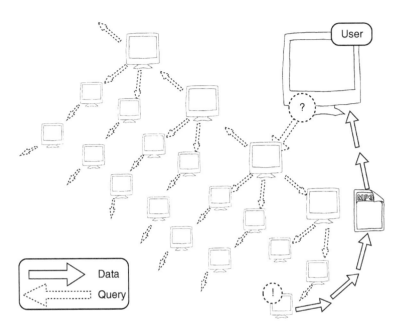

Figure 4.1 GNUtella network architecture

network. However, this was not present in Frankel's initial version and, unlike Napster, the program also did not come with an easy user interface – it was only later in its life that the program began to take shape as a serious rival to the Napster throne (Babenhauserheide, 2004).

Frankel and Pepper released the initial GNUtella build on 14 March 2000. The program was uploaded without AOL's knowledge to the Nullsoft website under a parody brand 'Gnullsoft'. The beta release included a small note:

> Justin and Tom work for Nullsoft, makers of Winamp and Shoutcast. See? AOL *CAN* bring you good things!
>
> (Jones, 2000)

By the following day GNUtella had been removed. When AOL became aware of the program it ordered its immediate removal and made a statement distancing itself from the project. The Gnullsoft page, devoid of a program, simply read 'temporarily down. come back later'. Frankel and Pepper were restricted from making any comment on the software and officially went silent. The following weekend, however, a user sporting Frankel's usual handle 'deadbeef' logged into a #gnutella IRC channel and answered questions about the banned software. In the session Frankel revealed his original intention was to release the beta, and then a final version complete with source code a few months later. With a freely available source code other programmers would be able to continue the GNUtella development. The idea was still tempting to Frankel, who mused on accidentally leaking the source code saying, 'I'd love to let it go and watch it develop into something much more' (Harmon, 2000).

Frankel lived out the rest of his time at AOL on a short leash and was steered back to WinAmp, discouraged from doing any interviews about his private project. Being Frankel, he did not take the censorship of his work lightly and continued to act out during the rest of his time with Nullsoft. In August 2000 he made an MP3 search engine but it was swiftly removed a day later. A month later he made a program called AIMazing which replaced the advertising in AOL's instant messenger program with an image of a musical heartbeat. After this AOL cracked down further demanding Frankel obtain permission before blogging. Yet even this did not deter him from his projects and he set to work on WASTE, a small program that created a 'darknet'. Darknets are small person-to-person networks that are fully secured so that only those invited to join a group will know of its existence. Once in, the group can communicate and trade files with relative impunity.

Frankel tried to placate AOL by offering it as a way for their two main offices to securely communicate across the country. However, AOL took so long to verify whether or not it approved of the project that eventually Frankel released it onto the net. As with GNUtella, AOL had it removed the next day. Soon after the removal Frankel considered quitting Nullsoft and eventually in January 2004 he announced his leave. Nullsoft still remains as an AOL subsidiary – its main duty still is to work on new iterations of WinAmp. Frankel moved on to create open-source music software[2] in his usual antagonistic style, creating such objects as the programmable guitar FX pedal system, the 'Jesusonic CrusFX' (Hu, 2004; Kushner, 2004; Mook, 2005).

GNUtella

Though Frankel eventually fell into relative obscurity, GNUtella took on a life of its own. Despite only being available for a few brief hours, Nullsoft estimated at the time that around 10,000 copies were downloaded before its removal. Nullsoft placed much of the 'blame' on tech news site Slashdot which posted a small announcement about an 'Open Source' Napster that was available on the Nullsoft website (Hemos, 2000; Jones, 2000). Although Frankel planned to eventually release the source code online there was little need. Within days the program had been pulled apart and reverse engineered, the primary credit going to Bryan Mayland (Kan, 2001). Less than a month after the release a GNUtella community website called WeGo.com was founded with the aim of continuing the development of GNUtella despite the AOL takedown. Through its disassociation with the program AOL claimed no rights over GNUtella, leaving it to fall into public ownership. However, as AOL had disallowed Frankel or Pepper from talking about their project there was no figurehead to champion the GNUtella flag, leaving the movement directionless; for a few days at least.

Gene Kan became the figurehead that Frankel couldn't be after his first interview with the Associated Press. A programmer from Redwood City near San Francisco, Kan was one of the initial developers that took on GNUtella as an open-source software project. After hearing about the program from a friend, Kan got hold of a copy and found it to be completely lacking in a user interface. There were no buttons or menus that most users these days see as the program in its entirety – GNUtella was all code, so he decided to put an interface in. There were others like Kan working on additions, refinements and features but there was a lack of organisation. Without any sort of leadership or centralised space in which to co-ordinate, Kan went to his employer WeGo and suggested it set up a community resource site for GNUtella. The company agreed and the WeGo.com GNUtella community site went live (Maney, 2000). Upon hearing about GNUtella, Associated Press reporter Ron Harris went looking for information and found the WeGo website. When he phoned the WeGo offices and asked to speak to someone about GNUtella the phone was handed to Kan – from that point on he became the face of GNUtella.

As well as fielding various interviews from reporters hungry to understand the GNUtella phenomenon, Kan was also working on his own implementations of the code. Along with colleague Spencer Kimball, Kan developed the concept of 'Infrasearch', a decentralised search engine. Search engines of the day were slow to update their records as they depended on automated 'crawlers'.[3] This was much better than the manual submission system that had preceded it, but Kan thought it could be even better than that. Although the crawlers meant that sites could be automatically added to the engine, they only logged a site's state intermittently, and if someone had added new content to their site, it would not be recognised until the crawlers came calling again. Kan's idea was to have a more decentralised, dynamic system of information search. Rather than having a central search server that needed to crawl the net for data, website owners would run some code on their servers that would both deal with indexing their site and would return information if it was queried. That way the updating of the search records was done on a site-by-site basis automatically whenever a change was made. If a user had a query, they would be able to use Infrasearch to ask all of these individual websites if they were relevant at that very second, rather than if they were relevant days ago when the crawlers last stopped by. This also allowed the interpretation of the query to be handled by the websites themselves, leaving them to decide if they were relevant to the query, rather than relying on a summary from a crawler. This meant that the returned information could be much more dynamic and contextual than a simple information directory. Kan and Kimball produced a working prototype based on the GNUtella code which showcased their contextual decentralised search model. In appearance it was much like Google, using a simple front page with a box to type a query that could be accessed by any standard web browser. If a query was typed in it would be sent out to a number of different servers. These servers had a variety of data sets and applications running on them so that there was a variety of contexts that the query would be matched against. Kan and Kimball's prototype consisted of, amongst others, an image database, a system that was able to ask questions of the 'Yahoo! Finance' database, such as stock quotes, an archive of news headlines and a system running a simple calculator that would evaluate all queries to see if they were algebraic expressions that it could answer (Borland, 2000c; Kan, 2001). With their prototype ready, Kan took the idea to Marc Andreessen, the original lead coder of the Mosaic and Netscape web browsers.[4] Showing an interest, Andreessen found investors for Kan's project and by June 2000 Kan was CEO of Infrasearch.

By late February 2001, Infrasearch had caught the attention of Sun Microsystems. Sun had already begun a project called JXTA (pronounced Jux-ta, in reference to Juxtaposition) which had the goal of producing a set of tools to aid the implementation and production of P2P applications (Borland, 2001c). At the time a general shift towards P2P was emerging within computing architecture. The initial arrangements of the internet across the 1970s and 1980s had relied on P2P systems as all users were considered to be equal and so the network architecture was designed symmetrically to allow both the consumption and publishing of information. However, with commercialisation in the 1990s came a shift to a broadcast model of network architecture. Network architecture shifted to the client/server centralised model of communications as the internet was seen as a platform for commerce. This centralised design was based on the assumption that home users would primarily be downloading more information from the internet than they would be uploading, meaning that the networks were designed to offer an asymmetric flow of data: data coming down to the user from the net was much faster than data that was being sent up. It is still the case that a home internet connection will have a much greater download rate than upload rate and that is further entrenched in the ISP's hardware, which often cannot cope with large amounts of information passing from the home user out to the net. However, with a P2P revival in the early 2000s many technology companies were looking to see what could be accomplished by linking up home computers through P2P networks and using them for data processing and publishing (Minar and Hedlund, 2001). Kan's decentralised and distributed search engine seemed like the perfect addition to any P2P platform and so Infrasearch was swiftly bought up and added to the JXTA project.

Kan continued to work for Sun until his unexpected death in June 2002. Many in the computing industry made statements expressing their sadness that they had lost him. Tim O'Reilly of O'Reilly Publishing praised Kan for his foresight in bringing P2P technology beyond file-sharing and into the core of internet architecture (Delio, 2002).

The JXTA project continued until 2004 where its various tech developments were integrated into Sun's other products: primarily its 'Java Desktop System' – which eventually became the Solaris operating system – and server system software. JXTA also became integrated into its work with corporate data-centres and communication systems with companies such as Verizon Communications (LaMonica, 2004).

Politically decentralised

Despite the popular mythology placing Napster at the forefront of P2P file-sharing, GNUtella was the protocol that set the model. Napster can be credited with introducing the western world to the concept of P2P file-sharing, of disseminating the practice of digital music curation out to a wide audience. However, GNUtella was the little-known bundle that defined P2P file-sharing. Rather than centralising the network in a set of servers like Napster had, Frankel's design emphasised the need to ensure that the network his software would generate would not be controllable by anyone. This decentralised model for P2P networking was derived both from Frankel's own counter-culture style values of what was important in the system's design, and the precedent set by the actions of the music industry in court. In the interests of economic exploitation, a group of individuals had identified themselves as the legal owners of the Napster network, and had exercised this power through the control of the indexing servers. This claim resulted in this group being held responsible for what took place on the network with legal threats against those individuals translating into legal threats against the network. These individuals and their servers were the lynchpin in the whole assemblage; target that pin and the whole structure tumbles down.

GNUtella had no lynchpin. With no dedicated indexing servers to seize and no owners to drag into court the network was untouchable. No owners also meant no exclusivity; developer communities were free to take Frankel's work and do as they wanted with it. With a dedicated community of development behind it the GNUtella model disseminated out into a variety of projects and software packages. Famous programs like Limewire, Bearshare and Ares Galaxy all operated the GNUtella protocol, and built upon it to further efficiency and stability. Napster's demise, far from ending file-sharing fragmented it into a plethora of software options and behind each one a decentralised network of individuals perpetuating the networks. Where the user base of file-sharers had been concentrated into one single network with an identifiable centre, after Napster it had been diffused infinitely out to a new market of file-sharing systems, each of which ran a variant of the GNUtella model.

The GNUtella model was founded on ideas of information free-flow, an avoidance of control and closure, and a dedication to providing the tools to allow anyone to continue the network. These values were injected into the design of the system, codified into agency through the assumptions the code made. With the persistence of the network came a persistence in Frankel's ideals which had been injected into the code through design. With the opening up of the model into a community project, its neutral approach to the information it allowed to flow, and its inherent discarding of centralised control the GNUtella model acted as an exemplar of Frankel's values and would plant that ideological seed into file-sharing communities. Slowly, file-sharing would become associated not simply with media accumulation, but with informational freedom, and a questioning of the apparent dominance held over the cultural commons by the incumbent media industries.

The greatest oversight in the popular narrative of illicit digital distribution is how influential Frankel's work was. His model of decentralised P2P file-sharing dominated the post-Napster years until the mass adoption of BitTorrent in the latter part of the decade. The GNUtella model defined file-sharing either directly through the utilisation of the protocol to run networks or through influence in design as others made their own variants of the elegantly stubborn rabble-rouser. Though it was often obscured by the vast array of different front-end software brands, in the back was Frankel's legacy keeping the network going. Frankel's decentralised design had saved file-sharing and ensured a robust persistence, however, in its myriad variations and implementations it would have consequences far from what Frankel had ever intended.

5
FastTrack: The Business of Piracy

The history of FastTrack is convoluted at best. It is a narrative that includes a variety of court cases spanning many years and multiple nations. Multiple companies with varying degrees of technology ownership and responsibility make pinning down its historical trajectory tricky. The FastTrack period can be understood as the boom of P2P file-sharing. Napster had introduced the habits of digital media consumption to a mass audience. GNUtella followed and established a background workshop of open-source P2P innovation. The sphere of P2P file-sharing was ready for someone to try to establish the P2P network as a legitimate method of media distribution. An audience of users had been established and the technology had been honed. This focus on the exploitation of P2P networks would provide the basis for the shifting of technologies developed under the illicit banner of piracy and into wider operation within the cultural industries.

Zennström and Friis

In 1997 Niklas Zennström met Janus Friis. Zennström was working for the then upstart (now behemoth) Swedish telecoms company 'Tele2' and had been tasked with starting up a small ISP business in neighbouring Denmark. Friis was working in customer support for a rival ISP and saw Zennström's ad for job openings in the Copenhagen papers. Friis went for the interview and got the job by devising a business strategy for the new ISP venture that impressed Zennström. From then on, wherever Zennström got transferred to by Tele2, he ensured that Friis got transferred too. Despite being in the ISP business, by

1999 they felt they were being left out of the innovations taking place in media tech and that, rather than working to make Tele2 bigger, they wanted to start their own venture. Friis moved into Zennström's apartment and the two tossed around ideas looking for the next big hit (Davidson, 2005; Roth, 2004).

Despite the correlation of its initial release in late 1999 with their time spent looking for a new venture opportunity, according to Zennström and Friis they were not looking to make the next Napster. By their account it was Zennström's experience running an ISP that led to the idea of a P2P media platform. The streaming of movie trailers and music was growing rapidly. With much of the services being hosted in the US, ISPs had the endless job of ensuring they had enough bandwidth to handle the distance. If the files were stored closer the issue wouldn't be as pronounced but they would still have the cost of hosting the files. However, if the users hosted the files then the costs would be minimal. According to Zennström and Friis, this was where the idea of FastTrack came from, though the account is refuted by the RIAA's then senior vice-president, Matthew Oppenheimer (Mackintosh, 2005; Roth, 2004). Their plan was to produce a P2P media-sharing system that was low on overheads but high on service quality by providing access to content at much faster than average rates. They would work out licensing arrangements with various studios and labels to keep everything legal and, if all went to plan, they would be at the centre of a revolution in media distribution.

Though they had business acumen and entrepreneurial vigour, neither of the duo had much experience with programming. They had the idea and knew how to get it off the ground – they just needed someone to build it. Zennström put out an online ad looking for programmers and a team of four Estonian game developers responded swiftly. The group who operated under the company name Bluemoon didn't know the programming language that the job required when they saw the ad, but within a weekend they had taught themselves and submitted a working design; the group were hired immediately. What they produced echoed GNUtella in its design. Quite when Bluemoon was contracted could not be ascertained but it is known that Zennström and Friis were drawing together their ideas in late 1999. The original GNUtella build was released in March 2000, and the first release of Bluemoon's product came a year later. Considering the time between the various events it is probable that Bluemoon worked whilst GNUtella was freely available to draw from and modify. It is also likely that it was at the peak of interest in the new P2P protocol, where forum discussions and specialist blogs would have been especially sensitive to anything GNUtella-related. However, though architecturally similar, Bluemoon's design, which Zennström and Friis dubbed 'FastTrack', was an improvement on the original GNUtella with some clever enhancements that would solidify the network's reign for half a decade.

Like GNUtella the traffic on the FastTrack network did not pass through central servers. Instead, the machines running the P2P software would negotiate between themselves to perpetuate the network. However, for GNUtella the lack of centralisation meant that, as the size of the network increased, it became increasingly sluggish at keeping track of all the machines and the content they hosted became difficult. FastTrack overcame this by being aware of the machines that made up the network and adjusting itself accordingly. The protocol would assign the more powerful and faster machines to be 'Supernodes', to act as network managers and to maintain indexes of the network. As more users joined the network, more Supernodes were produced ensuring there was always a healthy number of indexers to handle the load. When ordinary nodes wanted to find information their queries would be sent to the Supernodes. The Supernodes would scour their indexes which were perpetually updated as users logged on and off of the network, and returned search results (see Figure 5.1 for an illustration of the FastTrack network architecture).

When Napster had rapidly increased its user base, Jordan Ritter's servers had creaked under the strain and he had to build extra to keep up with demand. When demand rose for FastTrack, the protocol would simply convert more users into servers itself, at no cost to the company (Kazaa, 2002; Roth, 2004).

This enhanced decentralised network was impressively robust and echoed GNUtella in its decentralised anti-authoritarian ethic. When *Fortune* ran a story on Zennström and Friis, it positioned the Estonian programmers as the product of decades of top-down Soviet social engineering. The USSR's focused endeavour to develop an institute of cybernetics began in the 1960s and, although centres existed all over the USSR, Estonia's focus on computer programming produced a savvy computer-literate demographic. When the country declared independence from the USSR, this computer literacy was fused with

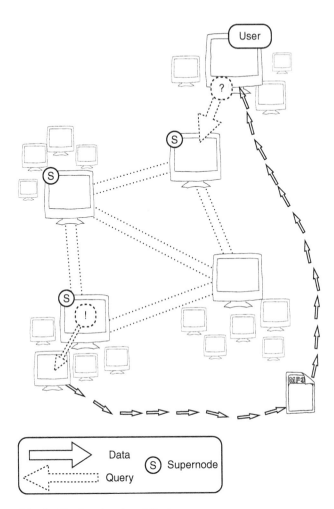

Figure 5.1 FastTrack network architecture

a sharp distrust of centralised authority. One of the Bluemoon programmers had been taught to program by both his parents who
worked at the cybernetics institute and was proficient at ten. According to *Fortune*, the FastTrack design was the product of an ideological
backlash against heavy-handed Soviet centralised governance. However, it may also have been an expression of ideological schemas often
present within bottom-up hacker IT cultures.

The developments Bluemoon made, especially the Supernode structure, were echoed in other GNUtella-based projects as part of the wider open-source community's goal of improving the GNUtella system. Whether the programmers produced FastTrack from the ground up or built on the existing GNUtella projects, these post-Soviet social characteristics were likely to have endeared Frankel's work to the team. However, despite the decentralisation and anti-authoritarianism that guided its design, for Zennström and Friis this was business. Once delivered to them the highly open and liberal design was packaged into a proprietary box, adapted for commercial exploitation. Zennström and Friis guarded the protocol closely. Rather than allow its code out into the world GNUtella-style they would license it to other companies to ensure a steady revenue stream. Their eventual vision was to have FastTrack act as the underlying architecture for myriads of different applications. As a P2P protocol it allowed the transfer of data amongst swarms of users, but this did not necessarily mean that data had to be media files. However, to sell their protocol they also needed some consumer software that would get them noticed and file-sharing was big. They hired some extra programmers to build their first product and in March 2001 released the FastTrack-powered file-sharing program Kazaa, under the company name 'Consumer Empowerment'.

The release of the Kazaa software coincided with Napster's demise, leaving a large opening in the P2P market ready to be filled. Although GNUtella had been released a year earlier, its status both as software still under development and as software without a central company behind it left it in the domain of the experts. For the everyday consumer, Kazaa was a free and fully functioning product with a veneer of legitimacy. Having demonstrated what was possible with Kazaa, Zennström and Friis began entering into agreements with other companies. US-based Streamcast Networks and Grokster Ltd were both eager to buy a licence to use the FastTrack protocol for their own file-sharing products. Streamcast released FastTrack client Morpheus whilst Grokster also released its own self-titled variant. As all three programs (Kazaa, Morpheus and Grokster) used the same protocol, they all connected their users to the same network. This 'FastTrack trio' came to dominate the P2P file-sharing landscape. Major download portal of the era, Download.com, reported that Kazaa and Morpheus had been downloaded more than 34 million times across the last months of 2001 and the amount of peers on the network had been steady at approximately 600,000 at any one time. At Napster's peak just before its imminent closure, analysts estimated that within February 2001 2.79 billion files were transferred using the Napster network. In August 2001 the P2P networks that had sprung up in Napster's wake had transferred 3.05 billion files, with the FastTrack trio playing a major role (Borland, 2001b).

GNUtella, the other major P2P system available to users had avoided scrutiny primarily because there was little in the way of a central representation for it. Though it had its evangelists and developers no central person or company took responsibility for it. FastTrack was centralised, at least in the legal sense, in the three companies: Consumer Empowerment, Streamcast Networks and Grokster Ltd. This centrality was necessary to generate revenue. Consumer Empowerment claimed ownership over the FastTrack protocol to license it and Streamcast and Grokster were looking to charge other companies to advertise to their users. Though the network was jointly perpetuated by the three software packages, they were also the network's gateways around which advertisements could be hung. To claim the rights to sell that advertising space it was necessary to be identified as having responsibility for the gateway. With GNUtella there was no profit motive and so no party or individual claiming rights over it. With GNUtella there was no-one responsible, and so no-one to call to court. With the FastTrack protocol, there were three.

As far as Zennström and Friis were concerned, they wouldn't reach court. Their original plan had been to keep the entire company legitimate. The aim was to harness newly emerging illicit practices, and develop a legitimate business around it. Part of this plan was to arrange licensing agreements with all the necessary studios and licensing groups. A few months after Kazaa's release, Zennström and Friis flew to the US having organised a meeting with some record label and movie studio representatives. Whilst there, Friis saw online that an RIAA document had been leaked. The document, which recommended the RIAA sue Kazaa's developers for copyright infringement, worried the pair and they sent their lawyers instead. Once the lawyers had negotiated an agreement that they wouldn't be served for the meeting's duration Zennström and Friis finally met the RIAA and Motion Picture Association of America (MPAA)[1] representatives. They received an onslaught of accusations about operating an international piracy forum and demands that they shut it down. The following day, Buma/Stemra, the music licensing and collection society for the Netherlands, dropped out of its negotiations with Zennström and Friis and threatened to sue as well. The pair quickly returned home, cautious about dealing with the major studios and about setting foot in the US again (Roth, 2004).

The US court summons of all three companies came shortly afterwards in October 2001. The case was brought again by the RIAA, but this time also joined by the MPAA because the FastTrack networks were facilitating video as well as audio transfers (Borland, 2001b). This was followed shortly afterwards by another suit brought against Zennström and Friis who were by then operating under the company name Kazaa BV. Kazaa BV was forced by the Amsterdam courts to cease its distribution of the Kazaa software until its legality could be decided. The company eventually complied, though this had no affect on the network, which was happily perpetuated by existing users of Kazaa and the products of Streamcast and Grokster. In January 2002 Zennström and Friis decided to distance themselves from the popular but risky Kazaa software whilst ensuring a steady income from their efforts. The arrangements at the time were shrouded in secrecy and misinformation as users, reporters and industry lawyers alike attempted to understand what had transpired. Originally Kazaa was owned by one company, based in the Netherlands. However, seemingly overnight, Kazaa had become the property of a company registered on a tiny island off the Australian coast and where there was one company, now there were four.

Sharman takes over

Kazaa had been sold to Sharman Networks, a company registered on the tiny island of Vanuatu, though actually operated via an affiliated management company in Sydney, Australia. As Sharman's CEO Nikki Hemming told it in 2002, she was tipped off about Kazaa's sale by CEO of Brilliant Digital Entertainment (BDE), Kevin Bermeister. Bermeister's LA-based company was working with Zennström and Friis to develop an advertising delivery network that used the P2P FastTrack protocol. Sharman was one of many companies bidding for the software and brand, but when the courts started closing in they were the only company willing to risk it. With the help of private investors Sharman bought the software, the brand, the web domain Kazaa.com and a licence to use the FastTrack protocol (Borland, 2002a, 2002b). However, Daniel Roth's (2004) account of the trade, based on his interviews with Zennström and Friis, presents the sale as more of a handoff to distance the Kazaa creators from their risky product. Although Hemming's company existed before the Kazaa sale with the purpose of investing in internet-based opportunities, Kazaa was its first acquisition. The expenses of the sale were financed by Zennström with the understanding that the loan would be repaid via Kazaa's profits. Zennström and Friis transferred the ownership of the FastTrack protocol to a new company they registered called Joltid and in partnership with BDE created Altnet, a company that would retail licensed music files via Kazaa now owned by Sharman. To finalise their revenue stream, Joltid took 20% of BDE's stock and secured a monthly license fee of $30,000 for the use of undisclosed software, presumably based on the FastTrack protocol.

A small relief came for Zennström, Friis and Hemming (her recent purchase's legality having not yet been determined) in March 2002. The Amsterdam courts ruled that Kazaa's developers and owners were not responsible for the actions of their users. The court accepted the company's argument that they were unable to directly intervene in the network and could not stop it now that it had formed (Gibson, 2003). The US took a different stance and decided that the RIAA and the MPAA's suit was valid, ordering all three companies of the FastTrack trio to court. Despite the ruling of the Amsterdam courts, speculation regarding quite how decentralised the FastTrack network was had arisen after various groups found themselves locked out of the network. Open-source software groups had, through reverse engineering, been attempting to produce FastTrack client software that would run on Linux operating systems (Kazaa ran on Windows exclusively). A group had successfully produced a working client that was able to hook into the proprietary network. However, in October 2001 it found its client suddenly didn't work. The programmers claimed that a 'security upgrade' released by Kazaa BV had forced all software on the FastTrack network to check in with a central server before connecting to the network and consequently as the open-source group had not paid for a FastTrack licence, their software had been blocked (Borland, 2001b).

A week before the US court order was announced a similar event caught previous licensor Streamcast off guard when it found that its Morpheus client was suddenly unable to function. Powerless to determine why FastTrack no longer worked, Streamcast quickly refitted Morpheus with the ability to hook into the open GNUtella network. Eventually Zennström announced that Streamcast had not paid its licensing bills and thus had not been provided with the new version of FastTrack to use in Morpheus, which led to incompatibility with the network. Streamcast was still uncertain quite how Kazaa BV had been able to orchestrate a complete shutdown of its software and made a statement that implied that Kazaa BV had more direct control over the network than it was revealing and that the upgrade story was a cover. Posted years later, a comment on a specialist telecoms blog[2] supports Streamcast's suspicions. The commenter self-identified as a programmer who had worked with Zennström and Friis on Kazaa. Known only as 'Julian' the commenter described the technical method by which Zennström and Friis had introduced a way of disabling the protocol to maintain licensing rights.[3] Though unresolved, the dispute between the companies left them all vulnerable. With a key issue in the courts being whether there was an ability to control the network, the infighting revealed that there may have been some degree of control held by someone somewhere, and for the RIAA at least, this was proof enough (Borland, 2002d).

The case officially began in March 2002 and by May, Zennström and Friis had announced that they lacked the funds to continue any defence and agreed to accept a default judgment, leaving their business partners to fight the case (Borland, 2002c). Having for the moment shed themselves of their past project they could look ahead to new applications of the FastTrack protocol. With their team of P2P programmers they spent 15 months developing their next big hit. One of the bigger changes in the telecom industry was the emergence of Voice-Over-Internet-Protocol or VOIP. VOIP took advantage of the rise of high-speed internet and offered the ability to route telephone calls over the net. Although not a new technology, the increase in broadband capacity meant that quality had greatly improved since the early 1990s. The technology offered smaller companies the opportunity to legitimately challenge the incumbent telcos by providing a comparable service whilst piggybacking on the pre-established communications infrastructure. Zennström and Friis wanted to take it one step further and produced a P2P VOIP service based on a variant of the FastTrack protocol. By routing the calls via users' computers rather than relying entirely on a centralised exchange system they could drop much of the overhead cost. On 29 August 2003 Zennström and Friis released Skype, and took the first steps towards yet again disrupting another well-entrenched industry by offering customers a global telephone network that charged the competitive price of nothing.

Grokster (Kazaa and Streamcast) v MGM

Zennström and Friis had left Grokster and Streamcast to defend the FastTrack protocol in the US courts, preferring to accept a default judgment rather than fight the case themselves. This initially looked to be a wise choice when in April 2003 the court came to the wholly unexpected decision. The judge ruled that developers of file-sharing software were not responsible for the actions of their users and that as long as an innovation had substantial non-infringing uses the tech was legal (Borland, 2002f, 2003).

The judge's decision hung greatly on the prior case of *Sony Corporation of America v Universal City Studios Inc.* (Borland, 2003). The case is well known within tech circles as the landmark case that established a safe haven for innovation in media distribution. The case was brought by Universal against Sony for its development of the Betamax home recording system. Similar to (and eventually surpassed by) VHS, Betamax allowed the public to record visual material at home. Universal objected, citing the primary concern that people could record and replicate copyrighted material such as the movie industry's films. The courts were sceptical of Universal's intentions and felt that media groups should not have the right to determine technological development to suit themselves. The US Supreme Court ruled in favour of Sony, arguing that even if a technology could be used for copyright infringement, if it had substantial non-infringing uses then the public should not be denied the benefits of such an innovation.

The decision did not have any bearing on the actual act of infringement; if an individual was using their new Betamax to produce and sell pirated films they were still liable. However, technological innovators were safe in the knowledge that they were free to produce media technologies without the copyright industries' oversight. If the opposite decision had been made, then outside innovation in media distribution may have plummeted as the fear of legal liability would discourage anybody without the copyright industries' blessing. As such it is unlikely that products that allowed media production outside the studios would have ever have been produced, forgone instead for safe systems of media distribution, with recording capabilities firmly discouraged. Beyond being merely about films and music, the decision's impact spread widely to ensure that the capacity to disseminate free speech and expression was available to the general public (Lee, 2005).

The Betamax case's simple result was that as long as an innovation had substantial uses that did not infringe copyright it would not be stifled, even if it did have some infringing uses. The Court recognised that as well as copyrighted material the FastTrack networks were facilitating the exchange of large quantities of public domain works. Another popular use was for independent bands to use the networks to spread promotional tracks. This allowed them access to a global audience without the need for the costly infrastructure provided by publishers and studios. The copyright industries asserted that the majority of FastTrack activity was infringement. However, to qualify under the Betamax protection the technology only had to be capable of non-infringing uses; it did not necessarily have to be primarily used for them.

However, the courts also had to consider issues of secondary liability for copyright infringement, that being the aiding or promotion of copyright infringement. Secondary liability comes in two parts: first there is contributory copyright infringement whereby the individual contributes in some way to the infringement. The second part is vicarious copyright infringement, whereby the individual has the right and ability to stop infringement but chooses not to. This was the downfall for Napster, where there was involvement of its central servers in every transaction. This involvement meant that it had materially contributed to the act of infringement (contributory) by providing hardware and had not applied filtering systems to stop copyright infringement (vicarious), even though central control meant it was able to do so (Von Lohmann, 2006).

In April 2003 the District Court ruled that Grokster and Streamcast's software was protected under the Betamax decision as having substantial non-infringing uses, citing the large amount of public domain works that had been distributed across the network. It also stated that the lack of any centralisation meant the two companies were not liable for either types of secondary infringement. This wholly unexpected ruling went against the Napster precedent, with the network architecture playing a crucial role in distancing the companies from the actions of their users. This use of technical design to route around copyright law was not lost on the Court, which recognised that in all likelihood the defence had structured their businesses in a way that avoided secondary liability (*MGM v Grokster*, 2003). However, tied by the definitions within the copyright Act, the Court was unable to act. The defendants were found not liable under either forms of secondary infringement. However, the RIAA and the MPAA, unwilling to be beaten so easily included a suggestion to the Court regarding how the FastTrack problem could be remedied.

> To justify a judicial remedy, however, Plaintiffs invite this Court to expand existing copyright law beyond its well-drawn boundaries. As the Supreme Court has observed, courts must tread lightly in circumstances such as these...
>
> (*MGM v Grokster*, 2003)

The decision was inevitably appealed by the RIAA and the MPAA but in August 2004 the Ninth Circuit Court of Appeals retained the decision, stating that even if all the companies closed up and deactivated their computer hardware, the network would still be running (Lee, 2005). Though the Court verdict was in FastTrack's favour it did not go without consequences for the individuals using the networks. Knocked by the Court's decision that the P2P systems were protected under Betamax, the RIAA resolved to focus significantly on the users of the networks than the networks themselves.

The idea was first announced by the RIAA in July 2002, though they stressed that it had not yet been put it into practice and was still merely a consideration (Borland, 2002e; Russell Perez, 2002). Some key cases against individuals had already occurred during the Napster years; however, fired by its failure in court, the group began a series of mass suits, targeting hundreds of file-sharers at a time. It was hoped that a sustained campaign of lawsuits against individual infringers would educate the public to see their side of the argument. These actions further ingrained the public perception that not only were the incumbent copyright industries out of touch with the changing face of cultural consumption, but also that they were aggressively working against it. In the court statements and campaign materials of the RIAA the representation of the innocent user victim began to subside. Before the court decision, network developers were luring in unsuspecting users and commandeering their computers for illegal acts. After the initial FastTrack cases the innocent victim gradually became portrayed as a heartless, selfish pirate. Where before little or no agency was ever ascribed to the users of the P2P systems, suddenly they had a selfish paradoxical desire for media and a grudge against creativity (see Reyman, 2010, for a deeper account of the use of language in the piracy debates).

Despite this change in approach to stamping out file-sharing the industry groups continued to pursue the network operators as well. In June 2005 the RIAA and the MPAA's appeal against the Ninth Circuit's verdict was heard. Each prior verdict had found that under the country's copyright laws the companies could not be prosecuted. However, when Grokster and Streamcast reached the Supreme Court they did not face the same law. Since the Ninth Circuit's verdict US copyright law had been altered with a clear view to reign in online copyright infringement. The change came through 'the Induce Act', which caused a stir amongst civil liberties campaigners and the tech industry, both strongly opposed to the changes the Act sought to make to copyright law. The Act was originally dubbed the 'Inducement Devolves into Unlawful Child Exploitation Act'; the long title was dropped but its content remained relatively unchanged.

Proponents of the Act championed it as a method to stop P2P network companies from inducing children to become criminals. The main proponent Senate Judiciary Chairman Orrin Hatch even evoked imagery of the child-catcher from *Chitty Chitty Bang Bang* luring children into danger with promises of sweets (McCullagh, 2004). Rather than overturn the Betamax ruling, which would have caused an even greater uproar, legislators had produced a new type of secondary liability called 'inducement'. Inducement stated that, if a company distributed a device with the clear promotion of using it to infringe copyright, the company was liable for any infringement committed. This addition essentially ensured that the 'intent' of the company, something which could be proved with circumstantial evidence, could be used as proof of liability. The Act was clearly targeted at overturning the Grokster/Streamcast ruling. Inducement was the expansion of copyright law that the media representatives had expressed a desire for in the District Court. However, opponents to the Act claimed that the broadness of the Act brought the legality of anything that could copy, such as Apple's iPod, VHS recorders, the PC and even a pen into question. As these, and many other, devices could be used to infringe copyright, the manufacturer's liability was based on how well a prosecutor could argue that the manufacturer had infringing intent. Under the Betamax decision manufacturers had a clear understanding of what was and was not liable for infringement claims; however, the Induce Act had overturned Betamax as collateral damage (Gross, 2004).

For Grokster and Streamcast, evidence of their intent was shown by their targeting certain audiences known for their infringing habits, such as ex-Napster users. The Court also pointed to their business model that depended on increasing the user base, and their failure to enact a filtering system (Von Lohmann, 2006). This newly introduced law overturned both prior rulings and sent the case back to the district courts, with the obvious looming reality that both companies would be caught on new secondary infringement charges. In November 2005 Grokster settled with the various studios, paying out $50 million and shutting down for good (Meyers, 2005). Streamcast refused to give in as easily and miraculously strung the case out until 2008. Judge Steven V. Wilson was dedicated to keeping the network going for non-infringing purposes; however, this required filtering systems, which were proving difficult to develop. Without any real revenue source the company eventually filed for bankruptcy, leaving the studios with little in the way of settlement (Healey, 2008).

Incorporating the competition

Two months after the final Grokster ruling, Sharman and BDE were found guilty of copyright infringement by the Australian federal courts. Just under a year later Sharman settled with the recording studios, paying out more than $100 million, much of which was paid for by Zennström and Friis personally. Sharman pledged to move away from illicit file-sharing and only distribute industry-approved content. Kazaa did indeed re-emerge years later as the legal subscription service Kazaa 2.0. However, Sharman has long since disappeared and the new service is registered to BDE (Deare, 2005; McCarthy, 2006; Pearce, 2004). Anthony Rose, Chief Technology Officer at Kazaa didn't make it to Kazaa 2.0. Though named in the lawsuit he was cleared of responsibility and when the BBC was looking to finalise its online television platform it looked to him. Rose arrived in late 2007, appointed as the Head of Digital Media Technology. His experience working with P2P distribution and digital media retailing made him perfect for the job. Rose also brought with him the P2P FastTrack principles and implemented a P2P system into the early versions of iPlayer. When the British public downloaded programmes to watch on their computers, the same FastTrack principles were at work. Eventually iPlayer dropped the P2P aspect, citing it to be unnecessary as the BBC was able to provide enough central server capacity to satisfy demand (BBC Press Office, 2007; Chibber, 2009; Lanxon, 2009).

Zennström and Friis' Skype continued to make ripples in the tech and telco realm for a couple of years until it was sold to eBay for $2.6 billion in October 2005 (Forrest, 2005; Reece, 2005). The company intended to combine it with its eBay marketplace to allow buyers and sellers a new way to communicate. However, despite an increasingly growing user base its financial expectations were not fulfilled. In 2007 eBay admitted that it had paid too much for the company, and valued it at $1.4 billion. In April 2009 eBay announced its intention to float Skype on the stock market, separating it from eBay Inc. (Clark, 2009). Zennström and Friis expressed a desire to buy the company and had gathered a consortium of investment groups to get Skype back. In a move reminiscent of their days with Streamcast, Zennström and Friis' company Joltid filed a copyright infringement claim against eBay. The claim revealed that when eBay paid $2.6 billion for Skype, it had not bought the rights to the underlying P2P technology; the core architecture of Skype was still owned by Joltid. Having revealed that anyone buying Skype would not even own the architecture that made it work, most of the buyers backed off. As a result Zennström and Friis' consortium bought back their company at a heavily reduced price (Johnson, 2009). Skype the software remained with Skype the company until 2011 when in May Microsoft announced that it intended to purchase the company for $8.5 billion (Microsoft, 2011). As for Zennström and Friis, they moved on to new things. The pair are now well known as savvy entrepreneurs in technology innovation. Friis' next venture Rdio is a free on-demand multiplatform ad-free streaming music service. Rdio is funded by his and Zennström's London-based venture capital firm Atomico, which aims to fund the next disruptive and 'transformative' internet innovations (Bradshaw and Palmer, 2010).

The business of piracy

What Zennström and Friis had developed was a proprietary P2P network, an attempt to exploit P2P activity by controlling the network access points. The FastTrack period represents an experimentation with the commercialisation of P2P file-sharing. The FastTrack trio sold the attention of the user base by placing adverts around the gateways to the network and inserting sponsored files into genuine search results. Zennström and Friis took commercialisation further, claiming ownership of the GNUtella model and licensing the technology out to other companies. However, to operate with the incumbent media industry's blessing the P2P companies needed content licensing as well. The open logic intrinsic to Frankel's model would not be so appealing to the labels, being intrinsically at odds with an understanding of IP that demanded exclusivity and restriction. The problematic nature of allowing your customer base to also be your warehouse meant the P2P distribution model would not catch on. The system was too architecturally close to Napster, and still carried with it the tinge of rebellion perceived in Napster and actually present in GNUtella. Allowing a model where the distributor role was taken on by the customer base subverted the established understanding of the top-down restriction of access that media retail was built on. Tarred by their experience with Napster, and hesitant to mess with their own business model, the studios' licences did not come easily. Instead, the P2P companies had to operate in a way that nullified the necessity of a licence, distancing themselves from responsibility whilst claiming enough control to derive revenue from advertising.

This seemingly contradictory state was provided by the network architecture. The FastTrack protocol was, through technical and legal design, decentralised and uncontrollable, yet conversely also proprietary and closely maintained. Frankel's model for decentralisation provided the FastTrack trio with enough disassociation to claim impotence when questioned about regulating activity on the network. However, it was their claims of ownership and exploitation that left them vulnerable. Their actions, motivated by the desire to exploit the network financially, were found to be proof of intent to induce others to use the FastTrack system for illicit trading. The technical design had been successful in decentralising responsibility to the point where any prosecution was futile in regard to stopping the network. However, there was still centrality in the claims over network access. By taking this stance of ownership the courts were able to circumvent the technical design issue and instead go directly to the intent of the company. The utilisation of Frankel's model had been successful as far as Frankel had envisioned it. However, layering a profit motive onto Frankel's model resulted in an expansion of copyright law in the US to circumvent the model. In its wake the Induce Act and the case of *MGM v Grokster* nullified the Betamax ruling and left the safe harbour of innovation companies in uncertainty.

The Induce Act's impact was to cement the dominance of the media content industries over hardware and software developers. Provable through circumstantial evidence, secondary infringement via inducement meant that developers of P2P networks had little defence. Those companies that didn't close soon after the ruling began negotiating with the major licensing groups and began work on a variety of solutions to control the networks. 'Legitimate' services such as Mashboxx (set up by Grokster's CEO shortly after the settlement) began to arrive on the digital distribution scene. These services presented themselves as P2P distribution with an ethical heart. They operated with label endorsement but this endorsement came at a price. The files that were exchanged on these networks were industry endorsed but also industry regulated. Rather than the open, malleable, replicable files which had driven the growth in P2P popularity, the networks were supplying files locked with DRM similar to the PressPlay venture before it. Attempts to legitimise P2P systems were also neutering them of their appeal. The only outlet for unrestricted digital media engagement, the type that individuals had become accustomed to and desired, would be those that were illicit and illegitimate. After the Induce Act, P2P systems continued; however, they would not be able to continue as legitimate, profit-driven enterprises. In the environment created by years of experimentation and litigation, all that would survive were collective, ideologically motivated networks.

6
BitTorrent: Revolution in the Network

Perfect

It was April 2001 and Bram Cohen had quit his job. Sitting at his dining-room table, laptop to hand, he was working on a personal project. Tapping away at the keyboard he reeled out lines of code onto the screen, stopping every now and again to pace the house before returning to his seat to tap some more. When Cohen had had a job it was with a dot.com start-up called MojoNation. MojoNation was looking to create a P2P network that could store encrypted chunks of files across multiple computers. The idea was interesting but the implementation was still clunky and complicated. It was far from suitable for public use and money was running out. This scenario was not unusual for Cohen. During the 1990s he had worked as a programmer for a variety of dot.com start-ups that had gone bust. Every time he saw his project never reach its audience, and it was becoming apparent that MojoNation would be no exception. Tired of never seeing anything through to completion, Cohen quit. He didn't have an income to speak of; instead, he was subsisting off of his savings and a well-executed regime of transferring debt across 0% introductory-rate credit cards. Being a man without an income it might be assumed that his personal project was seeking to remedy that – some potential dot.com hit that would make Cohen rich. But it wasn't; it was just an interesting project. Cohen had noted a problem with the way that the internet operated and, inspired by the work he had done with MojoNation, knew he had a solution (Roth, 2005; Thompson, 2005).

As prior P2P developers had noted, the contemporary internet was not designed for contemporary uses. Increasingly, files were being distributed across the internet by home users. Napster had clearly demonstrated a demand for music and the GNUtella model had begun facilitating larger file transfers. As much as bandwidth was a defining factor when it came to how fast files could be transferred, a contributing factor was the way in which contemporary ISPs had designed the architecture of the commercial net. When the internet was originally designed as the government- and university-focused system of information-sharing, all machines on the network were considered equal. Computers were given equal capacity to upload information as well as download; much of the back-end (what the home user doesn't see) of internet architecture still works in this fashion. However, between 1994 and 1999 the massive uptake of internet in the home meant that the once quiet networks of academia became a mass media information centre. The perceived use of the internet was not as a space for contributing information, but one of retrieving and consuming information, and the ISPs had to build accordingly. By providing higher speeds for information being downloaded by the end user, they were sacrificing the speed of any information the user uploaded. This 'asymmetric bandwidth' worked well for the majority of users and drove uptake of the web as a space to consume richer sources of information, such as audio and video (Minar and Hedlund, 2001). However, in environments where information transferred between home users, speeds would suffer as the transfer was limited by the upload rate of the individual with the file. The downloader may have been able to download at 2 megabytes per second, but if the uploader could only send at a tenth of that speed, that was what the downloader received. For relatively small files such as text, images or music which maxed out at an average of 4 megabytes per file, this wasn't much of an issue, but if you wanted to distribute larger files without paying out for server rental and high-capacity bandwidth there was little you could do.

For Cohen this problem wasn't political like it was for Frankel, nor was it a possible business venture as would have been seen by Zennström and Friis; it was simply an interesting problem. Cohen had Asperger's syndrome, a form of autism that in his case gave him above-average faculties of concentration and abstraction. This abstraction and concentration had been channelled into an incredible proficiency for writing clean, efficient code.[1] It also made it difficult for him to relate to social cues and he was often disarmingly frank. As a result, when Cohen asserted that he quit his job and started a project purely because it was an interesting problem, he meant it.

Cohen's idea to overcome the problem of asymmetric bandwidth was to have a large quantity of users upload a file at once. Although individually each one of them would be uploading at a fraction of the receiver's download rate, communally they would max it out, providing a much faster transfer than a simple one-to-one transfer. If the file was broken down into pieces, the downloader could receive different pieces of the file from different sources at any one time. Furthermore, if the software could ensure that the pieces were ordered properly after they arrived, it wouldn't even be necessary to download them in order. This would make things even quicker as pieces would be downloaded if they were available, regardless of whether they were the 'next' piece or not. As download order didn't matter, downloads could be stopped and resumed later, allowing them to be spread out across multiple sessions. Having files in pieces even meant that it was not necessary to have the entire file before you were able to supply other users with copies of the pieces you already had. As more users joined in the 'swarm' there would be more copies of individual pieces available and more sources to download from, making the network faster as the load increased, a complete turnaround in data distribution principles.

Though elegantly simple, whether it was actually possible to translate the idea into a working example was another matter. Technically minded friends were sceptical and concerned that Cohen had dedicated himself to an unachievable goal. However, bereft of social niceties Cohen simply told them that he was clever enough to do it. In an interview with *Wired Magazine* he explained: 'I can come off as pretty arrogant, but it's because I know I'm right...I'm very good at writing protocols' (Thompson, 2005). A few months later Cohen proved that he could do it and uploaded a prototype of the code onto the net. An announcement he made on a Yahoo! Group for 'Decentralisation' received one reply, 'What's BitTorrent, Bram?'.[2] Needing a decent set of users for a trial run, Cohen produced a Torrent download of free pornography and used it to lure participants. Word that there was a protocol that could transfer large files at high speeds with ease began to spread and the computer-literate communities of Linux users began to adopt BitTorrent for trading programs.[3] In February 2002, Cohen presented the project to CodeCon 2002,[4] a programmer-centric conference organised by Cohen and friend Len Sassaman (Thompson, 2005). Adoption of BitTorrent continued to grow slowly, and Cohen continued to work. In October 2002, Cohen released a publicly useable version. It was still rough and needed more optimisation but money was running low. Luckily, Cohen's work had attracted the attention of John Gilmore, a free-software entrepreneur and one of the first employees at Sun Microsystems. Gilmore lived near to Cohen and saw the value in a freely available protocol that allowed anyone to distribute large files. Deciding to help Cohen, Gilmore covered his living expenses so that he could focus on finishing the project (Schiesel, 2004).

The BitTorrent protocol that was released for general use differed from the other file-sharing systems. Previous incarnations, Napster, GNUtella and FastTrack, had come as an application in which to search for, transfer and store files alongside some community and advertising features. The protocol was in the back-end but the main focus for the user was the application, which sought to cement itself as a media hub. However, because Cohen's primary intention was that BitTorrent become a general-use protocol for any type of data, he did not specifically promote it as a tool with a particular focus. BitTorrent was neutral; simply another way of communicating data. He saw it as a publishing tool; something for people who produced (be it software, film, music, etc.) but did not have the money to support distribution. Cohen supplied software to handle BitTorrent transfers, but it was simple and focused solely on the task of uploading and downloading data.

We can use an example of one of Cohen's hypothetical users to understand how BitTorrent works in practice. An independent film-maker has made a documentary, they did it for fun and, at least at this stage of their career, are more concerned with getting a name than with money. Securing a DVD distribution deal looks impossible as his documentary is unlikely to have mass market appeal. The film-maker doesn't have the money to pay a professional company to host the video online for people to download, and the size of it would mean it would take a long time to download anyway. Instead, the film-maker turns to BitTorrent and uses the software

Cohen provided to make a 'Torrent' file for the film. This Torrent file is not the film itself, but a tiny file that has the information necessary to allow another person to download the film straight from the film-maker's computer. During the Torrent file's creation the film-maker designates a tracker that the file will use to co-ordinate all transfers. Though technical knowledge is needed to set up trackers, they are often inexpensive and require drastically less computing power than running a file-server. Trackers are also not limited to only managing one swarm. Due to the relatively small amount of work required to co-ordinate swarms, they often handle thousands of transfers at a time. This means that they are often run as free and open-community services, available for anyone who wants to use them to co-ordinate their uploads. The film-maker chooses a community tracker he likes the look of, gets the appropriate information from their website and then runs the newly made Torrent file in the BitTorrent software. The software connects to the tracker and announces the computer's address and that it is ready to provide a copy of the film. For now the computer sits idle, waiting for someone to request the film stored on its hard drive.

The film is available for download, but nobody knows about it. The film-maker puts the small Torrent file on his website, with the announcement that he wants people to download it and get his film. We can also assume that if he's particularly savvy he'll do some more marketing elsewhere (remember BitTorrent deals purely with distribution). A few hours later and someone has downloaded the tiny Torrent file from the website and opened it in their own copy of the BitTorrent software. After querying the tracker as to the film's whereabouts, the software forms a connection between the film-maker's and film fan's computers. The film starts being transferred in small pieces and at first the rate is quite slow. The film-maker only has a standard home internet connection and, like everyone else, his upload speed is slower than his, or the film fan's, download speed. However, a few minutes later a copy of the Torrent file is opened by another fan, and then another, and another. Their computers are also asking for the pieces of the film file, so the film-maker's computer sends them pieces as well. Up until this point in the example, BitTorrent has operated in a similar way to Napster; users know that a file is available, have asked a centralised server where the file can be downloaded from and have connected directly to the source to be sent it. However, this is where BitTorrent becomes both complex, but brilliant.

Rather than send the new downloaders the same pieces that it sent the first downloader, the software instead decides to send them completely different pieces. The goal of the film-maker's computer is to provide one full copy of the film to the entire swarm of downloaders. The job of the users in the swarm is to copy the pieces they have between themselves, making sure that they all have a copy. Each user is connected to many others at once, downloading different pieces from lots of different users, maximising their download capacity. After a few hours the swarm has increased to hundreds but the film-maker has only uploaded one full copy of his film into the swarm. However, because of all the swarm members downloading and uploading different pieces of it, connecting to 40 or 50 different people at a time to maximise their speeds, there are now many full copies of the film, which people are both watching and providing to the swarm members who are yet to have the complete file. To ensure that these users kept providing copies of what they had received, the BitTorrent software's download rate was directly tied to the upload rate, acting as a control to ensure that users gave as well as took. After a day or so the swarm is filled with other users who now have full copies of the film and the film-maker doesn't even need to provide a copy anymore; other people are doing it for him. Although a very active complex process, beyond the opening of the Torrent file little user engagement was required, with the software doing all the organising and co-ordinating. We can assume that after activating the tiny Torrent file the film-maker and the fans left their computers to the job at hand, and occupied themselves with something else (Figure 6.1).

The common understanding of data transfer on the net was that, when downloading something popular, speeds would likely plummet because the servers hosting the file would strain to fulfil the many thousands of requests. But Cohen's design had turned this on its head; instead of slowing under an ever-increasing mass of users, transfer rates would speed up as increasingly sources of file pieces became available. A real-world test of BitTorrent's capability came in March 2003 when the open-source software company Red Hat released the latest version of its Red Hat Linux operating system. Servers struggled under the deluge of eager customers and many

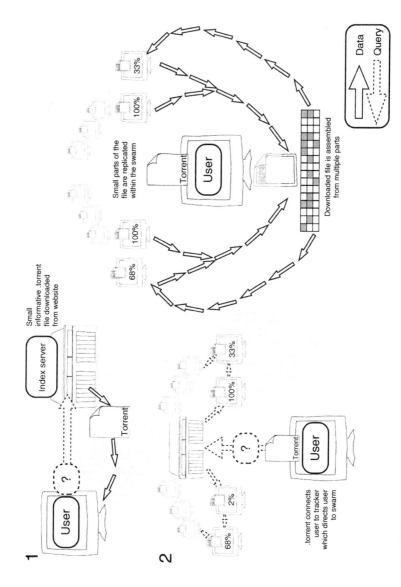

Figure 6.1 BitTorrent network architecture

were left without access. One customer, Eike Frost, who had got a copy, decided to try and ease the load by hosting it via BitTorrent. He posted an announcement on popular tech news site Slashdot (the same site that announced Frankel's GNUtella on its initial release) and the swarm began to form. Eike was running the BitTorrent tracker which was co-ordinating the Red Hat Linux swarm and so was able to collect information from the tracker's logs. Within three days of the announcement, Red Hat fans had transmitted 21.15 terabytes of information between them; the printed content of the Library of Congress would comprise approximately 10 terabytes. Frost estimated that had he hosted the full file and paid the traffic costs of providing it to the thousands of downloaders his bill would have ranged between $20,000 and $60,000. Having only hosted the minuscule Torrent file his bill was $99, the same he usually paid (Roth, 2005). The event was clearly a success for Cohen's code and demonstrated to a large community of software users that BitTorrent was a useful utility.

However, the protocol had also been put to use in ways that Cohen had not intended. Whereas for him the original idea was to use Torrent files to self-publish and transfer free and open software, it was clear to many users that the protocol would have great utility in filesharing. Music, films, TV shows and software were enjoying a new vitality with BitTorrent as most of these types of file were significantly large enough to make sharing on GNUtella- and FastTrack-based services fairly futile. Websites where people would upload Torrent files to a central, searchable index began to appear in droves and more BitTorrent trackers were set up to cater for demand, often being tied directly to the index sites. Inevitably, these indexes began to fill up with copyrighted media alongside the other files. Cohen was rather bemused; he'd never made BitTorrent with this in mind and so anonymity was never built into the protocol. People sharing copyrighted works were thoroughly exposed. Users were exposed on previous protocols as well, but BitTorrent upped the scale of identification. Identifying an infringing user on a P2P system is as simple as taking part in the network. Your computer had to know the IP address of the individual you were downloading a file from, otherwise you would never find them in the first place. Copyright enforcement agencies, with the blessing of the rights holders, would simply use the P2P software to download films and music, and make a note of the IP address of who had supplied it. Lists of these addresses would then go to court where the various ISPs who provided these addresses would be subpoenaed for the name and address of the subscriber. With a BitTorrent system, the process was essentially the same except when the enforcement agency took part in a download, it would be supplied with hundreds of IP addresses at once. This absolute transparency of users' identities made Cohen less liable for their actions. Cohen's clean, simple implementation of BitTorrent did not try to obscure these addresses or bury them out of sight; it simply strove to transfer data efficiently and this provided Cohen a safe level of detachment from the actions of the users. Cohen had given away his work, and others had used it to implement the protocol for their own projects, some legitimate, others less so. However, nothing in BitTorrent's underlying architecture, its presentation by Cohen or its features suggested how it should be used. BitTorrent was neutral, because Cohen's goal was neutral. This provided Cohen with a safe level of detachment from the tsunami of piracy that his protocol would soon facilitate.

The legitimate BitTorrent

Cohen's only concern was optimising his project, ensuring every detail was perfectly honed for efficient data transfer. By the end of 2003 he was still unemployed but donations from grateful BitTorrent users were keeping him afloat. However, BitTorrent's popularity was catching the attention of Gabe Newell, Managing Director of computer game studio Valve. Valve had become recognised as one of the top game studios with its popular 1998 title, *Half-Life*, which won more than 50 'Game of the Year' awards and received *PC Gamer* magazine's 'Best Game of All Time' award in 1999, 2001 and 2005.[5] The studio was in the process of producing the sequel, but also had another project it wanted to implement. Valve was designing a platform to sell and distribute PC games over the internet called Steam. Tired of waiting for the games publishers to tackle online distribution, Newell decided to take on the project. Rather than rely on physical distribution the company wanted to make the system entirely digital distribution, allowing customers to buy and then download PC games. Games at the time were significantly large, often the size of a DVD[6] and downloading straight from a server would barely be feasible. Newell contacted Cohen and hired him onto the Steam development team to try to overcome the problem. Cohen didn't stay with Valve long, barely a year; however, his influence in the Steam architecture is apparent. Having a completely distributed system where users provided copies of games to other users was not safe. It was perfectly possible to change code in the game files and then distribute them masquerading as legitimate copies, posing a big security risk. Instead, Steam implemented a system of resumable, broken-down files, which are downloaded from a range of company-controlled servers dotted around the planet.[7] The Steam software ensures that all the files match the description of what should be present, and if files get corrupted or deleted, automatically replaces them. Not only did this aid in the initial download, but updating the products also became streamlined, as updating could involve incremental alterations rather than requiring the user to completely replace the game data. Valve had said little about precisely what Cohen's role in this system development was. It's equally probable that Valve had already engineered such a system and brought Cohen in for optimisation purposes, as Newell stated that the company was actively looking for distributed publishing experts before finding Cohen (Schiesel, 2004). Steam eventually proved to be a successful venture, and in 2009 announced 25 million active user accounts and a 205% increase in sales over the previous year (Valve, 2010). With Newell's core philosophy that PC gaming was a not a product but a service economy, this success and dominance drastically changed the market of PC gaming's distribution and production (this is covered further in Chapter 7).

Rather than work with Valve, instead Cohen looked back to BitTorrent as a business opportunity. Having seen the success of his work, his father was hoping Cohen would try to benefit more from it. If his work was clearly good enough for so many people to be using it, why not get some form of payment? Cohen was hesitant; he hadn't made BitTorrent with the view of making a business out of it, and didn't consider himself corporate material. His initial offering at building the BitTorrent empire wasn't much; the main income source from BitTorrent was through exploiting the BitTorrent brand, selling official T-shirts and taking a more direct approach to asking for donations. However, when he met Ashwin Navin through a mutual friend in 2004 they quickly began discussing BitTorrent.

Navin formerly worked for Goldman Sachs and Merrill Lynch as an investment banker and research analyst, and then, prior to BitTorrent he worked for 'Yahoo!' where he was responsible for mergers and acquisitions. Navin clearly had the business acumen and head that Cohen didn't and he was convinced that Cohen should be doing much more than T-shirts. He was hired on as company president (Cohen retaining his position as CEO) so that Navin could handle the business whilst Cohen got on with the engineering. In September 2004 they registered BitTorrent Inc. and stopped offering the open-source BitTorrent code. The BitTorrent protocol and code was of course already released and roaming in the open-source wilderness; however, Cohen's company retained the right to exploit BitTorrent commercially. Programmers were free to use the protocol as they had done before but the company was ensuring that, when it came to offering BitTorrent services and partnership to other companies, BitTorrent Inc. would be the sole provider (Bulkley, 2006; Ernesto, 2006b; Thompson, 2005).

Throughout 2005, BitTorrent Inc.'s primary business model was through selling advertising space around a dedicated BitTorrent search box. The search hunted for Torrent files around the web; however, the company was always in competition with the community sites. The latter often managed to garner a dedicated user base by providing the very latest media. With only a search box these illicit but well-managed sites were tough competition. The primary business goal was to mimic these community sites, providing access to the latest films, TV, music and games via the BitTorrent protocol. To be legitimate would require the blessing of the major rights holders but luckily they were just as keen. In 2005 the big blockbuster movie was *Revenge of the Sith*, the third of the new *Star Wars* releases. In May 2005, *Revenge of the Sith* was being traded heavily on the illicit community BitTorrent sites, which got the attention of the MPAA who looked into where this new piracy system had come from. However, unlike its previous encounters with rogue programmers, it appeared from interviews with Cohen and the company's current model that BitTorrent Inc. was looking to operate legitimately. Cohen had never supported using BitTorrent for piracy, and continued to be vocal about BitTorrent's lack of anonymity. In July 2005 Cohen was contacted by Dean Garfied, head of legal affairs for the MPAA, and they worked out a deal.

The deal amounted to little at the time; BitTorrent Inc. agreed to ensure it did not link to infringing content and the MPAA agreed that it would be favourable towards a future arrangement with the company. With its reputation bolstered by this nod from the industry, the company sought investment. In September 2005 it managed to secure $8.75 million from Doll Capital Management; co-founder David Chao had been using BitTorrent to share family videos and was already intrigued (Berfield, 2008). The company had already taken small steps to try to change the BitTorrent image. Its talks with the MPAA had garnered it some kudos from the venture capital sector, but within the media industries the name BitTorrent was, despite Cohen's distancing, still synonymous with rampant piracy. Navin attempted to combat the often-made association of BitTorrent to Napster, highlighting Cohen's purpose of producing the protocol, its lack of promotion as an infringing device and its inadequacies for privacy. This collection of circumstances would protect the company from claims of 'inducement'. The company also announced that it would be working to stop unauthorised use of the BitTorrent name. Those that wanted to use the name for a piece of software or product would have to submit to a vetting process and pay a licensing fee (Borland, 2006). The announcement had little impact on the production of BitTorrent software in the open-source community, which continued as normal. However, by the end of 2006 it was clear that the announcement was not necessarily directed at the non-commercial developers anyway, but instead was to ensure a steady revenue stream from licensing BitTorrent to hardware companies. The aim was to integrate BitTorrent into various pieces of home entertainment hardware. The idea, reminiscent of MP3.com's plans for hardware integration, was that set-top boxes would be able to download media directly from the net and play it on the home TV. The result would be a closing of the gap between internet content delivery and the traditional home TV (Falcone, 2007; Lacy, 2006). Navin had been negotiating with various film studios since Cohen's initial MPAA meeting and the intention was that when the official BitTorrent Entertainment Network (BEN) was running, there would already be hardware in place that supported its integration, making it one of the first internet-based media delivery services available.

The BEN launched in February 2007 with the blessing of the major Hollywood studios, including Warner Bros, 20th Century Fox and

MGM. The service offered approximately 3,000 films and many more episodes of popular TV programmes. The network utilised users to distribute the paid downloads between themselves; however, in a similar fashion to Steam, they also hosted the files on servers which acted as members of the swarm. This ensured a stability of high speeds and also ensured that there was always a source to download from, even if no users were available to share. Though the original intention was that all content would be available for rental and purchase, Cohen and Navin reported that the studios were demanding too high a price for film purchases and so they were only able to offer rentals. Cohen, with his usual candour, stated his disapproval of the DRM that had been a necessity for the studios to get on board. He was critical of its impact on user experience and expressed a desire to strip it out of the system. DRM was inefficient and messy, an anathema to BitTorrent's streamlined efficiency. The company's biggest challenge was to draw BitTorrent users away from the illicit community download sites, and into their paid service. However, for many users DRM was a barrier as, in terms of usability, the content offered by the entertainment network was lacking. One unconvinced user interviewed by the *New York Times* stated:

> The sad thing is, it's not about the money... I'm not interested in renting a movie. I want to own it. I want total portability. I want to give a copy to my brother. Digital convergence is supposed to make things like this easier, but D.R.M. is making them harder.
>
> (BitTorrent user quoted in Stone, 2007)

The DRM limited the lifespan of the film files, making themselves redundant after 30 days or 24 hours once the file began to play. TV episodes, although bought by the user, were only authorised to play on two devices which were limited to computers running Windows or presumably BitTorrent's licensed hardware vendors. This meant that Apple Macintosh users, and Linux operating-system users (the core of technically savvy internet users) were out of the loop and the files could not be watched on the growing army of portable media devices, such as Apple's iPod. The pricing model was also deemed to be too steep; although the prices were comparable to other download services, users were donating their internet connections to distributing for the company without compensation (Needleman, 2007).

Cohen's technology was certainly revolutionary but the business built around it was far from groundbreaking. On offer were inferior files that did not have the functionality that was available on the illicit networks. Free open downloads from illegal sites could be played anywhere, anytime, kept as long as you wanted and cut up and messed with. Files from illicit networks could be owned and treated as property by the user. In contrast the files that BitTorrent Inc. was offering were clearly owned by the companies that had licensed them, and customers weren't being provided with an incentive to accept the compromise. Despite the breakthrough protocol behind it, the BEN was bogged down by the same rights-centric weight that had sunk previous legitimate services. The service, which had started up in February 2007, had its closure announced in November 2008, alongside the lay-off of half the company's staff (Stone, 2008).

The failure of the BitTorrent Entertainment Network can probably be attributed to multiple factors. Although the technology was significantly better in terms of efficiency and overhead costs the company had been competing against already-established online media distributors such as market dominator Apple, whose iTunes Store had been opened many years earlier before Cohen began working with Valve. In 2005 Apple had begun distributing TV shows and movies, and had a large pre-existing user base in the form of iPod owners. This market dominance in portable media devices meant that Apple had a large enough user base to make it work, despite very similar DRM still being a requirement for film and TV (Apple Inc., 2003, 2005, 2009). BitTorrent Inc.'s offering came very late to market, and though BitTorrent the protocol had a very well-established user base, it was with the illicit community sites, not with BitTorrent Inc. Arguably, when your service has to charge, it is difficult to compete with a service that provides the same content for free. However, as the interviewee for the *New York Times* expressed, it was not the price that differentiated the services, but the quality of what was on offer; the pirates had a better service.

BitTorrent the company still continues on, producing new more efficient iterations of the protocol, which are implemented into their official client µTorrent. µTorrent was a free client produced outside the company using the open code that Cohen had released before regaining control over it. The client was incredibly popular with BitTorrent users and had retained 50% of the user population; clearly superior to the official offering of the time. BitTorrent Inc. bought it from the original developers Daniel Ek and Ludvig Strigeus in December 2006 (Ernesto, 2006a). It is speculated that the proceeds from the sale helped Ek and Strigeus launch their next project, a streaming music service that utilises background P2P to ease server load called Spotify. BitTorrent the protocol also continues to live on in the incredibly successful online game *World of Warcraft*. Blizzard Entertainment, the game's creator, has long utilised the technology to distribute the significantly sizeable copies and updates of the game to its customers. Twitter, the hugely successful social networking tool of the late 2000s has also announced work towards integrating BitTorrent into its system. Twitter, which allows individuals to post short messages up to a central space for others to see, runs on a multitude of servers to ensure that updates are received by users globally in good time. To ensure this speed all of these servers need to synchronise on a very regular basis, which is where BitTorrent and project Murder come in. Murder (as in a murder of crows) is an attempt to utilise BitTorrent's distributed file-sharing system to keep these servers synchronised with as little effort as necessary. Though not fully implemented at the time of writing, the system should ensure that Twitter can scale as its user base grows even bigger (Github, 2010; Klinker, 2010). Finally, the most prevalent legitimate use of BitTorrent is in the back-end of Facebook, the internationally successful social networking website, which has already implemented what Murder is working towards (Ernesto, 2010a).

These ventures (Steam, Twitter, Facebook, Spotify, *World of Warcraft*), though successful enterprise uses of the BitTorrent protocol, are dwarfed by the overwhelming use of BitTorrent for more community-based file distribution, of both copyrighted and public domain media. These sites are often comprised of two elements, a website index and a tracker. The tracker, as already touched on in the example of the documentary maker, is the back-end of Torrent distribution. It is used to co-ordinate computers that are part of a Torrent swarm, ensuring that computers with the relevant file can locate each other, and that the distribution is done as efficiently as possible. The index is the front-end; a website where private individuals can upload the small Torrent files to be hosted, along with a description for search purposes. This allows others to easily find what files are being shared on BitTorrent swarms and obtain the small Torrent file, which contains the information to let them join the swarm. Often these sites are run on the understanding that the moderators will allow almost[8] anything to be uploaded, and that it is their users that are responsible for whatever they decide to make available. During the BitTorrent protocol's first years of release, there were a multitude of these sites which set up to provide central spaces for content distribution. However, many of them received cease-and-desist notices from various rights-holder groups such as the RIAA and the MPAA and quickly shut shop. The sites required a degree of legal centrality in the people that had registered the website names and operated the site and tracker. This made them particularly vulnerable to being shut down. However, through the utilisation of technological innovations, incongruity between national laws and simple acts of physical relocation, some of these sites have endured and represent the politicised illicit BitTorrent that Cohen never intended.

The Pirate Bay

In November 2003, Swedish citizen Gottfrid Svartholm was in Mexico working as a programmer for a security consultancy when he heard that the activist group Piratbyrån was looking to set up a BitTorrent tracker: he considered the request, assembled some old computer hardware into a cardboard box, and dubbed it The Pirate Bay. In five years' time he would be standing with three other men in the Stockholm courtroom where this book began, accused of undermining the economy of the Western world because of the decision he made.

There are multiple likely reasons why Sweden produced the climate appropriate to produce and sustain a site like the Pirate Bay. Thanks to a government policy of subsidising private computers since 1998, Sweden could boast the highest levels of access to a home computer in the world, meaning a highly technologically literate population. Furthermore, the above-average speeds in broadband of 40–100 megabytes per second were huge compared with the average single-digit speeds of other European countries. This meant that downloading media (particularly large files such as films) from the net was a viable option much earlier than Sweden's neighbouring nations. Sweden's copyright laws were also not as stringent as in the US, and did not consider online copyright infringement for personal use to be a serious enough issue to prioritise. This did not mean that Swedes were immune to charges of copyright infringement; in fact, the country boasted the largest amount of infringement warning letters of any other country. In the US, 300 letters were sent per million residents between July and September 2004; in Sweden it was close to 7,000 (Ekman, 2005).

With illicit file-sharing being akin to a national norm, this massive stream of infringement notices and consistent anti-piracy rhetoric from industry representatives produced a strong backlash. The Piratbyrån formed in August 2003 out of a group of anarchic hackers, programmers and artists. The Piratbyrån or Piracy Bureau (in satirisation of the nation's primary copyright enforcement group, Antipiratbyrån) worked as a political think tank that aimed to provide an alternative viewpoint to the dominant industry groups that were lobbying their government. Many of them had found that their own creative works were being impeded by the claims of the large copyright industries and felt a need to act. Though they utilised the traditional methods of disseminating their ideas such as conferences, papers and interviews, the group was not averse to using artistic presentation and technological innovation to also further its message (Torsson and Fleischer, 2005). With a significant amount of trackers being taken down due to claims of copyright infringement, the group saw it as necessary to not only set up its own, but also to be resistant to any attempts to have it shut down.

When Svartholm volunteered his expertise to build a tracker, the group's symbol of resistance was born. Comprised of some spare parts housed in an old cardboard box it was as ad hoc as the Piratbyrån hacker community. Svartholm chose the name as an unashamed statement of piratical intent – a safe harbour for piracy, but also a rejection of contemporary IP law. It was the kind of aggressive humour that became a core element of the Pirate Bay image. Running it through his employers' internet connection the tracker dominated company bandwidth, eventually leading to complaints. In 2004 Svartholm moved it home to Sweden. There, fellow Piratbyrån members Fredrik Neij and Peter Sunde assisted in getting it established with a better connection and they began to grow the site. Neij soon took over responsibility for maintaining the hardware and dealing with the ever-increasing traffic that the site would attract (Swartz, 2009b). Sunde was a member of the Swedish forum and demo scene.[9] As demos were often made as part of an introduction to a crack designed to bypass copy protections on software, the demo scene was as creative as it was illicit. The forums were filled with files being passed around and discussions of various copy protections and the ways to circumvent them. However, for Sunde the idea that his hobby was swiftly becoming a serious crime was ludicrous. That sharing knowledge could be a prosecutable offence jarred with his sense of ethics, a conflict that led to him becoming the 'official unofficial' spokesman for the site (Norton, 2006).

The site gained legal advice from Mikael Viborg who primed the group on Swedish IP law; the law that would, in conjunction with the BitTorrent architecture, protect the Pirate Bay as other Torrent sites fell. The site did not host copyrighted material; it hosted Torrent files, which pointed towards copyrighted material. The notion of contributory or secondary copyright infringement did not apply as it did in the US, making the site perfectly legal under their nation's law (Ekman, 2005; Norton, 2006). Secure in their understanding of Swedish law, site operators Sunde, Neij and Svartholm made it site policy to respond to cease-and-desist notices with aggressive humour. Posting the exchanges into the 'legal' section of the site, they ridiculed the very idea of IP and the pomposity of US companies that made demands of individuals in other nations. One of their first notices was from lawyers representing the film studio Dreamworks, regarding the availability of the movie *Shrek 2*. Dreamworks received a reply from the site informing it that Sweden was not a state in the US and that US law did not apply. The site also suggested that the Dreamworks legal team sodomise itself with a retractable baton. Legal threats did not seem to concern the Pirate Bay. As increasing amounts of Torrent sites collapsed alongside the once prominent FastTrack network, the Pirate Bay remained. It served its users with a dependable source of Torrent files and the politics of the Piratbyrån via the antics of the site's operators. By late 2004 the site had become an international ideological force of its own – much bigger than the Piratbyrån that had founded it. The site separated from the Piratbyrån, which moved on to other projects, leaving the site to operate independently.

Though the site continued to receive legal threats, the operators responded in their characteristic way and the site flourished. The Pirate Bay had become an international haven for file-sharers whose previous networks were either long shut down or deemed unsafe. Users within site communities would often report any difficulties they had with a download; increased reports of receiving letters from industry lawyers could kill a site quickly. As the Pirate Bay's user population increased so did the attention of the various international IP groups. Antipiratbyrån (the Swedish copyright enforcement group) was sending thousands of letters to ISPs regarding their customers' file-sharing habits, and individual prosecutions were taking place. However, the Pirate Bay was still a significant problem for the copyright industries. With its technical architecture of only hosting Torrent files rather than content, the site was difficult to prosecute under Swedish law. Furthermore, acting against the site had become politically risky. It was estimated that in 2005, 10% of Sweden's 9 million citizens were active file-sharers and with the Pirate Bay at the centre (Harrison, 2006). It appeared that the site was bulletproof. In typical Pirate Bay style, on 1 April 2006 the site played a prank on its users announcing that it had been raided by the Movie Picture Association. Two months later, on 31 May 2006, it wasn't a prank.

When the Swedish police arrived at Neij and Svartholm's ISP business, everything was evidence. Their company hosted the Pirate Bay, the Piratbyrån site, and a variety of other commercial customers, and the distinctions between the server boxes were a moot point. The police were looking for copyrighted material and any one of the servers could contain it. Systematically they removed all the hardware from the building in aid of exploratory evidence gathering. This hardware seizure was not only limited to site servers, but also the personal computers of anyone connected to the site, right down to the cables and webcams. At the time of the raid there was no case against the Pirate Bay administrators, but to produce a case, evidence was required. Svartholm and Neij weren't present at the time; however, when they did arrive they were swiftly taken into custody without charge. Their legal advisor Mikael Viborg joined them not long after as a suspect rather than counsel. Viborg's legal knowledge meant he secured himself a legal representative for the interviews, but Svartholm's request was denied during questioning (Grandwell, 2006; Viborg, 2006).

As the Western world woke up to find the site down, rumours started circulating until the prominent BitTorrent blog Torrent Freak broke the news that the servers had been taken. In Sweden there was a public uproar, with many politically minded groups, Piratbyrån especially, being acutely aware of the incongruity of the event in regards to Swedish law. The MPAA announced a victory against filesharing, declaring no space on the globe to be a haven for illegal copyright infringement. On the surface it appeared it was correct; the site was still non-operational, as was the tracker. In reality the situation was not so clear. Though no-one could obtain any more Torrent files, those files that they did have continued to operate as normal, forming swarms and distributing as they always had. Trackers by this point had become only partially necessary, useful for co-ordination and efficiency, but not absolute. Various technologies had been built into the BitTorrent system by groups outside BitTorrent Inc. that meant if a tracker went down (which, being enthusiastically run on a shoestring, they often did) the swarms would continue.

The two primary systems of decentralisation, Peer Exchange (PEX) and the Distributed Hash Table (DHT), operated in tandem to ensure swarm stability in the event of tracker loss. PEX operated in a similar way to the GNUtella systems in that once an individual had joined the swarm, the few other users that they connected to would provide them with a list of who they were also connected to. The swarm would continue to update each other's lists as more users joined, providing a massive directory of swarm members that could be drawn upon without tracker assistance. DHT worked in a similar way to bootstrapping in GNUtella, with the client software having a list of nodes that accumulated lists of all active Torrent files. These lists worked using hash tags rather than storing any clear information regarding what was being traded in the swarm, simply containing a numerical ID and a list of IP addresses. The DHT nodes were technical facilitators, lacking any information about what they were facilitating, be it the latest Hollywood blockbuster leaked two weeks before release or a piece of open-source software. The DHT nodes would update each other, ensuring that even if a user is the very first person in the swarm (the initial seed and source of the file) and only informs one node of their position, the others will get wind of it fairly quickly. Even without the support of a tracker or knowledge of who was hosting a file, PEX and DHT meant that a single user could shout into the abyss, and eventually someone would shout back.

It was for this reason that most of the world's Pirate Bay users didn't notice the downtime. If they didn't go looking for more Torrent files they would have been none the wiser. Regardless, the world wouldn't have to wait long. Whilst the police had been busy seizing hardware and dealing with Svartholm and Neij, Peter Sunde (the then anonymous fourth member of the group) was elsewhere in the building. As the police disconnected the server stacks one by one, Sunde was one step ahead backing up as much of the site as possible. Coordinating with community members Sunde reconstructed the site out of the backups and took the reconstituted data to a temporary site in the Netherlands. The Pirate Bay hardware was still in custody when the Pirate Bay site jumped back to life after a total downtime of approximately three days. All precedents showed that when a site or service was taken down by legal intervention it stayed down: the Pirate Bay hadn't. This was a significant moment for the site, a demonstration of resilience and defiance that showed industry power was not absolute. With no business aspirations but simply a community that operated under strong ideological cause, the decentralised ad hoc Pirate Bay would not be an easy target. The site administrators, now released from custody but charged with copyright infringement, changed the site logo to show their trademark pirate ship bouncing a cannon ball off of the word Hollywood. The backups had had their locations hidden; anyone attempting to look up the IP address of the new Pirate Bay servers found that they were located at hey.mpaa.and.apb.bite.my.shiny.metal.ass.thepiratebay.org; clearly theraid had not affected their sense of humour. Although downtime had been minimal, the group resolved that it was not good enough and put in place an automated backup and fail-safe system. If there was a next time, the backups would kick in within minutes and the site would continue to operate, hosted in another country (Ernesto, 2006c).

The main question of the event for the Swedish public was, 'Why had it happened?' In their view this kind of targeted, aggressive raid without prior evidence was not supported by their legal system. Reports emerged that Swedish officials had been in discussions with the US government and the MPAA about the Pirate Bay in April prior to the raid. The Swedish Justice Ministry profusely denied the talks had directly led to the raid and that they were simply general discussions regarding copyright. Swedish law had a barrier between ministers and police; ministers were allowed to brief the police on the broad direction they would like them to focus but direct orders were strictly disallowed. Public TV channel SVT reported that it had viewed documents proving that the US had threatened Sweden with blacklisting through the World Trade Organisation (WTO). Dan Eliasson, undersecretary of state in Sweden's Justice Department, later confirmed that the US had intended to place Sweden on the WTO surveillance list on the grounds that it was a danger to US copyright. Prosecutor Håkan Roswall who had ordered the raid addressed the allegation. Roswall stated that, when he had been summoned by the Justice Ministry, threats of blacklisting had been mentioned, but that he was also told that he should not interpret that as direction as to what he should or should not do. The situation was messy. That Piratbyrån – an independent political think tank – had, whether intentionally or not, also been wiped from the net by the raid just made everything look worse. Though investigations occurred little came of them (Ewing, 2006; Grandwell, 2006; Roper, 2006). Many Swedish citizens were unsettled by the event, perceiving that their government placed US corporate interests above their own rights.

Throughout late 2006 and 2007 the group continued to run the Pirate Bay as equal parts media portal, political activist hub and art project. In December 2006 the International Federation of the Phonographic Industry (IFPI) ordered Swedish ISP Perspektiv to block a Russian website called Allofmp3.com. The site illegally sold copyrighted music via a unique loophole in Russian law that allowed it to operate as a radio station. The site had a history of legal tribulations and allegations of underhand conduct, but when Perspektiv complied with the ban, the Pirate Bay administrators took offence. Regardless of the Russian site's activities they saw such actions as web censorship and in retaliation blocked Perspektiv from its own site, cutting off all of its customers. Through the Piratbyrån they announced that, although an ISP was perfectly within its rights to say what would and would not pass across its network, its customers also had the right to transfer to an ISP that does not engage in censorship (Smaran, 2006). Then in January they announced their intention to start their own country where copyright law did not exist. They focused their efforts on micronation Sealand – a disused World War II platform off the British coast that had been claimed by Major Paddy Roy Bates as an independent nation in 1966. Bates was a pirate radio DJ who wanted the platform to broadcast Radio Essex to mainland Britain from outside British territory. In 2007 Bates' son still owned the platform under the title Prince Michael of Sealand but was looking to sell. The Swedes couldn't resist the opportunity for a stunt and started a tongue-in-cheek campaign to raise the obviously unobtainable €750 million required. They never reached their target, but on the way they generated a lot of publicity that took the endeavour more seriously than they did (Chan, 2007; Ernesto, 2007b; Out-Law.com, 2007). Throughout the year they also ran a variety of specific media sites designed to facilitate access to media that was particularly timely, such as all the films at the Oscars, and another which listed all the Eurovision entries for the year. They promoted their favourite musicians on the front page and took the credit for Swedish artist Familjen's Grammy win in December. The site was a larger-than-life hub of political and media engagement, with a few pranks and stunts thrown in for entertainment.

Despite the fun, Håkan Roswall was still generating a case against the site and its operators. The servers from the raid were still in custody but evidence gathering was proving difficult. From the prosecution's perspective it was because the site operators had put too much security into their systems and cracking their way in was slow. In the site operators' view it was because there was no evidence to begin with. However, Roswall's work dug up a relatively unknown association with the Pirate Bay that caused much controversy. Carl Lundström, one of five heirs to the largest crisp-bread manufacturer in the world, Wasabröd, had made his fortune when the company was sold off. He used his share of the profits to start Rix Telecom, a broadband and internet telephony supplier. When Frederik Neij moved back to Sweden after the project in Mexico he worked at Rix, where he established the Pirate Bay using company servers and bandwidth with Lundström's permission. However, with this connection came difficult associations. An exposé by German newspaper *Der Spiegel* highlighted Lundström's political connections and funding of far-right nationalist groups and politicians. The report only worsened when allegations arose that Lundström not only funded nationalist groups, but also had taken part in assaults on minority groups. Speculations that the Pirate Bay, far from being a liberal haven, was actually a nationalist movement began to circulate. Sunde publicly denied the allegations, stating that they simply accepted initial assistance from the company. Magnus Eriksson of Piratbyrån also came to the site's defence publicly stating that the site only ever accepted bandwidth and server space in the company during the initial Swedish set-up and that, when Neij left the company, the site went with him (Ernesto, 2007a; Roettgers, 2007). For Roswall the association was significant enough to include Lundström in the case alongside Peter Sunde, Gottfrid Svartholm and Frederik Neij who, in January 2008, stood accused of copyright infringement, each facing two years' imprisonment and a $180,000 fine.

As harsh as the consequences were, the trial did not come swiftly. Though filed in January 2008, it took until February 2009 to start the trial and the site operated undeterred throughout. As usual journalists were able to view the trial to keep the public informed. However, Sunde was concerned, noting that many of the mainstream news sources which the journalists wrote for, were closely tied to or even owned by their opposition. Prior to the trial, as assertive as ever, Sunde demanded that the trial be open and accessible to the public. Their initial demands were to have seats reserved for bloggers alongside the usual journalists, rooms set up where up to 150 others could watch a video stream of the court proceedings, which would also be simultaneously broadcast on the net. A few days after the demands they got most of their wishes, settling for an audio stream handled by public broadcaster SVT. To compensate for the lack of video, SVT would send a journalist to live-blog alongside the stream to ensure as much information could be conveyed as possible. Plans were also drawn up for the site community to pitch in as well, ensuring that those members who were able to speak both Swedish and an additional language would live-blog the audio feed in as many languages as they could (Enigmax, 2009k, 2009n). The day prior to the trial two of the defendants, Sunde and Svartholm, were joined by members of Piratbyrån at the Stockholm Museum of Technology for a press conference. There the group asserted that this was not a trial against the Pirate Bay, but against four individuals: the site would therefore continue regardless of the outcome. When asked whether they feared the amount of money they were liable for in fines, they were dismissive, implying that the amount was so ludicrously high that they would never be able to pay any of it off, making it essentially ineffectual. They called the trial a 'Spectrial', a mash-up of the words spectacle and trial that implied that the trial was more about asserting rhetorical dominance rather than tangible impact; the plaintiffs were not actively seeking the end of the Pirate Bay, but to publicly punish the people that espoused the ideology behind it (Enigmax, 2009g).

The bravado exuded by the site administrators meant that on the first day of the trial the tone outside the courtroom was far from serious. Various supporter groups had arrived outside and were intent on joining in on the spectacle, setting up street bands, handing out sweets and waving flags. Inside the courtroom, as the bloggers blogged and twittered the courtroom happenings, the first day of the trial began. The prosecution's main purpose appeared to be to argue that the site operated as a commercial organisation, and that Lundström was a financier and shareholder in the company, thus establishing Lundström's reason for being named. The defendants and their supporters' moods were positive and Sunde even took the time to send a message through the Pirate Bay site to point out the technical ineptitude of the prosecution. Roswall had had issues getting his PowerPoint presentation to work and had eventually been ordered to forget it and rely on his papers; as far as Sunde was concerned, if this was the level of technical ability they faced, he had nothing to worry about (Ernesto, 2009h).

The second day in court appeared to further strengthen this image when half of the charges against the defendants were dropped. Roswall had explained to the court how BitTorrent operated, and had evidence which he believed clearly demonstrated that the tracker that the Pirate Bay operated had been involved in the transfer of copyrighted material. Roswall presented screenshots of a computer downloading a Torrent file from the Pirate Bay site and then using it to obtain copyrighted material. After the explanation Neij requested that he be allowed to comment on what Roswall had just presented and managed to neutralise his entire argument by pointing out that whoever had produced the screenshots had left DHT on. As it has already been explained, DHT is the technology that allows Torrents to operate without a tracker, instead relying on using other peers in the network to self organise. With DHT left on there was no way to prove that the Pirate Bay tracker had been used at all; all charges relating to 'assisting copyright infringement' were dropped immediately (Enigmax, 2009a).

On the third day the trial continued with the plaintiffs still looking to prove the other charge that the defendants assisted in making copyrighted material available was valid. Questions regarding the individual defendants' involvement with copyright infringement were the main focus of the prosecution, alongside justification for the size of the fines. Each member was defended by their individual lawyers who spoke with the intention of placing a distance between their client and the copyright infringement that took place via the site. Svartholm's lawyer simply argued that users provided the content and that he had no control over what that content was. However, Sony had already complained to the court that someone had the ability to remove content as misnamed and dangerous files were routinely removed from the listings; leading to the question of why that cannot be done for infringing files. Sunde's lawyer emphasised his role as site spokesman and argued that he had no other interaction with the site. One of Lundström's lawyers (he had brought two, one a copyright expert) used what affectionately became known to the site community as the 'King Kong' defence.[10] The defence was so named because Lundström's lawyer furthered the defence used by Svartholm's lawyer by focusing on a prominent Pirate Bay uploader that operated under the handle 'King Kong'. The lawyer argued that his client had no ties with the user King Kong and as such could not be considered as assisting in King Kong's actions. As with prior illicit-network cases, it seemed that the aim of the prosecution was to prove direct involvement with the transfer of copyrighted material, whilst the defence utilised the technological mechanisms of the code to distance their clients from it; a defence that had precedent in prior P2P cases, but had not yet fully succeeded. However, the defendants were still positive and Sunde was still confident in his characteristic way. After the trial concluded for the day the defendants went out for pizza where they happened upon the prosecution team doing the same thing. Sunde asked them if they could pick up the bill; the prosecution declined (Enigmax, 2009c).

When the trial resumed the topic of the day was the source of the content that had been named in the charge as being infringed on; in particular the availability of big studio content such as the latest blockbuster films and chart-topping albums. Lundström's lawyer, Per E. Samuelsson, questioned Svartholm on the source of the material. From the exchange it was revealed that much of the content was not from individual users but from the 'Warez' scene. 'Warez' groups (also known as 'the Scene') are anonymised communities that endeavour to get hold of, remove any restrictions from, and release the very latest films, music, games and software. In addition they produce software that allows the circumvention of copy-protection mechanisms and small programs that are able to generate new licence keys to authenticate software. It is speculated that the members of these groups are members of the media industries somewhere along the distribution line, allowing them early access to unreleased media. For example, despite the major concerns regarding the recording of films in cinemas via phones and hidden camcorders, many Scene releases are DVD-quality files that have been made using screener discs distributed to the press for review. These contacts mean that often Warez groups are able to achieve the highest kudos through '0-day Warez', the release of media not only on the same day as its official release but sometimes even weeks before. There are a multitude of groups which often fight between themselves, leaving taunts and slander against rival groups in the information files provided with their releases. This rivalry drives the groups to seek out and be the first to release the biggest commercial media for the kudos and status that it brings.[11] These revelations played well for the defendants as Samuelsson argued that as these releases were not produced solely for the site, but were actually leaks of a leak, the content could already have been distributed to millions before it was even listed on the Pirate Bay, a clear attempt to downplay the idea that the site was the hub of internet piracy.

The mention of these Warez groups clearly made an impact on one of the prosecution's lawyers, Peter Danowsky, who questioned Svartholm Warg further. Danowsky wanted to know if these Warez groups 'hired' the Pirate Bay to distribute their content. Svartholm answered that in fact these groups hated the Pirate Bay as much as the media industry did. Far from operating on principles of informational freedom, Warez groups operated as closed units, exchanging releases between their members. Zero-day Scene releases were for the knowing inner circle of the IT elite, kept out of sight of the majority of the population, both out of a sense of tribal community and to avoid garnering too much attention. However, the proliferation of P2P networks and leaks from inside their groups had meant that they were suddenly supplying millions of people with copyrighted material complete with text files and tags proclaiming which group was responsible, making them very big targets. The Pirate Bay clearly stood close to its mantra of informational neutrality; whether it was the work of the highest ivory towers of Hollywood, or the darkest corners of the Warez scene, if it was information then its distribution would be facilitated without question (Ernesto, 2009a; McCandless, 1997).

On the ninth day a specialist in research surrounding the music industry was brought in as an independent witness to comment on the site's impact on industry revenue. The expectation was that the witness would verify the claims of economic malaise made by the prosecution. However, when questioned by the prosecution's lawyers Professor Roger Wallis consistently replied that his research had shown no evidence to suggest that the Pirate Bay would be negatively impacting the music industry and that it may in fact be driving sales of tickets for live events. Wallis' reputation was brought into question by the prosecution, asking him multiple questions regarding his credentials in an attempt to discredit his testimony. When his time was over Wallis was asked by the judge if he wished to be reimbursed for travel expenses, to which he jokingly replied that the court could send his wife some flowers if they liked. The court declined; however, the Pirate Bay supporters who had received the information from their in-court reporters took it as an opportunity to express their appreciation. Supporters grouped together and a few days later Wallis and his wife had been inundated with flowers, chocolates and gifts estimated to have cost more than €4,000 (Enigmax, 2009o; Ernesto, 2009i).

As the trial continued similar arguments and questions arose in almost direct repetition of the previous days. Lawyer for the IFPI Magnus Mårtensson produced screenshots demonstrating the use of the Pirate Bay in the act of copyright infringement and again found the evidence useless when confronted about the use of DHT. Neij was questioned by Peter Danowsky regarding the ownership and control of the site in an attempt to discern exactly who was responsible for the site as a whole. Neij frustrated him with talk of a diffused anarchic community that had no discernible hierarchy or organisation, clearly not what Danowsky was looking for. When questioned about his involvement, Neij disclosed that he enjoyed the technical challenge, and that the site was the only place he had found where the challenge was available without having to suffer top-down management from a boss. Danowsky recalled back to the raid on the Pirate Bay, and the speech that Neij had made during the protests outside the Swedish parliament.[12] Neij had railed against the attempts to close down the site and, although not particularly inflammatory, it was the act of someone more politically engaged than someone who just enjoyed the technical challenge of network management. However, Neij countered, stating that the speech had in fact been written by Tobias Andersson of the Piratbyrån; Neij had simply delivered it. At the time of the questioning Tobias was sitting in the courtroom but when noticed was asked to leave due to his upcoming role as a witness later in the case. On his way out Andersson asked the courtroom if (despite his exclusion from the proceedings) he was allowed to listen on the audio feed, to which one of the judges replied, 'Well, we cannot stop you, can we?' (Swartz, 2009b)

As the conclusion of the trial drew closer the expectation of many of the site's fans was that the case would be thrown out. Having followed the case closely via the blogging and tweeting coming from the courtroom, it appeared that the plaintiffs had lost due to the disassociation of those accused from the site, which had been made possible by the technical architecture and fuzzy organisational structure of the site. This is why the guilty verdict that was pronounced on 17 April 2009 came as a shock to many (Swartz, 2009a). The four men would receive a year in prison and a fine for $905,000 each. As far as the P2P community understood it, the defence was solid, and the plaintiffs' evidence had been systematically discredited. The defence questioned the suitability of the judge that had presided over the case. Tomas Norström's objectivity was questioned significantly when the defence announced that he was a member of the Swedish Association for Copyright, and the Swedish Association for Protection of Industrial Property. They called for a retrial claiming that Norström's connections had invalidated his decision. The defence lawyers even began publicly speculating to Swedish media network SVT that Norström was not randomly selected as judges should be under Swedish law, but was in fact hand-picked for the trial. The court decided to review Norström's connections to determine if a retrial would be necessary. Another judge was appointed to the review, but was swiftly removed when critics pointed out that the new judge was connected to the same groups as Norström. Though prime evidence for conspiratorial murmuring, both Norström and his reviewer had been chosen from the branch of the court that specialised in copyright law; a necessity for the case but very likely to draw on individuals already active in the various copyright associations. The final choice of the court was to assign a group of three judges from a different division of the court to judge Norström's suitability. The verdict was positive for the courts; Norström's connections did not undermine his decision. Peter Sunde believed that one of the three judges who had investigated Norström's connections was also too closely affiliated with the lawyers for the plaintiffs; however, little came from his objections. A retrial was denied and the defence filed an appeal. With an appeal in the pipeline the site operators, though convicted, would not yet face their punishments and the site remained active (Ernesto, 2009b, 2009e).

Whether they were founded or not, the Norström incident had undermined the authority of the Swedish courts dramatically. The trial had driven an increase in membership to Sweden's niche political party, the Pirate Party. The group was originally set up by Rickard Falkvinge in 2006 to deal with the concerns of Sweden's citizens regarding IP law in their country. The large volume of lawsuits against individuals for copyright infringement had become a national issue and a change in Swedish law had made the sharing of copyrighted material online illegal. Falkvinge used policies established by the Piratbyrån to found the Pirate Party and swiftly gained enough support to become a recognised political party in Sweden (Falkvinge, 2011; The Local, 2006). After the verdict of the trial, and the subsequent undermining of the courts, the Pirate Party enjoyed a tripling in its membership. The publicity and new membership was so great that the party won two seats in the European parliamentary elections a few months later with 7.4% of Sweden's votes (Byfield, 2009; the *Times*, 2009).

Only a few weeks later perhaps the most surreal year in the site's history began when it was suddenly announced via a press release from a relatively unknown company that the piracy site was to be sold and turned into a legitimate business. Though in common pattern with previous P2P hubs, the Pirate Bay was ostensibly an ideologically rather than business-driven endeavour. The company was Global Gaming Factory (GGF) whose CEO, Hans Pandeya, was a relatively unknown entrepreneur. Pandeya intended to purchase the site and reinvent it as a legitimate licensed hub for media, utilising the community to distribute media whilst royalties were paid to the rights holders. The idea was reminiscent of Sharman and BDE's attempts to derive revenue from Kazaa. However, almost immediately after the announcement the bizarre nature of the sale began to unfold. It transpired that, prior to the announcement by Pandeya, trading of GGF's shares had been halted by market regulators after a sudden spike in stock value. The regulators suspected insider trading as little could account for the sudden gain in value that GGF's stocks were enjoying (Enigmax, 2009l, 2009p). The reputation of GGF continued to decline as, in tandem with Pandeya's repeated assertions that he would be purchasing the site, a variety of events undermined him. Despite managing to secure some recognisable names into the purchase their association ultimately did not help. John Fanning, majority owner of the original Napster supposedly approached Pandeya about joining his consortium, pledging $10 million to the purchase. However, after discussions between the two men the deal was never mentioned again. Wayne Rosso, former Grokster CEO did join Pandeya, but swiftly left the partnership after his confidence in the viability of the deal dropped. As far as Rosso was concerned, Pandeya didn't have the money that he said he did, and he wouldn't be able to raise it either. Pandeya set the date of the deal as 27 August regardless.

When the date of the sale came around an agreement was made that GGF would transfer $7.8 million to the current owners of the site, which surprisingly was not Sunde, Neij or Svartholm. Prior to the verdict from the Swedish courts the site founders had become embroiled in another case against them, brought by the Dutch anti-piracy group BREIN. The site operators had always emphatically denied that they owned the Pirate Bay site, claiming that it had been transferred to a company called Reservella in 2006. During the BREIN trial when the operators' lawyer was asked for proof of the claim that the site had been transferred to this mysterious company registered in the Seychelles, he responded that he could not. BREIN produced credit reports that implied Neij was the individual behind Reservella; however, that was refuted with the argument that Neij was simply working for the company to do the basic work to keep the site online. The trial was, at least on the topic of Reservella, inconclusive (Anderson, 2009). Despite the details of who exactly owned, and thus could sell, the site being less than transparent, Pandeya was resolved to complete the deal. However, Pandeya's ability to meet that deal appeared to be waning. Before the deal was made most of his investors had pulled out, leaving him severely short of the required funds. Then after the agreement, reports of Pandeya's motorbike and car being repossessed hit the headlines and Peerlialism, a P2P development company Pandeya intended to purchase for the venture, said that there would be no purchase as GGF had no money. A former GGF board member said that Pandeya already owed him in excess of 6 million kronor ($840,000) and that Pandeya was in debt to the Swedish tax authorities for 780,000 kronor ($110,400). Pandeya's message throughout was: 'The deal will go through' (Enigmax, 2009h, 2009j; Eriksson, 2009).

But Pandeya's deal didn't go through. With a diminishing investor base and an expanding parade of creditors the whole arrangement collapsed. Pandeya has insisted that the deal has simply been delayed; however, at the time of writing no further action has been taken. The viability of the deal is questionable anyway as with many of the prior attempts at corporatising these illicit networks, the value is derived from the community involvement. However, when the initial announcement came the community began its own project of 'Pirating the Pirate Bay', downloading as much of the site so that when the sale went through it could reinitiate the site from a backup and carry on as usual, free from Pandeya's interests (Enigmax, 2009d, 2009e; Ernesto, 2009d, 2009g).

Though the defendants had lost the trial in Sweden and the sale had collapsed, the site continued to operate. The verdict was against the four men, not the site, and with an appeal not far off the impact of the trial decision was yet to show. This did not stop various rightsholder groups from attempting to effectively remove the site from the internet. A consortium of broadcasters and film studios named the site's bandwidth provider, Black Internet, in a suit in Stockholm with a threat of $70,000 in fines. Grudgingly the ISP complied, calling for other ISPs to join them in supporting the Open Internet

Foundation, a free expression advocacy group. The delay in hosting barely lasted a day and the site resurfaced with another bandwidth provider willing to risk similar threats. Twenty minutes after the new host began serving the site it received a call and was subject to similar threats (Enigmax, 2009f, 2009m). The second ISP lasted a few months; however, with no funds to fight a court battle it also had to relent. In turn the site hardware was moved to the Ukraine with a new host. The Ukraine's internet infrastructure was less reliable than that of Sweden's, but other Torrent sites such as the well-known Demonoid had found it to be a safe haven for the moment. However, due to the network topography of the country, much of its traffic was routed through the Netherlands. The Netherland's anti-piracy group BREIN swiftly moved on this weakness and ordered the companies carrying the traffic to block the site severing access for many users once again (Enigmax, 2009b). It was a troubling precedent for some; the companies being targeted were not hosting or doing business with the site, but simply acting as carriers for another company's traffic. Rights holders did not need to threaten the groups directly involved in the continuity of a site, they simply needed to make it known that pressure would be exerted on anyone that carried its traffic (Ernesto, 2009c). A couple of days later the site was moved across national borders again, into the Netherlands. The site's new host, CyberBunker, was an ISP that had set up shop in a former NATO nuclear bunker and was particularly intolerant of demands to censor traffic, having already clashed with BREIN over MP3 sites in the early 2000s and coming out unscathed (Ernesto, 2009f). Whilst with CyberBunker the administrators reduced the infrastructure of the site by removing the dedicated tracker. Peer-exchange and DHT had advanced enough that they believed the site could operate without it. The tracker's stability had not been optimal since their legal troubles and many had moved their tracker usage over to open alternatives that had sprung up such as Open BitTorrent. These were all-purpose public utility trackers that allowed anyone to utilise them for their distribution purposes. With the announcement of the sale to Pandeya, the exodus of the community out of the Pirate Bay architecture had, alongside the backup movement, involved this tracker switch. The decision to remove the tracker came in tandem with the implementation of 'magnet links'.[13] These clickable links on the site took over from the usual habit of downloading a Torrent file first by launching the user's BitTorrent client and instantly hooking them into the swarm to download the Torrent file. This reduced the load on the index site, making it more flexible for relocation and reconstitution, and placed it another step away from involvement with the infringement by simply providing links rather than Torrent files (Enigmax, 2009i; TPB, 2009).

Six months later the site was forced to move again when Sven Olaf Kamphuis, owner of CyberBunker, received threats regarding a collection of films available on the Pirate Bay. The notice stated he would be liable for €250,000 per infringement of every film and could face prison for his role in hosting the site. Kamphuis, despite his emphatic support, was forced to comply and the site moved on (Enigmax, 2010a). The site's next and (as of writing) final host was its most interesting (even more so than a former NATO bunker). The site left the Netherlands to return to its native Sweden, despite its initial expatriation being due to its legal vulnerability. However, the site's new host would be able to provide it with a unique layer of protection. Taking advantage of their new positions in the Swedish and European parliaments, the Swedish Pirate Party took over responsibility for the hosting of the Pirate Bay. The unprecedented move meant that the site had now gained a new level of status. Not only was it the Pirate Bay, infamous space of online piracy, but also an extension of the Pirate Party's own political message. In an interview with Swedish broadcaster SVT, Sunde ventured that under the party's banner, attempts to shut the site down could well be argued to be political censorship (Anderson, 2010c; Benholm, 2010). In October 2010 the appeal was heard in the Stockholm courts and little of the arguments from either side changed. The defendants lost and received a similar judgment, reducing the prison sentences but increasing the fines; varying the sentences between the men based on the judge's understanding of the level of involvement each man had in the site's operation. Svartholm was not present and did not receive his sentencing due to being ill and out of the country in Cambodia. Months later it was reported that Svartholm was still yet to be sentenced, and as far as the courts, the plaintiffs and his lawyer knew, had disappeared completely.[14] The following December Lundström filed the final appeal to the Swedish Supreme Court and is still waiting to be heard (Enigmax, 2010b, 2011; Ernesto, 2010b, 2010c).

A piratical ideology

The story of the Pirate Bay is one of rhetorical conflict and decentralisation through technical and social means. Its underlying work, beyond the simple technical provision of copyrighted and non-copyrighted information, was as a tool of ideological dissemination. Attempts at codifying the ideology of the pirate have been myriad, though the best attempt is that of Berry and Moss's (2008) 'Libre Culture Manifesto' which, through 21 statements, argues for the value of culture free from ownership. The site's roots in the Piratbyrån activist group is an origin unlike prior distribution networks, which were produced either out of enquiry or entrepreneurship. First, beginning as one element of a wider campaign, the site swiftly became a significant force for rhetorical influence in the Piratbyrån's wider work to challenge the systemically ingrained assumptions of IP. It served as a centralised hub for those who already shared the beliefs of the activist group, but more importantly was a key platform to introduce these principles to a wider audience, expounding them through their actions as well as words. Through the site's defiant demeanour and approach to dealing with rights-holder demands it retained longevity where other Torrent sites had fallen under pressure. This stability and strength in the face of what seemed like insurmountable opposition positioned the site as a figurehead for resistance in the IP conflicts.

This stability was in large part due to the decentralisation of the Pirate Bay system, both technologically and organisationally. With the majority of the network infrastructure being handled by the users' computers, the site and the tracker were flexible enough to relocate and reconstitute internationally in response to legal attempts at dismantling. Further reduction of the infrastructure through the use of magnet links and the closure of the single tracker made this system even more decentralised and difficult to pin down. The non-hierarchical operation of the community and the ideological drive meant the site always had support if it needed to relocate quickly, even if the threat of legal action was looming as individuals such as CyberBunker's Kamphuis demonstrated. The site could also rely on the community to take its own initiative when it felt the site was under threat, as the preparations for a 'TPB diaspora' showed. This strong ideological foundation behind the site led to its most interesting element of support with the circular narrative that sees the site produce its own safe harbour. The political party whose success was derived from the targeting of the site ultimately used this new-found power to provide a stable, safe harbour. The site which had begun with the intention of acting as a political tool had circuitously become one.

In some respects the Pirate Bay is vulnerable: without a client-side search the BitTorrent structure requires some sort of external hub for swarm access, even if the rest of the infrastructure has been outsourced to third-party trackers and client-side computing. The key central element of the assemblage is thepiratebay.org, the entity behind the domain where individuals come to find their way into the swarms now under political protection. However, the index site is not only a swarm gateway, but the space of focus for the act and ideology of piracy, for both sides of the conflict. The necessity of this centrality is now questionable. In some respects the site has played its part, fulfilled its original Piratbyrån brief by disseminating the group's ideology. The site now sits as a quasi symbol of centralised media, be it the centre of an alternative media market, a hackers' market. The bizarre buyout that appeared dead before it began, the removal of the tracker and the implementation of magnet links point to a further dismantling and diffusion of P2P file-sharing, driven in reaction to the state and industry interventions. Comments from Sunde throughout the buyout period indicate a view to dismantle the Pirate Bay community internally, an act of further diffusion. In an interview with Torrent Freak after the announcement he indicates a need for the community to diffuse, that placing its hope in a single site is not the answer to its ideological considerations. He emphasises the need for change in the BitTorrent assemblage, for 'more trackers, less centralised systems and more people standing up for the community' (Ernesto, 2009j). As much as the representative groups hope to quash the act of file-sharing by toppling the figurehead, it appears that the end result may simply be a great diffusion of the ideology instead.

The rights holders presented themselves to be the guardians of culture, a top-down curatorship that fervently protected the copyright industries in the interests of the social good. In their view, if the economic element was removed from the equation, the copyright industries and so creativity as we knew it would perish. The site and its ideological underpinnings also saw themselves as cultural curators, providing a free, accessible platform for information dissemination, believing this informational free-flow to be the true way to foster creativity culture and a free society. Many were heavily invested in the site's welfare and expressed great gratitude to anyone willing to support them; exemplified by the particularly human moment of the trial where supporters inundated an independent witness with flowers in appreciation after their testimony. Thanks to the site's influence 'Pirate' has become an ideological position and the Pirate Party, bolstered by the trials and tribulations of the Pirate Bay figurehead, cemented this ideology into a political entity with the aim of implementing that ideology. Going from being simply a Swedish phenomenon the Pirate Party is now international, present in multiple countries and officially registered in countries such as the UK, Canada, Germany, France, Finland and Italy. The popularity of the party has spread both through its association with the internationally known Pirate Bay site, and through populist backlash against attempts to govern the use of the internet. In the UK, for example, the Pirate Party was officially formed in response to Britain's Digital Economy Bill, which was provisionally considering implementing filtering systems to control what could and could not be accessed online to curb copyright infringement (BBC News, 2011). Having seeded the habits, ideas and technologies of mass information dissemination it appears that now the site that initiated the swarm intends to dissolve into it.

It is this ideological aspect that makes the Pirate Bay story differ from its spiritual P2P predecessors. Though the FastTrack years would greatly define the industry's approach to file-sharing, the Pirate Bay is a continuation of the principles Frankel expounded through the GNUtella model. At the centre of a convoluted arrangement of technology, art groups, political parties and hacker communities sat an index site as a hub for the social and software network. The site acted as a focal point and catalyst for the rhetoric that sat in opposition to established precedent and has served much of the purpose Piratbyrån intended. However, despite the focus it has gained from its supporters and its detractors, its demise will not mark the end of the wider ideological issue of how to deal with the ruptures caused by digitisation. The true impact of the Pirate Bay is not the tangible, quotable losses of revenue to the media industries around the world, but the violence of the suggestion, a suggestion now diffusing into an even more difficult to contain entity, that when the

Western world is increasingly becoming an information economy, information should be free. As the incumbent industries grasp at these figureheads of an alternative media market, each time the figurehead collapses and slips between their fingers, fragmenting and diffusing into increasingly difficult to regulate entities. With each succession of piracy system, regulation has appeared to have only decentralised the problem further. How do you deal with a market like this? You compete.

7
Hacking the Market

If you had Coca-Cola coming through the faucet in your kitchen, how much would you be willing to pay for Coca-Cola? There you go. That's what happened to the record business.

(Doug Morris, CEO of Universal Music Group,
quoted in Mnookin, 2007)

Keeping it in the family

When Michael Robertson was looking to promote his idea of selling music as MP3s via his new venture MP3.com, he found the labels to be cold to the idea. They were disinterested, seeing little benefit in these low-quality compressed audio files. When Napster sought licensing, a similar situation occurred: told by the courts that they required a license to operate, they found the price set to be unattainably high and eventually liquidated whilst their only industry ally, BMG, was punished with liability for Napster's actions and their eventual consumption into Vivendi. When Niklas Zennström and Janus Friis' arranged meetings with music and film licensing groups in the US they found themselves not in negotiations as arranged but at the receiving end of accusations and threats. During the rise of media's digital distribution, the media industry was out of the loop and intended to stay there, a decision which at the time, made perfect sense.

The shift from cassette and vinyl to CD had been a sustaining boon at a time when profits were dropping. The CD, an insider innovation from Sony Corporation, revitalised the recording industry, which had found vinyl's price to have reached a market low at $8.98. Consumers had become comfortable with the price and any more was considered to be profiteering. However, the CD, sold under the banner of its clean digital sound and novelty of the new, meant that the standard price could be set at $16.95 with consumers willing to pay a premium for the format. Though the labels sold CDs under the banner of high-quality digital sound, what brought the customers flocking were the new capacities of the CD. They were robust, durable, portable and allowed quick skipping around the album without fiddly re-adjustment of the phonograph arm or repeated rewinds and fast-forwards to locate the right spot (Mnookin, 2007). Even if customers already had the music in another format, the CD, as a way of instantiating music, brought with it a set of capacities that made it worth having, and they sold in droves. The CD changed the expectations of what music should cost, resetting the perceived value of recorded music and with it upping the income of the recording labels. CDs cost the labels more to produce in the short term – inefficiencies and a lack of production plants being the primary cause. However, consumers were unaware of what it cost to produce these futuristic laser-read records giving the labels the opportunity to adjust price perception. Labels inflated the price to cover the cost of production and then some, pulling in more profit than the well-established but now mundane vinyl could.

The labels also took the opportunity to redefine artists' contracts, citing the cutting-edge technology as a reason to change well-established contractual habits. Costs to the label were added to the contract meaning that artists were required to pay a higher percentage to them for production and distribution. Under the vinyl system artists received on average 75 cents for every $8.98 record. Under CDs, even after the new deductions they received more, 81 cents per disc, but relative to the retail cost the label was taking the lion's share. Under vinyl, the artist received just under 0.08% of the sale price for every record. Under the new CD scheme the percentage was just under 0.05%. Control of the whole production chain from act discovery down to ownership of the manufacturing plants had meant a solid grip on vinyl production and the CD was no different. As consumers flocked to repurchase albums on CD, labels began re-opening their vinyl facilities and refitting them for

CDs. The recording industry had been on a low entering the 1980s, with CBS, one of the largest labels, dropping profits from $58 million in 1981 to $22 million the following year. However, as CD adoption went up and people replaced their vinyl collection with CDs, profits soared leading to an industry golden age across the 1980s and 1990s. By 1999 the profits from US sales alone were $12 billion and production efficiencies meant that the profit margins got even higher (David, 2010; Knopper, 2009; Mnookin, 2007). These were the boom years buoyed up by a persistent back catalogue conversion by music fans seduced by the format capacities and convinced that music media had reached the end of history.

It was clear that the labels also intended that CDs would be the be all and end all of media. Internal R&D was focused primarily with multimedia, hybrid data and audio discs, extending the CD not supplanting it (Knopper, 2009). At the beginning of the 1990s CD prices began to fall as market pressures pulled them down. The average price of a CD dropped from $15 to $10 and consumers' price expectations began to lower. However, then the average price rose again, and then again. Tower Records founder Russ Soloman saw retail prices raise a dollar each year, each time the labels giving various reasons regarding the costs of production. With complete control over the supply chain, no-one could argue with the price (Knopper, 2009: 33). Throughout the latter half of the 1990s prices had stabilised and showed little sign of dropping. In 2000 the US Attorney General's Office investigated this unusual phenomena and found that the biggest labels had colluded to raise prices. It was industry practice to pay retailers subsidies to help with the cost of advertising industry products. These subsidies were in the millions of dollars, meaning that any retailer without a subsidy would be at a serious disadvantage. This gave the industry leverage to set the prices at retail level by withholding subsidies to anybody that advertised prices lower than a set price. The retailer could still sell at a lower price but they were not allowed to promote it without losing industry backing. This manipulation artificially inflated the CD prices, keeping income up when it should have been falling. Similar attempts to control the market also came in the industry's attempts to close down the resale market on used CDs, sales that cut into industry sales and did not provide it any returns – all perks of monopolising the supply chain (Cisneros, 2000; Deutsch, 2002; Easley, 2005; Glusman, 1995;

Knopper, 2009). Compact discs had placed the labels in a significant position of strength. Even when their various methods of adjusting the prices had been deemed unacceptable, as a format the CD was a brilliant stalwart for industry interests. It is understandable that the industry would be less than happy to see it leave.

The common perception of the recording industry is that it was caught unawares by digital distribution, though that wasn't necessarily the case. By the time Robertson had approached the labels they were aware of the MP3 and that individuals were using the format for trading music online. In 1997 the RIAA's head of anti-piracy had found people trading MP3s over chat rooms, websites and file-transfer protocols. Though the labels had been warned back in 1990 by the Fraunhofer Institute that the MP3 standard could transform the CD into an incredibly open format, little attention had been paid to it. The internet at the time was just an emergent development with slow speeds and a small user base; it was unlikely to catch on that fast (Knopper, 2009). When the RIAA discovered this activity it sent cease-and-desist notices to the offending online spaces and the activity swiftly stopped; problem solved. However, as the practice grew in size with P2P networks arising the issue became more pressing.

Doug Morris, a 72-year-old industry veteran and then CEO of Universal Music Group asserted to *Wired Magazine* that the industry was aware of the possibilities of digital distribution, but it didn't know what to do. There were no technologists in the industry, and it wouldn't have known one if it saw one; at least that's what Morris thought. Morris was a veteran music man, entering the business as a songwriter in 1966; he also produced, started his own label and oversaw artist distribution. He later became CEO of Warner Music US in 1994 and then CEO of Universal in 1995.[1] In his interview with *Wired* in 2007 he represented the well-entrenched element of the music industry. He knew what was happening on the internet, but he was a music executive, not a programmer. He was in the business of making music people wanted to buy. His challenge wasn't satisfying the consumer's format desires, it was to find and produce music that would sell. He asserted that the industry's detachment from digital distribution couldn't have gone any other way. However, the interview portrays a man still bitter about the transformations forced upon his territory and the difficulties they've brought him. Other industry insiders who worked with Morris believed that when digital distribution came around, Morris' lack of knowledge and engagement with the subject was probably more wilful ignorance than helpless confusion (Mnookin, 2007).

His staff, primarily those in Universal's new-media department, were more accepting of the situation and desperate to get his attention to the possibilities of digital distribution. Throughout the 1990s IT entrepreneurs like Michael Robertson were courting with the major labels, looking to sell them the new channel of media distribution and found themselves to be just as successful as Robertson was. Formats like Liquid Audio and Real Networks' RealAudio were developed specifically with industry needs in mind, providing built-in encryption and rights controls. However, the other major labels were just as receptive as Morris was and even these tailored rights-centric solutions were turned down just as Robertson had been. Despite expansive licensing discussions between Liquid Audio's Gerry Kearby and Sony's executive Al Smith, the reality of Sony's intention was to never let its content get online. In a brief moment of honesty after months of back and forth negotiations, Smith said to Kearby,[2] 'Look, Kearby, my job is to keep you down. We don't ever want you to succeed' (Kearby quoting Al Smith in Knopper, 2009: 120). The CD had kept the industry well since the mid-1980s and it had no intention of letting go of its channel control. Licensing to vendors outside of the well-established distribution chain had the potential to undercut CD sales and the labels had grown to such a size, and their executives had become too comfortable, to take such risks.

The technologies brought to the recording labels by people such as Kearby and Robertson were what Christensen (2006) refers to as 'disruptive' technologies. In general terms, disruptive technologies are entrants to a market which offer different capacities to the incumbent products available. They are often cheaper to produce and (in the initial stages) poorer quality than established products, but offer a capacity or capacities that make them more desirable than what is currently available. The incumbent in the market, in this case the labels, instead will focus on technologies that will sustain their business. These can be simple incremental improvements on their current product such as multimedia CDs, or radical sea changes, such as Sony's MiniDisc, but they will be developed with a view to sustain current profit margins and to complement the current industry

structure. Often, these new disruptive technologies will offer capacities their market isn't asking for and are too small to further grow
large companies that have reached market dominance. The rational decision for any company is to wait it out to see if it takes off.
If demand improves to a viable level and the tech gets to a point
where it will provide return on investment then the company will
take interest. However, at a lower production cost to the original
product the disruptive technology allows space for competitors to
emerge and easily undercut. These small competitors who lack the
overheads and demands of the market leaders can serve the fringe
market without going out of business. This fringe market eventually
grows to the point that the incumbents will take interest. However,
by that point it is too late and the incumbents have been undercut, often finding that consumer expectations for their product are
now defined by these rapidly growing new competitors (Christensen,
2006; Easley, 2005). This works in a completely free market without
restriction, but when IP gets involved the process is not so clean-
cut. These entrepreneurs with their cutting-edge technologies kept
coming to the labels because they still retained dominance of the
production of music through their control over the IP. Without their
co-operation no business could even begin to compete. The process of disruptive technology was stalled at the first hurdle because
the opportunity to compete had been blocked by the incumbent.
Robertson, though inconvenienced by their lack of interest, had not
been dissuaded and instead sought to woo unsigned artists to the idea
of digital retail. However, his drive for more popular music led him to
the My.MP3.com system where the uncertainty of the law gave him
an opportunity to offer owners of music CDs a digital equivalent;
his intention being to make a business from providing the capacities of digital distribution rather than the content itself. Robertson
also kept extensive logs, designed to demonstrate to the labels that
My.MP3.com encouraged sales of CDs. He wanted to convince them
that MP3 could be an asset to their retail system rather than competition (Levy, 2006). For his persistence he found himself at the end of
an industry lawsuit. The court, having concluded that My.MP3.com
required licensing as well, Robertson was again at the labels' mercy.
The eventual conclusion meant the dismantling of the labels' competitor after high licensing fees siphoned off Robertson's funds before
Universal's eventual refusal to co-operate finished the company off.

Had the recording industry involved itself with Liquid Audio or MP3.com, the history of digital distribution may have played out differently. Though it would still have been relatively late to digital music distribution, it was yet to be happening on the scale that Napster would bring in the near future. The opportunity was there to work with the entrepreneurs at the industry's door and begin to define what digitally distributed music was and how customers could engage with it. Rather than being perceived as being in conflict with customers' desires for the capacities of digitally distributed media, the labels could have been at the forefront providing those services. They could have also begun the uptake of digital distribution with a price tag on the files, attributing them economic value from the outset. However, there was little drive for the labels to do so; MP3 trading was, as far as the labels had seen, small scale. It was not their customers trading these files; their customers were in the shops buying CDs. For whatever reason that these individuals chose to trade these low-quality audio files, they were not a big enough population to be of any concern. Any move to digital distribution would be a move to relinquish distribution control out to third-party technologists, and with such lower overheads it may have cannibalised CD sales. Consequently, the opportunity to define the MP3 as a product, an extension of the recording labels' format line-up was not taken. Instead, the labels chose not to be the providers for this emerging new set of consumer demands, and in some cases actively worked against those interests with actions such as their work to control who was licensed to develop digital music technology (the SDMI) and their case against the Diamond Rio MP3 Player. The market was open for a competitor, in the sense that there was a new set of habits and expectations emerging around engaging with recorded music. However, the market was also to some extent closed. With the labels unwilling to license their catalogues out for other companies to distribute digitally, the recording labels had effectively vetoed digital distribution; apparently a stalemate had been reached.

A hacker's market

When corralled into governments, universities, or large multinational companies, and forced to follow rulebooks and wear suits and ties, they at least have some conventional halters on their freedom of action. But when loosed alone, or in small groups, and fired by imagination and the entrepreneurial spirit, they can move mountains – causing landslides that will likely crash directly into your office and living room.

(Sterling, 2002: 66)

When Shawn Fanning was developing Napster, he was not doing so with the intention to form a business. Though that drive would come later via his uncle, the initial impetus to develop Napster came from the desire to solve the problem expressed by his room-mate, and that he had encountered himself. His approach to solving this problem could be characterised as obsessive. Many descriptions of Fanning's work on Napster talk of irregular sleep patterns and an unshakeable focus on the work at hand, a focus so intense that it drove him from his place at Boston University to his uncle's couch where he could work with less distraction. As *Time* magazine's rather hyperbolic feature on Napster put it:

> He didn't need friends, family, financing – he almost went without food. He was self-sufficient, gaining sustenance and strength from the work, as if by his hands he was creating his own manna. And if the idea could nourish him, he reasoned, then how many others could feed on it as well?

(Greenfeld et al., 2000)

When Bram Cohen had found his problem he reacted in a similar manner; ditching his job to sit at his kitchen table and code for months on end. When Cohen was done with the project, feeling he had completed it as best he could, he gave it away; months of his life used and debt accumulated to solve a technical problem, the results of which he chose to post on the internet for free, and he fully intended to leave it at that. Fanning's project was also given away for free, out to the w00w00 contributors and then later on out to the wider public as word spread. Justin Frankel developed GNUtella entirely with the drive of giving it away and of relinquishing control over it. Frankel's work on WinAmp and GNUtella followed a similar pattern; developed because he felt the software was needed, for practical (Winamp) or ideological (GNUtella) reasons, and he had no qualms about giving the results of his labour away for free. For these developers of computer code, the goal was not to produce a product, but to solve a problem. This approach to labour is in no way uncommon to communities that are heavily involved in the act of programming and has a long intricate history.

Dubbed by many inside and outside of these communities as the 'hacker ethic', it is a mutable set of principles that often defy codification; though this has not stopped people from trying. One of the first attempts to do so comes from Stephen Levy, who derived his set of principles from his detailed history of computer researchers at MIT in the early 1960s (Levy, 2001). Levy believed that these individuals, responsible for so much of the initial development of computer technology had a closely held set of beliefs within their community derived from the academic working environment they were in, alongside the difficulties of working with the great hunk of computer machinery that was the TX-0, an experimental computer designed at MIT. From interviewing these early computing researchers Levy developed a set of seven 'hacker' principles.

(1) Access to computers – and anything which might teach you something about the way the world works – should be unlimited and total.

Always yield to the hands-on imperative.

(2) Essential lessons can be learned about the world by taking things apart.

Any barriers to taking things apart, be they physical, algorithmic, or legislative are deeply resented.

(3) All information should be free.

Free exchange of information allows for greater levels of creativity.

(4) Mistrust Authority – Promote Decentralisation

Free exchange of information and thus creativity is best supported in an open environment without hierarchical controls. Bureaucracy and arbitrary rules impede tinkering and innovation.

(5) Hackers should be judged by their hacking, not bogus criteria such as degrees, age, race or position.

Status can only be attained through action.

(6) You can create art and beauty on a computer.

There is beauty in code.

(7) Computers can change your life for the better.

Computers have a huge potential to improve just about anything.

(Adapted from Levy, 2001)

Other researchers have their own positions regarding the ethic's origins. Söderberg (2008) and Himanen (2001) make the case for the academic sphere's values and working habits such as volunteerism, the valuing of knowledge over money, and informational free-flow as being a significant element in the formation of the hacker ethic. Similar historical considerations of this hacker community such as Markoff's (2005) history of the personal computer and Sterling's (2002) comments on hacking history place 1960s' counterculture at the fore. A sudden university influx of those avoiding Vietnam conscription and a fascination with the perception-expanding potential of computing technology meant an odd convergence of computing hardware and liberal counterculture values. Sterling's (2002) brilliantly detailed account of the history of phone hackers, from the birth of the US telecommunication companies up to the early 1990s points at the 'Yippie' movement as the origin story for the more anarchic element of the hacker culture; the underground groups more likely to be cracking into a corporate server bank than building an open-source word processor. A sub-group of the 1960s' counterculture, the Yippies was perhaps the most anarchic faction of the wider countercultural movement. Its anti-Vietnam protests were not through demonstration but through avoidance of paying for using the telephone system, which had had a federal surtax imposed on it. Believing that paying for the phone service was directly funding the overseas campaign, the group sought to circumvent the requirement to pay in a practice that became known as 'phreaking',[3] exploiting technical (usually restricted) knowledge of the phone system to bend it to its own ends.

The group organised around the *Youth International Party Line*, a countercultural 'zine that mixed ideological rhetoric with technical documentation and guides on hacking the phone network. As knowledge of the phone networks increased through experimentation and stolen Telco technical manuals, so did the capabilities of those who began to treat the phone networks as their own personal playground. The veneer of political protest slipped quickly and the practice became one of convenience and entertainment coloured with a vague anti-establishment sentiment rather than direct action. Phreaks would appropriate corporate phone accounts for straight phone calls or use unused company voicemail systems for message drop boxes. They would often find their way into corporate conference-call systems to set up their own conferences of 10–12 people, chatting away much like social networks are used today. To keep the conference line open new people would drop in as others dropped out, all the while the fee clocking up on the company account. As the system became increasingly digitised turning into networks of servers, file-stores and bulletin boards, these phreaks also digitised.

This subculture became increasingly identified as hackers[4] by law enforcement agencies, who had been drawn into dealing with computer crime as Telco's became more and more frustrated with the abuse of their networks. No longer knocking around on conference calls, these groups drifted off to bulletin boards set up on home-run servers or sometimes set up as hidden colonies in the servers of unsuspecting companies. Proprietary technical information was still desired but was now found on the networks themselves on company file-stores, rather than in the refuse bins behind the company offices. It was deemed that this proprietary information should be shared freely, allowing these groups to continue their tinkering and play around the networks. Servers were hacked into and documents were retrieved to be added to the growing archives of the various bulletin board systems (BBS) that hosted the chatter of enthusiastic hacker groups. Though their actions could be interpreted as a statement of freeing information, disregarding the concept of information as property, it's probable that the real reasons were less heroic. The documents were the spoils of snooping around corporate servers, and were shared out across bulletin boards for bragging rights. Rather than the lofty ethic of informational freedom, more often documents were obtained to gloat and boast, to establish proof of skill and to solidify a position in the BBS hierarchy. Stolen Telco documents were for bragging rights; to pull out when arguing with fellow hackers to establish one's technical prowess and to slap doubters into submission.

Though less glamorous than auspices of informational liberation, the lineage of phreaking within contemporary hacker culture shouldn't be overlooked. It was the subculture that retained the anarchic attitude, the prankster nature and the darker elements of the wider hacker sphere that inevitably fed into the choices and actions of some agents within the history of digital distribution. This unseen anarchic element is still prevalent within wider hacker culture. Warez groups such as those whose work was leaked onto the Pirate Bay are one of the better known elements of underground hacker culture. Warez scenes are the source of the great majority of the new-release copyrighted content on piracy sites. They operate somewhat like gift economies, with status and kudos being given to individuals able to provide their particular insular group with new media content on the day of release or before, in a convenient and unrestricted format (Rehn, 2004). The underground prankster streak is also visible in contemporary 'hacktivist' groups such as Anonymous, which use their technical skill to campaign against – or harass – various companies, organisations and individuals that they feel have wronged society (Anderson, 2011; Coleman, 2011; Whitney, 2011).

The various takes on the history of the hacker ethic, though different, complement each other well: Levy's focus draws you towards a conclusion that the hacker ethic was derived from working with a big old chunk of computer history, a necessity of pursuing personal interest with this emergent technology. Markoff draws attention towards the view that the computer labs of the 1960s and 1970s reflected the politics of its time: anti-Vietnam, countercultural values laced with psychedelics and a desire to expand consciousness. Himanen and Söderberg point to the academic origins of computing technology, the relationship between the values of academia and the values of the computing sphere, both groups dealing primarily with knowledge and skill than raw materials and money. Then, of course, there is Sterling's specific focus on the Yippies, and the darker lineage of hacker culture. The best conclusion is that all authors are simply focusing on one aspect of a much wider historical picture, one that includes the both separate but interacting groups of academic researchers, home-computing hobbyists and anarchic activists who have all played a part in developing the wider values of the hacker ethic.

The attribution of a single set of values and political ideals across a wide expanse of individuals that we can loosely group as being information workers or programmers is blunt at best. As we have already seen there is a variety of histories to hacker culture, each of which equally valid but none of them standing as the single history at the exclusion of all others. Furthermore, we are not talking about well-organised and codified institutions, but a mass of disparate individuals each with their own biographies that will shape their values and ideals. However, there is something to be said for the ideals that appear to be shared across the different lineages of hacker history. Coleman and Golub (2008) argue that it is possible to consider a singular hacker ethic, but only if we remain aware that it is more of a sensibility shared across a variety of hacker genres between which individuals can fluidly move. Their work draws upon three lineages of programmer culture: amateur cryptography; free and open-source software work; and the hacker underground, to examine if there is a shared set of values present across each genre of hacker culture. The authors conclude that the heterogeneous genres of hacker culture express long-standing liberal ideas of freedom of expression, free speech, privacy meritocracy and individualism that have been reworked in their relations with computer technology. As such, despite the lack of one singular hacker value system and ideology, it is possible to talk of one with an understanding that it is the liberal foundations behind the overlapping, contradictory ever-shifting genres that those that may be identified as hackers move between. It is worth considering that the hacker ethic is, as Coleman and Golub argue, a fusion of technology and long-held US-style liberalism; the result of liberalism extended and augmented by the expansive reach and agency inherent in the manipulation of computing technology.

Of this amalgamation of hacker genres, the one whose practices have had the most study is the field of Free and Open Source Software (F/OSS). It is one of the more prominent groups that operates in close adherence to the hacker ethic today and its practices have interested those in management and organisation science as well as those interested in work and labour more generally (Kogut and

Metiu, 2001; Lakhani and Wolf, 2005; Shah, 2005; von Hippel and von Krogh, 2003). F/OSS communities develop and maintain software that is made freely available to the public as an alternative to proprietary packages. These free packages are also licensed in a way to allow anyone to edit or adapt the software if they deem it necessary. These free-software projects can run from small, simple single-function scripts all the way through to office suites, media production suites and entire computer-operating systems. These projects are often well supported by the community of developers and often rival paid proprietary software in functionality (for a comprehensive consideration of F/OSS communities, see Alleyne (2011)). Lakhani and Wolf's (2005) study of the motivations behind F/OSS developers found that by far the strongest motivator was the intrinsic creativity in solving a problem – the sense of satisfaction derived from working with a specific purpose. The majority of their survey[5] participants reported their work on the F/OSS projects to be on par with the single-most creative thing they had ever done and that they often found themselves so engrossed they lost large amounts of time when they should have been doing something else. Few were directly paid for their work by the project, though many reported working on the project during their day job, finding the project's programming work to be more alluring than their paid programming work. The strongest motivator to take part in the project was the drive to produce something that would fill a perceived user and community need. If there was a gap in the market that had not been filled, or had not been filled in a way that the developers felt was of most value to society, then they would engage in that project.

When the music industry left the market open through its lack of participation, user need and desire took over. This, of course, would not always happen; if a drugs company refused to release the patents for, and to develop, a much-needed drug, it is not likely that those who desire the drug would simply begin developing it instead. However, this user group was a special case in that those who had adopted digitally distributed music were the technically savvy, the early adopters and technical tinkerers. They took interest in what they could do with the technology because of their predisposition to find new technological developments attractive; they were hackers. As such, the user community that was unserved by the music industry was the same community likely to have been called upon if the recording labels had decided to embrace the technology. They had the necessary skills to produce the services they desired, and they had the tools as well. Programming is a highly skill-reliant form of labour. When producing new innovations, the tools of labour (the personal computer) can largely remain untouched, whilst it is the skill and intellect of the worker that drives the development of new products and services (Söderberg, 2008). Whereas with optical and vinyl media a whole host of physical tools and resources were required to operate a distribution system, the tools and resources for a digital system were already in the hands of those most qualified to produce one, with little investment on their part. The task of producing products to easily find, share, use and produce MP3 files was taken up by the community that most desired the products, and the community best suited to do so.

These groups come together in virtual spaces to form collectives of 'peer production' (Benkler and Nissenbaum, 2006), collaborations of hundreds or even thousands of individuals operating as a collective that freely shares knowledge and skills in aid of a common enterprise. There is little in the way of organisational management and though a degree of leadership emerges, often the projects are broken down into modular pieces where individuals can choose to dedicate their efforts, forming smaller units within the larger collective. These 'private collectives'[6] (von Hippel and von Krogh, 2003) form a powerful market rival to private enterprises that cannot hope to employ as many individuals as a F/OSS project can attract, nor could a private enterprise motivate them in the same way. Lakhani and Wolf's survey has already suggested that money is not the primary motivator to a F/OSS contributor, in line with the broadly agreed principles of the hacker ethic that favour the free distribution of information, not its financially driven exploitation through exclusion. Benkler and Nissenbaum suggest that the act of contributing to projects like these is rewarded by the virtuous nature of the endeavour. The sense of industriousness and creativity, coupled with the projects' inherent altruism and the social benefits of feeling part of a strongly united community are highly motivating. These arguments regarding the non-monetary rewards of peer-production projects are echoed by Himanen (2001) who argues that these projects fulfil a variety of social, creative and ethical needs. These F/OSS collectives of exceptionally able individuals, working in their spare time, for no pay, are able to produce highly user-centric software that can, due to the cost of production (close enough to zero), give away their labour for free.

However, this meant that rather than develop and design the products with commercial aspirations in mind, they were developed under the principles of the hacker ethic. As far as these communities of developers saw it, principles of control and exclusion were a negative force when developing programs for the greater good, where conversely they were an absolute essential in the sphere of information business. Lakhani and Wolf's research also found that the hacker ethic's belief in the freedom of information and a distaste for exclusionary practices hold as true today as they did in the early years of the 1960s. Alongside user need their surveys showed a strong drive amongst the community to contribute to the public domain. This drive flies in contradiction to our wider societal understanding of IP and the legal framework for IP, where metered exclusion is the accepted way to derive value from an information product. Yet in making a stance of ownership and thus rights of exclusion this position also opens up the owner to a degree of responsibility for the product. Where Frankel produced a system and then severed all ties to it, he walked away from all issues regarding its use. The Pirate Bay operated on an incredible level of disassociation of responsibility from the site through its operation as a non-hierarchical community project, where no one individual claimed ownership. Both have been relatively successful in their longevity despite their illicit nature.

However, FastTrack, as a similar but proprietary system, sought like other information products to derive profit from licensing its use. This meant the exploitation of FastTrack carried with it the responsibility for that product, ultimately leaving whoever was responsible culpable. However, with developments in digital distribution, where it was clear that to develop these systems legally had been vetoed out by the incumbent recording industries, this organisational arrangement and approach to IP of 'informational liberalism' was a boon to actually releasing, establishing and sustaining the systems. The design of these systems also carried with it a bias towards informational liberalism, in direct opposition to informational exclusivity. Friedman and Nissenbaum (1997) argue that information systems, rather than being value neutral and rational, can carry with them the values of its developers through the assumptions that govern its design. In the original digital distribution systems this bias was a reflection of the hackers' subcultural values, whose drive to produce the best software they could, relied on the definition of 'best' being informed by the hacker ethic, rather than business considerations. These systems treated all information as neutral, whereas later systems built with industry in mind treated data as having restrictions, owners and necessities of financial remuneration. This value-led design also applied to the MP3 format, which was produced under the assumptions of the hacker ethic, rather than concerns for informational exploitation, leading to its inherent openness which aided in its widespread adoption and prevalence within the P2P networks.

Confronted by this new type of market opening up without them, and the open standards of the MP3 so at odds with their own interests, the record labels were forced into engaging with digital technologies. Easley et al examined 128 record labels during the early part of the 2000s to determine whether piracy had had a role in their experimentation with digital distribution and online services. They found that those labels most affected by piracy moved to engage with the internet sooner than those who had been less affected. However, much of what the companies did was only focused on establishing a presence online – many were yet to set up a website – rather than providing a realistic alternative to the MP3. The majority of labels that had suffered high exposure adopted the practice of providing streaming clips of the songs via the Real Audio proprietary format. A significantly smaller amount dabbled with providing some songs for free as full downloads, but retained the proprietary 'Real' format that was at odds with the open standard of the MP3 (Easley et al., 2003). Overall the authors found that the illicit distribution of a label's content drove it to consider the internet as a useful utility for sales, but by 2003 it had not driven the majority of the labels to embrace the digital market, instead opting to use online space as a way of driving physical disc sales. After acquiring MP3.com, Vivendi Universal dropped the download element of the site that had attracted so many users, and instead used it as a marketing platform to sell CDs through an affiliated distributor. The move was somewhat innovative; the distributor CD Baby was (and still is) a site where independent artists could sell their own CDs (Hansen, 2001b). The affiliation continued MP3.com's work of marketing unknown and unsigned musicians, but Vivendi's approach was firmly towards the physical distribution model.

Those labels that did attempt to do digital distribution found a great deal of difficulty in making their own services successful. Label-run services such as PressPlay (which used the tech no longer needed at MP3.com) and MusicNet operated as subscriptions, requiring monthly payments for access to the label's music catalogues. Users had a monthly download and streaming limit, with the downloads rigged to be unplayable after 30 days, requiring the user to return to the service to regain the tracks. Restrictions were placed on how the tracks could be used; you could only burn ten songs to a CD per month though not all songs were burnable in the first place and users were restricted to using certain software for playing the songs (Spring, 2002). The labels' approach was entirely rights-centric, focusing on ensuring at all costs that users would not begin to develop the same distributive capabilities that the labels had held exclusive rights to for so long. However, in their attempts to ensure they were not providing users with the base materials for piracy, they overlooked what had drawn users to the digital format. As Walt Mossberg of the *Wall Street Journal* put it, PressPlay and MusicNet reflected the 'false lesson of Napster' that the labels had learned; that all people are thieves (Mossberg, 2002). In comparison with the MP3 format these subscription services seemed unnecessarily restrictive and in no way matched the capacities of the digital music already available from the illicit services. Whether the labels believed they were providing a truly competitive service or were simply making a token gesture to placate the courts is unknown but the services did not last.

Although in Michael Robertson's day prior to Napster users had expressed that MP3s were for music access, not for ownership, attitudes had since changed somewhat. Napster meant that users had cultivated large music collections on their hard drives, archives of music that began to draw the title of 'music collection' away from their CD racks. Users still wanted to collect music, just as they had with their CDs, but now they also wanted their collections to have all the capacities of the MP3 format. These new services undermined the users' ability to own their collection by encoding restrictive and destructive rules into the files. It seemed to many that the only way to get digitally distributed music with all its appealing capacities that they could 'own', was to avoid the industry-sanctioned digital services, and to buy and rip CDs. CDs being just another platform that held digital music had become a prominent leak in what was once the industry's robust and secure distribution system. Though it would eventually attempt to plug that gap it was clear that even if legally it had the power to determine what music went online and how, in practicality it had lost all control.

Although a rational decision for self-preservation, the recording industry's opposition to, and lack of experience with, digital distribution left the market open to an outside competitor, a 'hacker's market'. Though legitimate competitors attempted to formalise the digital distribution market, the recording labels were concerned about licensing their music to these outsider vendors. By vetoing the option to distribute their music online these recording labels had seemingly put a stop to digital distribution. However, the users who desired the capacities of this new distribution format were also the same population who had the technical skill to develop what was missing from the music mediascape. These users developed their own ecosystem of software, both for the distribution of content and for its use, but did so prioritising usability and access over rights and finance. Cost was not an issue for these developers. They were divorced from the overheads associated with the development and generation of new music products. Replication and distribution costs (bandwidth, hard-drive space, CPU cycles) were shouldered by the users, primarily because they were too small to matter. With informational freedom taking the fore these programs were made freely available on the internet so that those who were equally interested but unequally skilled in programming could also engage in digital distribution. The user base grew, increasing the variety of available content and the files flew around the networks, traded at the same price that it cost them to produce; nothing. This community, operating on a basis of user need and an ethic of free information had set the standard for the recording industry to live up to and had generated a burgeoning new market of demand for digitally instantiated music. Not only had it set the price but it had also set the standard of what a digital commodity was, what you could and could not do with it, a standard based not on business but on ideology. Whilst this coup on the recording industry's territory would leave it with the almost mantra-like consideration of the digital age, 'How do you compete with free?', it would overlook how the capacities of digital distribution were an equally, if not more important element than the price, 'How do you compete with open?'

8
New Media Gatekeepers

Bring in the technologists!

The music labels were in a bad way. Piracy was increasing as new, more complex P2P networks like GNUtella and Kazaa were developing in the wake of Napster. They had attempted to engage with the digital marketplace, but through either ignorance or apathy, their services MusicNet and PressPlay were failing to provide what the hackers market was. The services had been designed by lawyers with a rights-centric focus that overlooked what it was the customers expected from a music experience. People were frustrated with the music industry; they saw their lack of engagement with the digital market-place as a sign of increasing irrelevance and the offerings of MusicNet and PressPlay only made to strengthen that perception. However, it was not only the consumers that were frustrated by the indus-try's lack of engagement with the capacities of digitally distributed music.

Apple Computer Inc.[1] was well versed in designing for the user experience, but the lack of viable legitimate online sources for music meant its burgeoning flagship product, the iPod, was not achieving the heights of customer satisfaction that Apple CEO Steve Jobs felt it could. By 2002 the second generation of iPod was already in the works; the first generation having been fairly successful despite only being compatible with Apple Macintosh (Mac) computers. The iPod was reliant on the iTunes software to move music onto the device and at the time the only sources of music for iTunes were CDs that users would convert into files through the software, or the illicit hacker market. What Jobs thought was needed was a way to buy music directly in iTunes, to eliminate the need to go and find the CD or to engage with the illicit P2P systems. The music industry was aware of the problem too, but it was still yet to agree on a file standard that all the labels would accept. AOL Time Warner and Sony were leading the standards consortium but getting nowhere. They approached Jobs hoping to get him involved in coming up with a secure file format that all the labels could agree on. Jobs agreed but simultaneously Sony pulled out. Sony had dominated the delivery of music in recent decades with the Walkman and the development of the CD. It already had its own proprietary format and intended to push that instead.

Though the labels were looking to Jobs for a file format, he decided to take it ten steps further. In his opinion the majority of people 'stealing stuff' on P2P didn't want to, but there was no legal alternative. People didn't want to rent their music from PressPlay or MusicNet; they wanted to own it (Isaacson, 2011). Apple put together the plans for its iTunes Music Store and took it back to the labels. Jobs' first target was Warner Music whose CEO, Roger Ames, was scheduled to meet Jobs regarding a new way of securing CDs to plug that prominent leak in the chain. Jobs ignored the planned topic of the meeting and instead barraged Ames with his vision for an online music store, a strategy that did not fail to impress. Though Ames was first, the primary target was Doug Morris at Universal; as far as Jobs saw it, if they could turn Universal's head the other labels would follow.

Getting a meeting wasn't hard; Universal's parent company Vivendi was floundering and concerns were abounding regarding who would purchase its stable of labels. Rumours were circulating that Apple intended to purchase Universal, something that Universal would welcome. As mentioned, Morris was aware of his company's lack of technological acumen and being linked to Apple could only help the matter. Jobs' clincher to convince Universal and the other labels was twofold. First, he would present the full plan, giving them the whole picture of how the entire retail ecosystem would work. Where other companies brought slices of the picture to the labels, Apple presented the entire package – software, pricing, fee structures, marketing – and could deliver it. The second selling point was the lowered level of risk involved. The iTunes Music Store would only be accessible via the iTunes software, which itself was only Mac compatible. Though the second generation of Apple's iPod would eventually become Windows compatible it was never Jobs' intention to allow the iPod out of the Apple ecosystem. The iTunes Music Store would have a tiny market – the small slice of the computer market that owned both a Mac and an iPod. To the labels this small potential market was a positive selling point. If the iTunes Music Store ended up being a monster in their eyes, only a small proportion of the market would be infected, with the much larger Windows user base being walled off (Isaacson, 2011; Levy, 2006). This experimental sample was vital considering that Apple, though offering a retail system, was making seemingly ridiculous demands.

There was a gap between the sphere of the media industry and that of IT. Jobs loved music and believed himself to be a highly creative person (Isaacson, 2011). He also understood IT; more specifically he understood hackers, and the hacker ethic. Though he was now head of a multinational computer company, he had started out rigging computers together in a garage and messing around with the Homebrew Computer Club. Jobs understood what made hackers tick, and he understood what riled them (Hertzfeld, 2005; Levy, 2001). Jobs didn't want to associate the Apple name with another MusicNet or PressPlay. Customers would keep the files they purchased, not lose them after 30 days. They could share them across the computers in their house, move them to their iPods (of course) and burn them to CD to play in other devices. To placate the labels certain limits to these activities had to be included, but Jobs kept pushing in the interests of user experience whilst the labels were pushing in the other direction. Jobs recognised that it wasn't the price that put people off the labels' cursory attempts at digital retail, but the experience they had with the files in comparison with the open-access MP3. His aim was to negotiate the labels down to a level of restriction that the average user would barely, if ever, bump up against in their day-to-day use.

After long negotiations, the labels eventually agreed to license their content to the store. Even Sony, which had left the consortium, was brought back into the fold. Sony, which had originally been the consortium's technology developer, had a rocky relationship with Apple. The iPod was increasingly threatening to Sony's Walkman market. Furthermore, as other labels had signed on to the iTunes concept they broke off from Sony leaving it with a rapidly decreasing market for its file standards. As its list of collaborators dwindled rapidly it eventually had to follow the rest of the industry into Apple's plan (Isaacson, 2011; Levy, 2006).

The store launched in April 2003 carrying more than 200,000 songs, covering content from all the major labels. It was a feat that until then had been unheard of. After a week the store had made more than a million sales, more than all the legal downloads that had ever occurred (Levy, 2006). The labels were delighted by the success. People were purchasing music online in droves, and profits were still being made. Apple had brought them the solution. As the success of the store continued Apple decided it was time to roll out the iTunes software, and thus the Music Store, to the much larger population of Windows users. The labels had little choice but to agree; iTunes was the only place people were willing to buy music online. If the labels tried to say no the fallout from angry consumers would end any chances they had to convince the world that they were willing to adapt. However, this placed Jobs and Apple in a very strong position. When he and the labels had bashed out the details of how to secure iTunes music the decision had been made by Apple to develop the technology internally, rather than to use any pre-existing DRM system. Apple's FairPlay system was utilised across all songs on the iTunes Store to ensure that the labels' concerns of rampant copying were placated. However, the system was also proprietary; Apple refused to allow other companies to use the system meaning that the only software and hardware that could play the iTunes Music Store tracks, was theirs. With the iPod's increasing dominance in the marketplace, and the imminent release of iTunes for Windows, Apple had tied up the online music market. The labels' desire for content protection had given Apple the excuse to set in place mechanisms that would drive people into their arrangement of hardware and software. The blame for such draconian demands went to the labels, whilst the benefit went to Apple. Apple had become the lynchpin in the music industry's distribution chain; as Doug Morris put it, Jobs had placed the labels in 'golden handcuffs'. Apple had saved the industry from the digital quagmire, but in one motion had usurped them at their own game (Levy, 2006; Mnookin, 2007).

Today, Apple holds the title of top music retailer in the US with 28% majority of the music market, and 70% of the digital market.

Its closest rival, online retailing giant Amazon, holds just 12% (NPD, 2010a). Apple's success lay in recognising the need to balance the open standards expected by customers, with the rights-centric attitude of the music labels. It was only by providing an experience that competed with the piracy networks that Apple was able to form a profitable business around the digital distribution of music. Consumers were looking for legal distribution systems that gave them the same capacities of ownership and engagement that the open MP3 standard had allowed them for so long. However, these capacities were in conflict with the understanding of IP that held that control and exclusivity was the only way to derive profit from information. All the music Apple was selling was available on the piracy networks for free, yet people were willing to pay for it. When Morris was asking why people would pay for Coke if it came out of the tap, Jobs was looking at the bottled water market. Apple had taken the same content available for free on the hackers' market, yet made the process of acquisition – the ease of payment, the imagery, the marketing – and the services surrounding the content, worth paying for. Apple had enticed users rather than corralled them. By offering them, not a product, but a service that rivalled the user experience of the MP3 around that product, it had managed to compete with open, and compete with free. To be successful Apple had to meld the capacities of the hacker market with the demands of the incumbent industries, a set of factors seemingly at absolute odds with one another. The solution ultimately was, for Apple and all other digital vendors, to treat media like software.

Codes of control

In 2005 Sony BMG decided to wind down the practice of selling CDs. It still pressed them, shipped them and retailed them through stores, but it wasn't selling the CDs. Instead, it shifted its business away from the sale of discs and moved into the realm of licensing 'content'. However, a problem arose when Sony did not make this explicit to its customers who, as they had habitually done so for many years, continued to exchange money for the discs under the assumption that they were buying them. The discs worked fine in legacy CD players; however, when inserted into a computer the disc made its unusual status known. An end user licence agreement

(EULA)[2] was displayed on the screen which outlined the terms of the contract that Sony and the customer were about to enter into, and defined how the user could and could not engage with Sony's property. Rights of access were tied to physical commodity ownership, meaning that if the customer lost the original disc they were contracted to destroy any copies they had made. They were also tied to the customer's economic solvency, asserting that access would be revoked upon the customer's bankruptcy. Use of the property was also closely defined; the customer was only allowed to put copies of the property onto a personal computer located in the customer's home. The property was not allowed to leave the country of purchase, in either physical commodity or digital file form. Using it as a backing track for a home-made video, sampling it or mixing it with other music whether for commercial purposes or not, was also disallowed. Using the music for anything other than listening was disallowed (von Lohmann, 2005).

The EULA hinted at (though did not fully disclose) the second half of Sony's rights management system used to define the terms of access and engagement with the content on this new breed of disc. The consumer had agreed to install updates to their computer; failure to do so may result in loss of access. Updates to what exactly? Though only alluded to by the EULA, the CD had, upon insertion, installed a rights monitoring system into the consumer's computer – a piece of software buried deep into the user's operating system designed specifically to monitor and control how Sony's content was used. This algorithmic EULA enforcer would ensure that the consumer having, it presumed, agreed to the terms in the EULA would be unable to renege on that agreement. This system of DRM was the architecture that would ensure adherence to the legalese set out in the license agreement. The XCP system (Extended Copyright Protection) would ensure that only a certain number of digital copies could be made and that only a certain number of copies of the album could be burned. The system also frequently communicated with Sony's servers regarding the use of the property.

Sony's goal was to gain a tighter hold on the redistribution of its IP via P2P distribution networks and CD burning. P2P networks essentially existed on users' computers; they were the material site of the immaterial network. To get a tighter hold on the network it had to get a tighter hold on these computers. However, to achieve this Sony took liberties with the consumer's property and privacy to ensure protection of its property. Upon insertion into the computer, the DRM system would embed itself into the computer operating system without notice prior to the display of the EULA. Even if the user did not accept the agreement, by the time they had read it, the enforcer was in place. When Sony's strategy was eventually uncovered by programmer Mark Russinovich he noted that, to surreptitiously install the monitoring software, Sony had used a technique more often affiliated with those looking to compromise a computer's security. The system needed to be near undetectable, able to communicate without the user's knowledge and was almost impossible for the average user to remove without damaging core system files. Sony's DRM system was a 'rootkit', a collection of code that once embedded allowed high-level access to a computer without the user or the operating system being aware of it. When Russinovich shared his discovery on his blog, it was quickly picked up internationally by the press and uproar from consumers and civil liberties groups ensued. Eventually, Sony was forced to reveal the extent of its software's invasion, release a patch to disable the software, and recall the XCP-enabled CDs, offering replacements to disgruntled customers (Russinovich, 2005a, 2005b). Why did Sony go to such great lengths to define how its customers engaged with its commodities? The arrangements of selling media on discs had been amicable so far, so what changed?

Sony's rootkit fiasco was both an attempt to deal with the difficulties of a consumer base able to easily replicate your property, and a more cynical power grab seeking to better direct the normative shifts that were occurring alongside the digitisation of media. The public reaction Sony suffered was primarily due to the underhand nature of its rights enforcement, and the security hole that it left in consumers' computers; a hole that not only allowed Sony backdoor access, but anyone else for that matter. However, Sony was not alone in the broader attempts to utilise both legal and technical code to define cultural engagement, nor in its shifting from sales to licensing. In terms of ensuring control over property replication, in literal terms, ensuring the sanctity of the copyright, the CD had become a prominent leak where it was once the solid wall. For music distribution, the physicality of the CD alone had been enough to dissuade replication for everyone but the most determined consumer. Consumers owned CD readers, not CD writers. CDs were impenetrable cultural conduits, to be played and enjoyed, not copied, ripped, transmitted or converted; purely objects of consumption. However, as the tools of replication and translation became available to consumers the simplicity of the 'physicality based' protection system of the CD became its vulnerability, facilitating largely open access to the IP it was conveying. The digital versions of songs being traded across P2P networks and home-burnt discs did not originate from an obscure source in the distribution chain; the commodity was the source. The backlash occurred because Sony was redefining the property arrangements of a commodity that consumers had already become comfortable with. Without the DRM Sony could have included the EULA but few would have taken any notice of it, secure in their own understanding of what property ownership meant. Sony's rootkit was an attempt to apply further layers of security to a medium that had become vulnerable and to ensure adherence to the redefined relations of media access. However, though the method was invasive Sony was doing little more than employing the same twofold legal and algorithmic rights architecture as those vendors that sold only digital copies.

The outputs of the copyright industries are IP, meaning that rather than being a tangible physical property, their dominion over that property is based on the exclusive right to both economically and creatively exploit it. Owners of this type of property have typically had three (Winston, 2006) options of how to sell their property to others. First, they can choose to sell the IP, transferring their exclusive rights of exploitation to another individual or group in return for payment. This is likely to reap a large lump sum but will then exclude the seller from exploiting those ideas and expressions. Instead, they may think to the future, and rather than sell all their rights to another company, they may choose to license the property to them. For a smaller fee another company can be given the right to exploit the IP under certain terms set by the property owner. The owners won't receive as much money, but they'll retain dominion over the ideas and expressions of that property. The option that the majority of the copyright industries have taken is to sell products that embody their IP. Record companies sell media that allow consumers to experience the IP, that is the song, film or book, but do not convey any rights of exploitation with that sale. By selling a copy rather than the IP the consumer is transferred ownership rights over that instantiation such as the ability to control access to, retain exclusive use of or resell the copy. IP laws were produced to reflect these forms of property exploitation, aiming to produce a balance that would encourage innovation and creativity. It allowed copyright industries to distribute their IP, allowed the population to experience it, but retained industry dominance over it despite revealing it to the world. In theory, without such rights the only way to ensure that no-one would simply get a copy of your work and exploit it for themselves was not to show anyone at all (Winston, 2006). This arrangement operated effectively so long as the average consumer was excluded from the production process. As a creative industry you could happily distribute your physical commodities that embodied the IP, because the vast majority of the population were unable or unwilling to unseat message from the medium, the intellectual from the property. IP law existed to protect you from your competitors, not from your customers. Crucially, as far as the law was concerned, a licence and a sale were distinct; with a licence you entered into an extended agreement with a company and were bound by contract. With a sale your relationship ended with the exchange, and you exercised all property rights over that commodity you had purchased. Separate copyright law restricted you from replicating the IP that the commodity embodied, but the commodity was yours.

Now there is an increasingly prevalent fourth option for exploiting IP; licensing a commodity that embodies IP. The advent of software development, and its slow mutation from its hobbyist roots into a business endeavour meant that a market developed around information products. These products brought confusion to the exclusivity of sales and licences. In its infancy the protection of software as property under US law was uncertain. Development costs were high, yet the ease of replication made it particularly vulnerable. The general redundancies taken for granted in other creative sectors – that even with a will to replicate a product the consumer would be hard pressed to find a way – did not so easily apply to software as too many of the enthusiasts had access to the same tools of production. The most famous example of software piracy was the distribution of Altair BASIC by members of the Homebrew Computer Club, a hobbyist hacker group (its most famous members being Steve Jobs and Steve Wozniak, founders of Apple Computer Inc.) that spent their time tinkering with home computing during its infancy. Unlike contemporary piracy this was done by physically reproducing the reel of punched paper that made up the code for BASIC and handing them out at meetings, the original reel being 'borrowed' by an unknown club member from an Altair marketing event (Markoff, 2005).

Software was a fledgling industry. Its product was difficult to understand and its place within contemporary IP law less than concrete. Rather than rely on the courts to apply public legislation to software, those seeking to recoup revenue from their efforts began to enclose a license agreement with the copies they sold that asserted that the software itself remained the property of the developer, and that the user was being issued a set of rights to use that software, not to own it. This worked in the developer's favour in the realm of enterprise software. A business customer may buy some software for use in their company, and have it installed across hundreds of machines. Technically this is possible with only one purchase; the software doesn't degrade as it is 'stretched' across multiple machines – each replication is of identical quality and utility. However, this is considered unfair by the software developer. The utility value of the software for the licensee can expand infinitely, yet the compensation to the developer, as a reward for their efforts, is static. Where they could have sold 500 copies they have only sold one, something that wouldn't have happened if they were selling something physical and tangible. Instead, by utilising licensing, the business customer had to have a separate licence for each instance of the software, rather than each physical copy; or better yet, purchase an enterprise licence and perhaps receive a discount for the metaphorical 'bulk' purchase. The EULA was able to act as an artificial limiter on the replicability of the data medium, closing down the capacity to reproduce it outside of the set boundaries of use by requiring contractual agreement from the purchaser. However, getting the user and the producer to form an agreement for every sale was difficult. Enacting a license agreement between a corporation and a consumer without those entities necessarily engaging with each other meant a new form of license agreement had to be introduced. Known at the time as 'shrink-wrap', 'click-wrap' or 'browse-wrap' licences these agreements asserted that by using the software the individual had agreed to those terms. Often the process of agreement between the customer and the licensor was little more than the removal of the shrink-wrap plastic from the box that contained the media.

Nadan (2004) asserts that it was the very nature of computer operation that led to this reliance on the licence. If a customer was sold the title to an instantiation of software, then though the user would have the right to resell that instantiation, they would not have the right to copy it; that right remaining with the copyright holder. However, without the right to copy the IP instantiated on the physical medium, the new owner would not be able to use the software at all. The primary trigger that invokes public copyright law is the act of replication. For example, after purchasing a book an individual can use it in many different ways without ever triggering the law. It can be read, resold, loaned or gifted to another individual, shelved, used as a door-stop and so forth without ever invoking copyright law. These are the unregulated uses of IP on which the law has little to say because the user is not infringing on the exclusive rights to replicate that are secured by the rights holder. There are also uses which do infringe on those exclusive rights, but which are allowed by law. Under US law 'fair use' rights allow for the copying of IP if it is for a variety of uses such as backing up, quoting for criticism or replicating for educational purposes. The law differs slightly under UK law, which refers to similar rights as fair dealing. These exceptions to copyright law exist because it is considered a public good to be able to replicate IP under these circumstances (Lessig, 2005). Replication of the property outside of this fair-use spectrum is considered to be an unlawful infringement. However, due to the technical realities of the data medium and the operation of computers, replication is required to perform what were once unregulated uses. If I want to listen to a song, my computer must replicate it into its RAM (a type of memory analogous to short-term memory in humans) to play it. If I want to move it to another hard drive, the computer does not move those magnetic inscriptions on the hard drive, it repeats them and then erases the old ones. Computer technology requires unimpeded replication for basic operation, every time triggering copyright law on grounds of unlawful copying. To circumvent this issue it was considered necessary to license rather than sell digital commodities. A sold product that embodied IP would constantly invoke copyright law if it was in the data medium, but a licensed product could circumvent the problem by allowing replication for certain uses in the licence.

This allowed the rights holder to define what copying was allowed and what copying was not, necessary for the realities of the medium, but problematic in the scope of control the rights holder and vendor had over the use of the product. Previously unregulated uses now had to be allowed by the licensor in the agreement. Under these conditions, the licensing rather than sale of software meant that the end user was – so long as they desired to use the software – forced to enter into a contractual agreement with the developer rather than own the property that they had paid for. This placed the licensor in a significant position of power; with complete control over the definition of how the product would be used, they could choose to customise exactly how their product would be engaged with.

As the interests of the developers grew, so did the licensing terms and restrictions placed on the use of the software allowing them to retain greater control over the life of the product after the transaction. Increasingly, rather than license with the intention of ensuring that previously unregulated uses remained effectively unregulated, the licences became increasingly expansive to enable the vendors greater intervention in the post-sale life of the goods they had already 'sold'. One such boon of the ability to privately regulate your products was to circumvent the right of the licensee to sell on their software, as one would with a book or CD. By eliminating the possibilities of a second-hand market and having greater control over the price of their product the click-wrap licensing greatly boosted the software industry's profits and cemented its position in the economy. This proliferation of the click-wrap was justified by pointing to software's inherent weakness in copy protection; software was essentially streams of code, designed to run on a system that itself could produce the same streams of code, intended to be run by people with an expertise of how to write streams of code. Unlike the CD, the expertise and tools to produce and utilise code was distributed fairly across both the producers and the consumers. There was no safety in physical impenetrability.

During the 1990s a series of court cases in the US tested the validity of these privately constructed licences that appeared to circumvent public legislation, some falling on the side of the developers, others on the side of the consumer, leaving the viability of the licences in a degree of limbo. This led to considerations of a new article of the US Uniform Commercial Code (UCC), known as Article 2B (UCC2B), in the late 1990s. This snappily named addition to the UCC would have asserted the validity of private EULA contracts for electronic information products and services, reinforcing the ability of developers to define their own terms of sale and engagement with their customers. The possibilities of UCC2B led to a great deal of controversy over what should be done; from a consumer rights point of view legislation that gave the go-ahead to license around the law was bad news; however, it was also bad for business as well. The purchase and implementation of new software in business settings would be an increasingly costly affair as poring over the licences would be a vital necessity before installation. Commenting on the possible impacts of UCC2B, law professor Pamela Samuelson considered that its implementation could 'herald the shrinkwrapping of information of all kinds – books, magazines, CDs, movies – you name it' (Samuelson, 1999: 33). Though UCC2B never came into force[3] the propensity for private licensing continued and Samuelson's predictions came to fruition regardless. Though there had long been a legally defined qualitative difference between the IP and the object that embodied it, rights holders' attempts to apply restrictive licensing to media instantiations did not begin with the software industry. Book publishers and the recording industry have both attempted to have a say in the post-sale life of their IP objects long before the computing age. In books, the 1908 US case of *Bobbs-Merrill Co. v Straus* arose when publisher Bobbs-Merrill attempted to sue a bookseller for selling its books at less than $1, something that the licence imprinted in the books prohibited. The courts decided that though Bobbs-Merrill retained its rights to multiply and sell its books, those rights did not extend to the limitation of the resale. Victrola Records used to have a note on the jacket stating the owner was not authorised to use the recording on more than one machine, nor sell it on (Samuelson, 1999).

These early attempts to control the post-sale life of commodities failed, with the US courts reinforcing the rights of the consumer regarding the ownership of property if the transfer had obviously been a sale. In fact the failure of Bobbs-Merrill in court was eventually cited for the creation of the 'first-sale' doctrine in the US that limited the reach of IP owners after the initial sale, making attempts at private licensing pointless. Regardless of the law, these demands were largely ignored by their customers who simply assumed the same property rights as anything else. Actual enforcement of these licences was near impossible, especially against individual consumers. Even in the world of software the licensing terms of operating systems such as early versions of Microsoft Windows were overlooked by many users who unknowingly broke the terms of use by installing one copy on multiple machines. However, today increasingly these terms of service enforce themselves through DRM, like that which was on Sony's XCP discs, through internal and external regulation. Internal regulation, the inclusion of protection schemes into the software such as the requirement of serial codes was a stalwart of anti-piracy measures in software. Without a proper serial code software would be limited, have internal measures to deny user access or disallow installation altogether. However, this form of regulation had a fairly big loophole. As much as the software code itself could be replicated, so could the serial code. Each instance of software could only check that it had a correct serial, not whether that serial was active anywhere else. However, now internet connectivity has introduced a new form of external regulation, monitoring user activity and software use to ensure adherence to the EULA. Windows ensures it checks in with Microsoft servers, ensuring that only one copy has been registered with its particular serial code. Without a unique serial, the software is able to (fairly) confidently initiate further internal regulation and shut itself down. Computer games phone in to external servers to say that they have been installed, or even refuse to operate unless they are continuously connected to company servers, even when the gameplay has nothing to do with being online (Lowensohn, 2010). The connectivity of the internet has brought with it a form of licence monitoring that has significantly bolstered licence enforcement. Previously, users would be able to (knowingly and unknowingly) break the licence because of a lack of external regulation. Now with the ability to make users accountable for infringement through surveillance, post-sale regulation is in its element.

The digitisation of previously object-instantiated media has meant that the same considerations the software industry had faced (easy replicability, increasing decentralisation of production and reconstitution) has become a reality for other copyright industries: their content swiftly coming under the banner of 'information' with its instantiation in the data medium. Previously they were secure in their habits of selling IP objects with their inherent capacities that restricted the average consumer from separating the intellectual from the commodity. However, when moved to the medium of data, those capacities changed and thus so did the affordances of the commodity owner, but crucially the affordances to the rights holders also changed in tandem. The prevalence of licensing over selling in the sphere of software had already cracked open the gates to reinstate habits of private licensing and a space to define the terms of a consumer's access and use in the media sphere as well. This gives the right holders a legal stakehold in the post-sale life of their cultural commodities. Equally, the medium of data also has also allowed the algorithmic enforcement of that legal stakehold, codifying legal claims of intervention into actual intervention. The enforceability of the EULA is increasingly augmented as digital commodities are able to regulate themselves and allow regulation externally through surveillance intent on making the user accountable for their previously unregulated actions. DRM has been invoked multiple times throughout the previous chapters, precisely because of its key role within the history of illicit and legitimate distribution networks. As the algorithmic enforcer of rights-holder will it is a powerful benefit derived from digital distribution. As much as the copyright industries may lament the passing of their old distribution chain the affordances of DRM are greater than any previous attempts to micromanage their products. Though DRM has been characterised here as an enforcer of the EULA, DRM can act alone, without the licensing arrangements of the EULA due to legislation both in the US and the EU. The validity of DRM is enforced by the Digital Millennium Copyright Act (DMCA) in the US and European Directive 2001/29/EC in the EU, which forbid circumvention of DRM measures. Hacking around DRM, producing a tool to allow others to circumvent that DRM, or distributing the tool or the knowledge to allow others to circumvent DRM is prohibited. Whether you are circumventing to exercise legally protected rights of engagement, or to allow you to indefinitely replicate and pirate does not matter. Though intent has become a key element in determining the legality of distribution networks, it is not a factor in anti-circumvention legislation, which is simply a blanket ban (Boyle, 2009). And what is the result of this legislation? Any regulation of your property is upheld, as long as you can write code to enforce it. Algorithmic code and legislative code merge, allowing rights holders to write the law in machine language.

The original justification for these kinds of blanket protection measures was the ease of replicability, the need to ensure the sanctity of copyright. However, DRM has now expanded to regulate product engagement beyond copy protection into audience regulation.

As much as it is occurring in media products this approach to enforcing legal claims of ownership encompasses online services as well. Sites such as YouTube use algorithmic recognition systems to monitor what is uploaded to their archives. If the system believes it has matched some audio or video in the upload with something in its list of copyrighted material made available by the major studios and labels, it will assign the rights of that upload over to the company that owns the rights. The company can then choose to block the content, or use it to begin harvesting statistics about its viewers and place advertising around the video to generate revenue from it (YouTube, 2011). This system can at times be controversial as individuals may upload personal videos with copyrighted soundtracks (or even copyrighted music unintentionally in the background) which will then cause the user to lose the rights to the video. The algorithmic system does not differentiate between the user who is uploading industry content to profit from it themselves (by receiving ad revenue for posting a popular music video) and the user who wanted to express a certain sentiment with some music or just happened to have music on in the background of filming. Considerations regarding what should and should not constitute content that should be blocked are ongoing. Parody videos that reproduce copyrighted content in full but with alterations for parody, satire or commentary also find themselves blocked (Axon, 2010).

The development of DRM has unfolded in tandem with illicit distribution networks. Whether rightly or wrongly the ease of illicit distribution of digital media has been the justification for both the further development of DRM and for its support in national and international legislation. A kind of dialectical arms race, DRM is used as a justification for the necessity of an open hackers' market, whilst the hackers' market is used as a justification for DRM. Boyle (2009) argues that the calls from the media industry for stronger copyright protection and the justifications for DRM are two separate matters. For him copy protection through legislation is a justified measure, a way of ensuring that the medium of data does not entirely overrule the economy of the creative market. However, for Boyle, DRM is unjustified; a reduction of public liberties for private gain. Yet DRM is part of the three-part system of legitimate digital distribution, and whether justified or not, is inherent in digital retail. The infrastructure of private licensing and algorithmic support in tandem with a retail platform make up the digital distribution 'ecosystem' and have been the foundation behind the legitimate digital distribution of media. This foundation has been present both in the services that have been rights-centric and restrictive, and the services that have attempted to mimic the open capacities of the hacker market. Though the data medium has allowed users greater capacities in the way they engage with and use media, the data medium also allows for these systems that work to limit those capacities and to make the user accountable for their actions. This intervention relies on the services and ecosystems built up around digital commodities. These ecosystems make the enforcement of the licence terms possible whilst also using the arrangement of licensing over ownership to make the paid services desirable through the provision of services around the information products. As such the loss of user ownership in the digital retail market has meant an intertwined set of affordances and restrictions for media producer and media consumer alike.

Competing with free

This section is not about media rights holders. It is important to clarify that rather than talking about rights holders we are discussing digital distribution vendors, the companies of technically minded individuals, comfortable with the digital realm in a way that many of the incumbent rights-holder industries aren't. This is about the usurpers of the media industry's distribution chain dominance. These vendors of course may also be rights holders. For vendors such as Valve, which operates Steam,[4] a digital PC-games outlet, it is the rights holders to a number of the products on sale via the Steam distribution platform. It can also be the case, as it was with Apple's iTunes Store, that the rights holders do have a say in how the vendor operates, but only insofar as negotiating the initial arrangements of the vendor's distribution architecture. In Apple's case it was because it required the outputs of the highly concentrated recording industry and so was required to bend to its demands. However, now as a highly successful vendor that is dominating the market, Apple is in a position where it is able to tell the recording labels what terms the labels must accept, having placed them in the aforementioned 'golden handcuffs' (Mnookin, 2007). With the dispersal of creative capacity (the technological means to produce cultural works hitherto concentrated within the copyright industries) has come the dispersal of sources of cultural commodities. Independent artists are able to operate without major labels or studios backing them, seemingly liberated from the gatekeepers of cultural production. However, now artists are confronted with the new cultural gatekeeper, the digital vendor. As such this section is primarily concerned with digital vendors, the intermediaries who distribute and sell the rights holders' IP, the retail outlets of the digital culture economy. It is these entities that through their role as distributors define the ways in which culture is disseminated and how consumers engage with cultural works as information products.

The market of digitally distributed media can be considered as a three-part system of interlocking elements that allow the regulation of digital products. We have already covered the history of the EULA and the importance of its algorithmic enforcer, DRM. However, in media these two elements of regulation are often dependent on a third element, the distribution platform. There are now many legitimate digital distribution platforms competing across the media market, though concentration of market share is particularly high with clear market leaders. Apple's iTunes Store dominates the US digital music market and there is a clear shift towards data- rather than disc-mediated music. In the US, the digital market has grown overall by 13% and retail sales of discs plummeted by 20%. With Apple at the forefront it holds a dominant position in defining the shift to digital distribution in music (Smith and Fowler, 2010). In the sphere of PC games,[5] purchasing habits are also moving towards the digital outlet. In the first six months of 2010 the US market saw a total of 11.2 million game purchases via digital distribution, 3 million more than physical retail boxes. At the forefront of the digital sales is Valve Studio's service Steam, the same service that utilised Bram Cohen's expertise on BitTorrent-like data distribution, which holds market dominance (NPD, 2010b). The digital distribution of books was relatively late to the commercial sector, despite a long history of illicit network trading. The lack of competitive e-readers that would allow customers to engage with digital books in a similar way to their paper copies delayed the transition. Amazon, utilising a similar strategy to Apple, grabbed market dominance – 90% market share in 2009 – via the simultaneous launch of an eBooks store and the dedicated Kindle reader, which was the first e-reader to gain mass market appeal. Each of these outlets operate an ecosystem that relies on the threefold system of licensing and algorithmic restriction wrapped in an online distribution platform that acts as a virtual storefront for the vendor. To illustrate the affordances and controversies regarding these distribution ecosystems, we can draw upon the prior examples of the most successful media vendors in their respective fields, Apple's iTunes Store, Valve's Steam PC-game store and Amazon's Kindle eBooks store.

Ownership

The consumer/vendor relationship has typically become characterised as a subscription rather than a transaction, a continuous contract whereby the consumer agrees to a set of terms in return for access to elements of the vendor's media catalogue, access that is typically made via the vendor's software storefront. If this system seems familiar it is not dissimilar from the model tried by the labels with their PressPlay system; a digital distribution model of music retail where users subscribed to content rather than purchased it outright. However, PressPlay made the subscription relationship explicit through restricting the capacities of the music files to the point that the consumer was acutely aware that they did not own the music they were paying for. Contemporary digital retail is much quieter in this regard by striving to maintain the illusion of ownership. Rather than the vendor and the customer entering into a simple transaction and then the two being free to disassociate from one another, the customer is legally tied to the vendor and often, due to the architecture of the distribution system, required to return to the vendor to engage with their purchase. In the case of Steam, the customer is entering into a 'Subscription Agreement'.

> Steam is an online service ('Steam') offered by Valve Corporation ('Valve'). You become a subscriber of Steam ('Subscriber') by installing the Steam client software and completing the Steam registration. Additionally, as a Subscriber you may obtain access to certain services, software and content ('Subscriptions') available to

Subscribers. Conclusion of this contract between Valve and you takes place as soon as you access the Steam service after accepting this Agreement.

(Valve Corp., 2011b)

Steam customers do not purchase individual games; they pay for a licence to access those games. Under section 'D: Ownership', the agreement states: 'All title, ownership rights and IP rights in and to the Software and any and all copies thereof are owned by Valve and/or its licensors' (Valve Corp., 2011b). The key part is 'All title and ownership rights', which establishes that at no point will the customer be entitled to exercise publicly defined property rights over the products that Valve is conveying to them via its distribution platform. Architecturally the customer is required to have the Steam client software on their computer to access the products they have licensed, the software itself incorporating the retail end of Steam's operation. Similarly for iTunes software purchases:

The software products made available through the App Store (the 'App Store Products') are licensed, not sold, to you.... You acknowledge that the license you purchase to each Apple Product that you obtain through the App Store Service is a binding agreement between you and Apple.

(Apple Inc., 2011)

Again, the applications sold on the iTunes store for its iPod, iPhone and iPad products are licensed to customers rather than sold. For music and film, Apple characterises the arrangement as a sale rather than a licence; however, the sale differs from that of a physical sale in the legal code laid out to define the terms of a user's engagement with those purchases. This is done by requiring the individual to agree that the iTunes store service 'permits you to purchase or rent digital content ("Products") for end user use *only* under the terms and conditions set forth in this Agreement' (Apple Inc., 2011, my emphasis). Further on in the document under 'Use of Purchased or Rented Content' it then states that the user agrees that whether or not the products are protected by security technology, they will not use the product in a way that does not comply with the 'Usage Rules', which are then listed below. The agreement is structured in such a way that though transactions are characterised as purchases, with the transmission of title, the process of purchasing via the store platform results in the customer agreeing to restrict their use of their purchase in accordance with the vendor's demands. As such the customer enters not into a licence but an ongoing usage contract. For some products this is a formality, with little practical implication; for others it restricts the ways in which a user can engage with their purchase. In the case of film purchases it is only possible, due to the legal terms agreed to and their enforcement by DRM, to watch those films from within Apple's iTunes software, or Apple's media devices.

Amazon's Kindle operates a similar arrangement:

> Unless otherwise specified, Digital Content is licensed, not sold, to you by the Content Provider...you may not sell, rent, lease, distribute, broadcast, sublicense, or otherwise assign any rights to the Digital Content or any portion of it to any third party, and you may not remove or modify any proprietary notices or labels on the Digital Content. In addition, you may not bypass, modify, defeat, or circumvent security features that protect the Digital Content.
> (Amazon EU S.a.r.l, 2011b)

Amazon MP3s' terms of service for their music store also explicitly states in the Terms of Service that, though the user is granted rights to use digital content, legal ownership is not one of them.

> Except for the rights explicitly granted to you in this Agreement, all right, title and interest in the Service, the Software and the Digital Content are reserved and retained by us and our licensors. You do not acquire any ownership rights in the Software or Digital Content as a result of downloading Software or Digital Content.
> (Amazon EU S.a.r.l, 2011a)

What can and can't be done with the digital content is systematically laid out within the Terms of Service. One such side effect of this ability to reach beyond the 'sale' of the product is achieving what the music industry longed for in the days of optical disc sales; the closure of the resale market (Glusman, 1995). The loss of title rights means the loss of resale across all media sold through the digital market place. Though rights may be granted to share those files with family members or across a set number of devices, the actual capacity to sell on media if you no longer have any desire to own it has been eradicated. This is not entirely by design, it is an inherent difficulty in the data medium's replicability to really guarantee that if a file is sold on, a copy has not still been retained by the previous 'owner'. Tested in the realm of software with *Vernor v AutoDesk*, the enforceability of restrictions on media resale has already been affirmed in court (Anderson, 2010b; *Vernor v Autodesk*, 2010).

However, beyond simply the aspirations to, and methods for, market dominance, this licensing arrangement fundamentally changes the relationship between the consumer and the vendor. They are placed in a continuous relationship whereby the consumer's access to cultural goods is directly tied, not only to their continued contractual relationship with the vendor via a personal account, but also the wellbeing of the vendor. Amazon's Kindle illustrated this perfectly in 2009 when many Kindle users found that one of their e-books had disappeared from their illusory virtual shelves. Publisher, MobileReference specialised in producing and formatting public domain works into e-books and had licensed their version of *1984* to Amazon to sell on the Kindle eBooks store. However, the title in question had not yet reached the public domain in the US, something that MobileReference only realised after it had submitted its e-book to Amazon. Upon discovering the oversight MobileReference informed Amazon that it in fact had no right to submit *1984* to Amazon and the latter in turn pulled the product from its store. However, not only did this stop Amazon from continuing to sell unauthorised access to the copy, it also reversed all prior transactions, refunding customers accounts and deleting the e-book from their Kindle readers (Fisher, 2009). Amazon's Terms of Service did not state this as policy explicitly; however, because the content was licensed to the customer rather than sold, when it transpired that Amazon no longer had the licence to exploit the e-book, it followed on that the licence between Amazon and the consumers was nullified also. The rectification of the licensing bungle was translated via algorithmic enforcement into a real removal of the unlicensed content, revoking access and deleting copies. This extension of reach through the symbiotic relationship hardcoded into the walled arrangement between the Kindle store and Kindle reader meant the Kindle store could reach out and affect the contents of Kindle readers. The abstract private contractual code was enforced by the algorithmic code via the proprietary walled-garden retail outlet that the consumer was legally and algorithmically tethered to.

However, this arrangement of licensing rather than owning media can also benefit a consumer if approached differently by the vendor. Valve's interpretation of its subscription model is that when a user purchases access to a product, the operating system that they access it on should not matter. Offline boxed retail of games meant a consumer would purchase one copy of the game per operating platform, that is Windows or Mac. As the consumer was purchasing a physical instantiation of code they had to choose which of the different sets of code they were going to purchase. If they wanted the ability to play the same game on different platforms, they would need to separately purchase the two sets of code, essentially paying twice to access the same experience. Instead, when purchasing access to a game via Steam the user is given access to it across both Windows and Mac platforms if the code for those versions is available. This initiative called SteamPlay (Valve Corp., 2010c) has taken the usually back-end technicality that a product is licensed not bought and brought it to the foreground as a benefit to the consumer. Other platforms such as the Sony PlayStation, Microsoft Xbox and the Nintendo Wii, despite still technically only licensing the product when consumers purchase a boxed disc are not given access to other platforms of the game, as the customer is licensing a particular version of the experience. This arrangement is in these vendors' interests, who all retain their own walled-garden system of game licensing and often seek to secure exclusive rights to popular games to encourage the purchase of their consoles. Valve, however, is not stopping with dominating the PC market and has already secured the rights to operate Steam on the Sony PlayStation (Valve Corp., 2010b). This has led to the application of the SteamPlay system between the console and the PC platforms for Valve's latest release, *Portal 2*, which provides customers with a serial code for the PC and Mac version if they purchase the boxed PlayStation copy (Valve Corp., 2010b).

Post-sale engagement

The term 'digital distribution ecosystem' with its organic horticultural connotations works well in relation to another oft-used phrase

to describe an assemblage of tightly controlled interlinking products and services; a 'walled garden'. Apple has the iTunes Store, the
iTunes media software and its range of hardware products that all
have varying degrees of dependency on one another. Apple's hardware demands the use of the iTunes software to move data on or
off and manage the user content, something hard-coded in both the
legal and algorithmic code that comes with the devices. Even if the
individual wanted to modify the product to allow the hardware to
work with different software, the code (legal and digital) forbids it.
Though the user may own the physical device, proprietary licensing
forbids them from tinkering with the software that operates it, which
remains Apple's IP. The hardware is directly linked to Apple's iTunes
Store, enabling the user to purchase file access directly on the device,
but to the exclusion of all other retailers. Consumers can purchase
music outside the Apple walled garden, but it must still be imported
into the iTunes software before it can be used with the Apple hardware. Though now not the case, in its early incarnation when there
was very little competition to the iTunes domination, music files purchased from the iTunes store could only be played in the iTunes
software or by Apple hardware, and iTunes was the only way to move
data to your hardware. As for third-party applications, whereas it is
possible to use non-iTunes purchased music on Apple's devices, it is
not possible to use non-iTunes applications, which can only reach
the device via the iTunes store and Apple's often-criticised opaque
vetting system that filters what can and cannot be loaded onto their
products.

All applications available for Apple hardware must go through
the walled garden and allow Apple to take its share of revenue.
Illicitly it is possible to circumvent this arrangement though Apple
will often undo these illicit options through software updates. This
intertwining of legal and algorithmic code helps to produce the
walled-garden effect that closely controls both the access to and
engagement with the catalogue of content offered via the distribution
platform. Amazon operates a similar system with its Kindle store and
Kindle hardware, whilst Steam requires the use of the Steam client
software to access the games purchased. This arrangement of inter-
connected devices and services is the platform for digital vendors
to provide a variety of services beyond simple retail. Some of these
platforms are more guarded than others, but all are developed with

the vendor as the key gatekeeper, and provide them with the ability to alter the platform's legal and technical architecture, and thus the terms of user engagement, as and when they wish. These platforms, by architecturally making themselves necessary for engaging with media, act as the hubs from which the vendors can both provide extra services to compete with illicit piracy networks, and grant themselves greater degrees of involvement with the customer's media engagement.

Under consumer pressure both iTunes and Amazon have introduced DRM-free channels for rights holders to distribute their products through, allowing media purchased in their stores to be used in competitor products. These channels are not strictly as open as their offline counterparts. iTunes still watermarks the files with user information so that people are dissuaded from sharing what they have purchased. The legal code, the terms and conditions, still encompass the non-DRM products and retain some rules regarding the usage of those files, including a provision that Apple can redefine those rules as they wish without notice. Doctorow remains sceptical about Amazon's DRM-free e-books, claiming that without explicit statements from Amazon, it is still uncertain whether access to DRM-free e-books could still be revoked at any point, and whether the use of Kindle e-books on non-Kindle readers is allowed (Doctorow, 2010). Despite being supposedly DRM free, these digital products remain the subject of contractual regulation between consumer and vendor. The contract can be changed at any time and though the consumer can refuse to agree to the new contract, they can only do so by not using the vendor's services; but if your media, laden with DRM, requires those services to be accessed, the consumer has few options.

With your media closely tied to the vendor's walled garden, both legally and algorithmically, the vendor's options for media alteration and surveillance increase. It is standard software and game industry practice to release patches and alterations to games after they have been released. Although testing is done before release it is incomparable to the sheer variance in the hardware configurations and playing habits that the game will be subjected to after it goes public. Usually companies will, after receiving feedback from their users via support requests and forums, fix bugs and change features to improve the quality of their product by releasing a patch. The user would then be required to download the patch from the official website (though it is often hosted on other enthusiast sites) and use it to update their game. With Steam the necessity for a user to be aware of patches and then take the time to implement them is removed. Instead, when changes are made to games purchased through Steam, the client software automatically updates the files on the customer's computer. This is seen to be a positive selling point for the Steam platform, a convenience that standard boxed copies of games do not have. However, the Steam platform also does not allow the user to opt out of these updates and if the software is aware that an update is available, will not allow the user access to the game until the patch has been applied. Rather than owning a fixed version of the product, the consumer must accept that they have paid for access to a product which can be altered long after payment was made. This is often for the better; few would complain about having a buggy game fixed up and often new features or extra content are welcomed. However, sometimes these updates can alter the game considerably in such a way that users may consider the game to have been 'broken', not in terms of its basic operation, but in balancing and design where the addition, removal or editing of certain game mechanics changes the experience of engaging with that product.

A more controversial element of this capacity for post-sale alteration occurred when Sony's PlayStation 3 gaming console (PS3) received a series of firmware updates. Although users purchased the PS3 hardware, the firmware, the code that runs the hardware remained Sony's property that was licensed to the user to use to run their machine. The PS3 when it originally shipped had the capacity for users to install alternative operating systems onto the device. It was not a major selling point for individuals but it had become a popular option for many institutions to install Linux onto sets of PS3s for setting up processor clusters for research (Anderson, 2010a). However, Sony, concerned by the possibilities of using the alternative OS option for software piracy, removed the option with a firmware update. It stated that the update was voluntary; however, choosing not to update the firmware would disable the device's ability to connect to the PlayStation network (Sony's online store and hub for many PS3 services) as well as play games or play Blu-ray discs, effectively making the device unable to perform the functions the vast majority of users purchased it for (Kuchera, 2010). By interlinking online services with offline functions, choosing not to sell but to license the operating code of the device, and by bringing the capacities of using the device into the boundaries of the walled garden, Sony was able to effectively enforce its desire to have the functionality removed from the devices it had already sold and users had little recourse. This post-sale alteration of products is currently a software-based phenomenon, though the legal and technical architecture is present for this practice to occur with other media too. There is potential for new forms of music, literature and other creative products to be alterable after the fact, constantly changing based on refinements or re-considerations by the authors. The cultural product does not have to be fixed.

A related capacity of the walled-garden approach is the ability to collect and utilise use/r-generated information. Content produced by users has been under great scrutiny primarily due to its perceived primacy in the shift from the first iteration of the web to the second, or Web 2.0. In digital distribution platforms such as Steam, iTunes and the Kindle store, user-generated content is prevalent in forums, reviews, shared playlists/wish-lists, recommendations and community groups, all officially supported by the platforms themselves, which utilise this behaviour to add value to their services. However, perhaps too quickly overlooked is the equally if not more important data produced by users without their direct engagement. The data produced through the use of the services, the collection of which is also built in to the platforms. To designate between the two I use the term 'user' generated for the former, and 'use' generated for the latter, but collectively they are referred to as 'use/r' generated. Use-generated data has been used more effectively for the provision of new services and features alongside existing product and service development.

One of the more established use/r-generated data systems is the recommendation engine. This system, having a total knowledge of your purchase history on a particular platform, will recommend to you other products based on the purchasing patterns of other consumers. These systems have their roots in 'bricks-and-mortar' retail, with one of the first implementations being put in place by Blockbuster Video as a film recommendation service based on past rentals. Amazon has perhaps the best-known recommendation system and that also has been primarily applied to its stock of commodities. The benefit to the vendor is that it may encourage consumers to purchase more, having presented to them a product which has a higher than average chance of appealing to them. By utilising the data produced not only through users' purchasing histories, but also their browsing habits whilst on the platform, the systems aspire to model human preferences and desires, injecting a degree of heterogeneity into the mix to compensate for the unpredictable elements of human decision-making (Ansari et al., 2000). These principles have also been effectively applied to music in discovery and community sites, such as Last.fm, which utilise the masses of data collected not from transactions but by user action. With the Last.fm software installed on their computer, users' listening habits are tracked and archived into Last.fm, which utilises that data to provide personalised radio stations that deliver music the system believes the user will like. Apple has a similar facility that it calls Genius that consumers can use to find similar music to what is already in their collection. Furthermore, the Genius service can, given a song already in the user's collection, construct a playlist of songs that are in some way similar. This facility assists users in engaging with their increasingly expanding music collections but requires the contractual engagement with Apple to operate. This arrangement ensures Apple a high sample of contributors to their Genius system and though users can choose to opt out, the useful service that Apple provides in exchange for your data is often enough to convince the user to opt in and provide a full database on the user's library contents to Apple, whether its contents were purchased from Apple or not. Based on both the Terms of Service agreement and Apple's privacy policy, contrary to popular cynicism, it does not appear that Apple sells the collated information on to third parties, though the data can be used internally for Apple's own purposes such as product development, advertising and the provision of services, though how this is achieved is opaque to the consumer.

Valve also collects data from its users, but takes a different approach. Apple's Genius function does not monitor habits, only collections. According to one of Apple's engineers Genius does not collect data on listening habits (i.e. user frequently listens to artist 'A' followed by artist 'B') but on the user's collection itself (i.e. user owns a large amount of artist 'A', and a comparable amount of artist 'B'). Utilising complex modelling algorithms Apple was able to utilise this fairly simple data set (essentially a snapshot of the library contents) by collating it across its huge user base. This allowed it to extrapolate consumer preferences based on the assumptions that individuals follow similar patterns in their aesthetic tastes (Mims, 2010). Valve, rather than operate on assumptions, instead collected more nuanced data to take advantage of its capacity to alter products after they had already been licensed. Being a game developer alongside a digital distribution vendor, Valve has a greater interest in exactly how its products are used than perhaps merely a retailer would. One of its more successful games, *Team Fortress 2*, demonstrated the extent to which Steam was being utilised to collect usage data from its customers. A couple of months after launch, Valve published a page on its website that presented the statistics the company had produced by collecting the data players had generated by playing the game (Valve Corp., 2011c). The game was an online multiplayer 3D game where two teams in a closed map attempted to achieve various goals whilst having to fight off the opposing team. Teams would often start at opposing sides of non-identical maps which theoretically had been designed so that though non-identical the maps were balanced for fairness. The statistics showed Valve and, through its transparency, its current customers, which maps gave certain teams unfair advantage, where the hotspots for getting yourself killed were on the map, where stalemate situations would occur (where neither team made any progress until time ran out) and a variety of other statistics based on the collection of data from the game's player base. Valve used this information to modify the game in the pursuit of a better playing experience, whilst also retaining it for reference for future game design. *Team Fortress 2* was not alone in its role as a data collector for Valve. Other Valve titles, even those that were single-player titles (and thus did not necessarily require the user to connect to online servers) began to collect information with the view that, whereas before the company would rely on verbal customer feedback and forums, now it could see how its customers played the games and identify problems with game design ready to alter it accordingly (Valve Corp., 2011a).

The collection of use/r-generated data and of the post-sale alteration of content can also aid in the use of the distribution platform for marketing. More generally the necessity of the user to return to the same piece of software or website to engage with their media collections is a useful boon in itself to integrated in-platform marketing. The comparable analogue situation would be the necessity to stand in a record shop before you could listen to your personal music collection. Steam will often provide separate window announcements of new deals, sales and new product releases once the user is accessing the client software. iTunes utilises the Genius function to provide a sidebar that informs the user of other media similar to what they are already engaged with that can be bought from the store, whilst Amazon's past-purchases recommendation engine also provides the user with suggestions for another purchase. This targeted form of marketing can become less intrusive to the consumer who, rather than being bombarded by useless information may begin to treat the adverts as a feature of the software, a way of discovering new content. No longer is it an imposition of the company on the user, but a service provided to them.

The capacities of the data medium that have significantly reduced its overheads have also brought new opportunities for marketing and sales events. Rather than waiting for significant events in the gaming market to occur to stimulate interest in its platform, Valve will often manufacture events on a weekly basis. With little in the way of production costs the company is able to announce massive price reductions on products to stimulate interest, sometimes selling collections of games at 10% of their usual price. These sales may last from days to hours, and Valve's ability to alter the price of a product worldwide instantly offers it other opportunities for engaging with its customers. The company is generally well liked by its core customers and often takes the opportunity to engage with those who play their games on a regular basis. During October 2009 the company decided to put the aforementioned *Team Fortress 2* on sale, dropping the price from $19.99 down to $2.49 for a limited period. The sale was announced on the game blog, which often provides a comical fictional account of how Valve is operating the company. After the sale began an emergency announcement on the blog stated that its accountants predicted the sale would bankrupt them and so the price would have to be raised to $2.50. Then a few hours later another post announced that due to massive success they would again roll the price back, to $2.49. This close integration of distribution platform and game marketing went down well with its core of fans who often appreciated the game developer as much for its humour as for its products; not to mention the free marketing it got via the 'blogosphere' (TF2 Team, 2009a, 2009b; Walker, 2009).

Valve's marketing director has expressed that keeping the development of marketing materials in-house means the final adverts often connect to the user community much better than something produced by a marketing agency (Sacco, 2011). The company, who has an in-depth understanding of the product as well as its fan base, is able to integrate the in-jokes, the sentiment and the character of the product into its adverts in a highly effective manner, just as it did in its *Team Fortress 2* blog. The company has taken this dominance of the distribution platform and the capacity to alter products after sale even further for its marketing of the sequel to its popular game *Portal*. In March 2010, prior to any official announcement of a sequel, 'owners' of *Portal* suddenly noticed the game began receiving alterations from the Steam servers, despite being relatively old and untouched for years. Those who played the game again found that the world had been slightly edited. Small radios now littered the game world, emitting audio static, whilst the ending of the game had been altered to imply that the game's story was not over. More adventurous owners of the game searched around the files that made up the game on their hard drives and found a series of audio files, each one containing initially indecipherable noises. Valve was counting on some of its fans having some of the hacker ethic (and skill set) behind them. Users found some of the audio files to be Morse code and others to be encrypted strings of code. When translated some of the messages turned out to be useless, though others had intriguing information such as phone numbers and login details. The remaining sound files, when converted into images, revealed corrupted photographs produced by the game's fictional corporation Aperture Science, which provided further hints at what might be in store. From the variety of information gathered from the images and the Morse code messages, users put together enough information to dial into a BBS (like those of the early phreak and hacker days), which was supposedly the corporate servers of Aperture Science. On the BBS were more documents and images hinting at a sequel. The BBS also contained a progress bar that seemed to be counting down to an official announcement. As the bar reached its final stages Valve released a press release for *Portal 2*, with some characters underlined (Valve Corp., 2010a). These characters made up another username and password for the BBS, giving users further information and titbits. When Valve CEO Gabe Newell received an award at the Game Choice Awards a week later he alluded to the BBS marketing the company had been doing, and offered to take some time to answer any fan questions. However, at that point the presentation screen behind him appeared to crash to a blue screen at which point he ended his presentation; the blue screen contained further cryptic information for BBS users.

Eventually the marketing campaign became more transparent to those customers not yet integrated into it. A variety of third-party games by independent developers (i.e. games developers that were not attached to a publisher) began to be secretly updated with *Portal*-related content. As customers played these updated games some found themselves directed to an Aperture Science website. Eventually the relationship became more explicit as Steam began selling all the altered games together as a discounted bundle. A few days before the scheduled release date of *Portal 2*, the Aperture Science website announced that the game was almost ready, but required extra CPU power to aid in the launch. The site showed a list of the third-party games, and the amount of customers playing them at that particular moment. A countdown timer to *Portal 2*'s launch was also shown, implying that the more people there were playing the games, the more time would be shaved off the release countdown. Valve's marketing strategy had been to produce an Alternate Reality Game (ARG) to draw its fans into its fictional world. ARGs utilise the real world in real time to produce game scenarios for individuals to 'live' through for a period of time. The use of ARGs is not new to marketing; the popular game series *Halo* used an ARG as part of its viral marketing campaign for the release of the second title in the series, whilst TV show *Lost* also used an ARG to further integrate its fans into its fictional world. However, Valve utilised its ability to tamper with people's media after they had purchased it to start off the ARG marketing campaign. Rather than being produced by a marketing department or external agency, the ARG was treated as an extension of the game and was developed by the game designers. It was as much conceived as a way to expand the game world, the fiction and depth of the game, as it was a marketing opportunity. Valve's director of business development stated that it was this integration of the marketing with the product being marketed, as well as the post-sale malleability of its customers media collections that allowed Valve to produce this experience for its customers, and produce a relatively cheap but high-impact advertisement for its new product (Tito, 2010).

Much of the focus of this section has been on Valve and its Steam platform, though it is for good reason. The company is in the enviable position of having gained significant dominance over the PC games market with its platform. Furthermore, Valve is also the rights holder to a number of products on that platform, many of which are held in high regard amongst critics of the medium.[6] Perhaps most importantly, as game designers they are at ease with what can be done with data and are acutely aware of how the most prominent elements of their customer base are likely to embody some degree of the hacker ethic. Valve's approach to rights management and of playing with the products under its control echoes this ethic similarly, and is used to great effect when engaging with its customers. For some distribution platforms such as iTunes, this kind of interaction with its customer base would be difficult. With a rhetoric that emphasises ownership over subscription the platform does not lend itself to post-sale tinkering with products. Valve, and the software products themselves, however, are much more comfortable with post-sale alteration and tinkering than say music and film. With the increasing prevalence of the streaming, cloud-stored subscription model in industry discussions, these possibilities for post-sale alteration of products and redefinition of consumer engagement may increase. The ability, both legal and architectural, is already in situ for most mediums; however, whether consumers are ready to allow their personal collections to be altered at a company's whim is not yet understood, and in fact is in desperate need of further research.

The new media gatekeepers

The development of legitimate systems of digital distribution was both driven and heavily influenced by the open capacities and demands established by the illicit hacker market. The amalgamation of services and networks played a significant role in both the impetus to form a legitimate online market, and in influencing the design and standards of those services. As we saw in the previous chapter, industry resistance to new forms of distribution outside its well-established and regulated chain of command was an appropriate response when faced with a disruption that was unproven to be able to support its already established infrastructure. However, its lack of engagement effectively placed a veto on competitor groups attempting their own implementation. The IP monopoly it held over the 'content' that would run through those systems was an impediment to patterns of legitimate disruption.

With the legitimate option vetoed no-one was moving to provide the tools and systems to engage with media in the ways that a growing core of people were becoming accustomed to. The groups most engaged with the innovations in digital media were also the groups best placed in skill and knowledge to develop digital distribution systems. Operating under a broad ideology of liberalism fused with the capacity to write their own software and information systems, these groups took on the responsibility for fulfilling their own media distribution desires. These illicit systems spread quickly as the tools of distribution were composed of the same base materiality as the content they were designed to transmit. This fast spread of digital distribution tools meant that the standards, habits and expectations of digital distribution were defined by the operation of these illicit systems and the capacities they allowed. The choices made about what these systems would and would not do were informed by the fusion of liberalism and information technology, broadly known as the hacker ethic.

When it became apparent that the option to veto out digital distribution had passed by, the incumbent industries were left behind, attempting to compete with the hacker market and the expectations it had ingrained into the ever-expanding user base. The values and assumptions these incumbents brought to their designs were inherently at odds with the hacker ethic, being focused on ownership, rights of access and exploitation. In collaboration with the corporate genre of the programming communities, the incumbents developed their own digital market. These vendors of digital retail implemented a three-part system of regulation: licensing, algorithmic enforcement and the distribution platform. The success of the various incarnations of legitimate services has been heavily reliant on how this three-part system has been utilised. The most successful have been those that utilise regulation to retain control over user engagement whilst also mimicking the capacities of the open standards set by the hackers' market. This three-part system has also been invaluable in developing new capacities and services around the rights holders' content that encourages further user engagement with the media. These regulatory systems, initially invoked to protect against the capacities of data and the values of the hacker market, have opened up a broad shift in media engagement that focuses on access, subscription and service rather than ownership, product and retail. The other side of these regulatory developments is the alteration in the power of the rights holders and vendors to define user engagement. The digitisation of media distribution, though often characterised as a cross to bear for incumbent industries, has delivered an architecture of control, making the apparent liberalising of media engagement into a system more closed than before. Where it was once the case that the unregulated use was in the majority, now the unregulated use has become almost non-existent as the data medium requires regulation for all use. These new systems of legitimate digital distribution were driven by the dialectical relationship between the incumbent industries and the hacker ethic. The conflict has not only furthered demand for digital distribution but also led to the development of more efficient technologies of distribution and algorithmic regulation. In turn these new architectures of media delivery have fundamentally altered our relationship with the vendors – the new media gatekeepers who now define and regulate how we experience our cultural products.

9
A History of Digital Distribution

A digital culture industry

> Bohemias. Alternative Subcultures. They were a crucial aspect of industrial civilisation in the two previous centuries. They were where industrial civilisation went to dream. A sort of unconscious R&D, exploring alternate social strategies.
>
> (Gibson, 1999)

The dream of digital distribution was born in the illicit network. The shift to digital distribution in the contemporary cultural industries was driven by the conflict between the market of illegitimate distribution networks and the incumbent rights-holder industries. Without the illicit networks' innovations and dedication the contemporary digital media market would not exist today. The decisions made about what this market should look like and how it should operate were influenced by re-appropriation of the open standards and expectations set by the illicit networks and the capacities of the data medium. These open standards and capacities, drawn from the liberal hacker ethic of the communities which contributed to the production of the illicit market, were fused with the rights-centric assumptions of the media industries. A capitalist logic was applied to the technologies developed by subcultural groups that were communally and ideologically driven. Hacker principles were appropriated and the capacities of the illicit market were simulated by newly developed media vendors, to cater to an audience matured on illicit networks.

As much as the conflict pushed the development of legitimate digital distribution platforms, it also furthered the development of the illicit networks. What began with the Napster assemblage of central servers and central ownership, has extrapolated through various iterations of technological progress into the self-sustaining, 'trackerless', 'indexless' swarms with wide ideologically driven support networks. The conflicts between the incumbent industries and the hacker market discouraged legitimation and drove them to further decentralisation. What remains is an illicit hacker market that has managed to propagate and survive a decade of sustained attempts to shut it down. Together, the illicit and the formal markets have entered into a recursive relationship, each reacting to and feeding from one another; each side pushing the other to improve and develop in response to the threat the opposing side presents.

Much of the power in the provocation brought to the creative economy by such a small collection of individuals has derived from the technology with which they operated. As the products of the incumbent industries began to be represented in data through encoders and decoders such as the MP3 format, they became subject to having those representations manipulated by code. Code is action, intention and agency (Mackenzie, 2006). Code does things and makes changes occur. In a society that is increasingly informational, the design of that code has great impact upon the operation of that informational society (Berry, 2011). The design of code, the actions it performs and the assumptions it reinforces through the performance of those actions conveys the values and ideology of the author/s. Code conveys the agency of its authors ad infinitum and thus can convey the ideology of its authors ad infinitum. The code is not the source of agency; it is the amplifying conduit of agency.

As much as this has been a history of the distribution of media it has been a history about the distribution of tools. The networks of distribution were only possible through the wide replicable dissemination of tools to a large user base. As the users began to run the code, the networks formed and the agency of the author/s was enacted by every system that executed the lines of code. The agency of these few authors could be expressed by hundreds of thousands of systems and in doing so have much wider consequences than if the author had not had the code to transmit their will. In an informational society where virtual spaces such as illicit online networks can have significant impact outside of them, the capacity to write code is the capacity to write reality. These individuals were free to define how media would act when instantiated in data form, and to define how it could be disseminated. Driven by a wide-reaching hacker ethic, these individuals chose the capacities of digital media, designed systems that would disseminate indiscriminately, and defined digital media from a user-centric perspective.

What followed was a conflict that would see the appropriation of digital distribution from the illicit sphere into legitimate markets and a diffusion of the illicit networks through greater degrees of decentralisation. The presence of the illicit networks forced the incumbent industries to adopt digital distribution. In turn the incumbent industries, through their legal sanctions, forced the illicit networks to innovate – forced them to develop new technologies of decentralisation and circumvention that would ultimately be integrated back into the legitimate marketplace. The consequences of coming second to digital distribution was that the precedent was set by a wholly different arrangement of interests. Unrestricted access and unencumbered user-centric usage defined the experience of many users' introduction to digital distribution. Users' expectations and habits had formed in tandem with these standards and the illicit networks demonstrated that the cost of distributing media digitally could be driven down to virtually nothing. Under these conditions the media industry's own standards of what was acceptable when distributing digitally came into direct conflict with the norms and expectations that had been established without them.

Balancing the open capacities of the hacker market with the rights-centric perspective of the industries that required exclusivity and media exploitation has been difficult, with initial offerings of legitimate services tipping the scales towards industry interests. However, the persistence of the hacker market meant there was no monopoly on the dissemination of media. Users were not forced to rely on legitimate services through the retention of exclusivity. They had to be attracted by the provision of an ecosystem that both mimicked and surpassed the affordances offered by the products of the hacker market. It was a lesson hard learned by the incumbent industries, which eventually relinquished much of their distribution systems to third-party vendors that better understood the informational sphere and the ethic behind it. Vendors such as iTunes, Steam and Amazon have diverted the flow of distribution through their own gates and now hold much of the control over customers' access to media; and to rights holders' access to customers. Though the rights holders still own the rights to distribute the media, the digital vendors have cornered the market through the development of attractive retail platforms.

To retail through digital distribution these vendors have had to utilise licensing and subscription rather than direct-sale models. The incongruities of IP law and the data medium have meant that the direct sale of digital media would result in repeated copyright violation. The consequences of this necessity have been twofold; the reduction of legal ownership of digitally vended media, and a variety of capacities and services that revolve around an ongoing relationship between the vendor and the customer. Much of what the illicit marketplace offered revolved around the provision of media that had the capacities of ownership. The eventual consequence of this has been the emergence of the long-term post-sale relationship between these third-party vendors and consumers. This has dramatically altered the structures that define media engagement and the vendor–user relationship. Previously, much of the distribution of media was managed from top to bottom by the largest media conglomerates. The new intermediary of the digital vendor has taken much of the control from the rights holders over the retail of their media. The digital vendor has combined the user-centric and rights-centric approaches to media, where the user experiences the user-centric, but the vendors and the rights holders benefit from an underlying rights-centric ecosystem. The result is long-term involvement in users' media engagement, and a shift towards media access rather than media ownership. Users no longer buy media; they subscribe to it, and are licensed access to media collections, which allows them a simulation of ownership.

The wider consequence of this newfound system of regulation has been the erosion of unregulated use, with all use now being either allowed or disallowed by private legislation. This private legislation has been further entrenched through the development of algorithmic enforcement, made possible by the data medium and presented as necessary due to the continuation of the illicit markets.

Alongside these internal developments, alterations to public legislation in the US and internationally have been designed to deal with the illicit markets. Despite the popular view that the media industry has lost out with the shift to digital, the public has found themselves in a position of greater restriction through the restructuring of the media delivery system. At a time when the tools of media production and systems of distribution are opening up to those outside the media industries, the enclosure of the majority of cultural industry products is tightening. This may lead to the development of an 'amateur' market, the further domination and concentration of media production, or most likely, a position between the two. The impacts on the cultural domain have been considered by law scholars (Boyle, 2009; Lessig, 2005, 2008) but the rise of amateur markets, either through artists' individual production, promotion and distribution, or through tools that aim to make careers outside the primary industry gatekeepers possible, is sorely in need of further research.

However, the shift to digital is not a simple polarised gain for the incumbents. Alongside this extended relationship between consumer and vendor is a wealth of facilities and capacities that benefit the consumer and provide new forms of media engagement. New ways to discover media, cross-media convergence, greater access and drastic price reductions come part and parcel of the long-term relationship between vendor and consumer. Marketing becomes more effective not only because it can be algorithmically targeted, but also because it becomes a part of the media. Marketing campaigns can be enjoyable, interweaving and subtle; experiences as entertaining and engaging as the media it seeks to sell. The most successful campaigns are playful and innovative, asking for their users to contribute as much as they consume, rewarding those that display curiosity and creativity. Media that alters post-sale can respond to the creative consumption expressed by its users. Communities form around the products and the products in turn begin to reflect their communities, with the best integrating the subculture of their fan base as much as they alter in response to the use/r data they've collated. The playful, curious tinkering so prevalent in the hacker ethic, the qualities that brought about the disruption, now begin to play out as a marketing and business strategy in itself.

As much as the principles of the hacker ethic have disrupted the well-established arrangements of the media industry, some of them have been appropriated by industry, and in turn have allowed it to develop and survive the expectations of its new audiences. The principles of communal development, technical exploration, openness and ease of use have been taken on by those vendors and producers to varying degrees, altering the formal mediascape in the process. Though the dream of digital distribution began in the illicit networks, with the slow development of formal systems of digital distribution, the incumbent industries have also gained the capacity to write reality. Through both legal and algorithmic code they are working to define what the cultural sphere should look like in their own interests. Where code was the tool through which disruption and reformation came, it has now become an equally useful tool to those that were disrupted.

Whilst there have been, and are continuing to be, these practical direct alterations to media engagement, the process is still in a state of flux. The wider conflict now revolves around the question of what the realm of digital media is, and what it should be. As much as some elements of the hacker ethic have been appropriated for business, it has also continued on an ideological and politicised trajectory which, thanks to digital distribution, has disseminated widely. Though the illicit piracy networks brought media to their members, they also introduced many to a set of ideals through both covert and overt methods. The illicit piracy networks were the ideals of the hacker ethic made material; community-centric spaces of informational free-flow and open access. Many who were previously unaware of these ideals came to find a new means of experiencing media wrapped in the values of the hacker lineage. As well as expressing their ideals in their design some networks, such as the Pirate Bay, also expressed them overtly. This mixture of media access and rhetoric introduced a wider audience to a counter-argument against the assumptions of IP.

Issues of copyright that had previously only been of concern to large businesses have become everyday considerations for individuals who suddenly had the tools of media production and distribution. As the population affected by IP law diversified, the conceptualisation of the purpose of IP has also altered. Neither the industry population nor the user population's conceptualisations of IP is intrinsically correct or incorrect, it is an alteration as the population alters. Spaces such as the Pirate Bay became the figurehead for the radical denouncement of IP; a bizarre merger of intense mass media consumption and fervent anti-copyright sentiment. With legal challenges both against the networks of distribution and the users of those networks, anti-IP sentiment has intensified. This led many users into further debates and considerations regarding much wider issues than simply the distribution of media. Questions regarding the value of making cultural expression property propagated, and a set of challenges inspired by the hacker ethic came to the fore. The incumbent understanding of IP argued that authors were inspired, that creativity was inherent and thus whatever an author produced was wholly theirs. However, the hacker ethic, drawing on a history of programmers riffing on and wholly reusing other people's code, saw creativity as imitative. Both sides claimed a desire to curate the cultural sphere and to protect 'creativity'. For one side the way to accomplish this was to protect the author's right to protect their creation, to allow others access on their own terms. For the other side the protection of creativity in the wider communal sense relied on the opposite; the open distribution of all creativity for all to draw from and imitate. The question became less about how to engage with media and more a grand rethinking of cultural production.

As the debate has intensified in courts around the world the hacker ethic has become formalised and settled in familiar organisational forms such as the Pirate Party, Creative Commons, the EFF and the UK-based Open Rights Group. 'Pirate' has become equated with a set of ideals and challenges not only to IP, but also, as the conflicts led media industries to prosecute sites and users, surveillance and censorship. Now the ideological conflict is played out in courts and governments as these groups represent the hacker ideals in response to attempts to better regulate the internet as a whole. Government initiatives such as the UK's Digital Economy Act, the EU's Intellectual Property Rights Enforcement Directive, and the multilateral Anti-Counterfeiting Trade Agreement seeking to regulate the internet in the interests of the incumbent rhetoric of IP, are met with opposition from the rhetoric of the 'pirate'. What began as a rights-centric versus a user-centric approach to media engagement has extrapolated into a much wider debate that is, still at its heart, gathered around these two opposing approaches: the privileging of the exploitation of media, or the privileging of the access to media. As we've seen in the case of the market solution to this conflict, the two are not irreconcilable, but on this wider political stage a balance is yet to be achieved.

The history of digital distribution and its focus on the illicit protocols was an attempt to draw attention to the role of the illicit and the disruptive in the generation of our contemporary digital culture industry. Through the conflicts, individual choice, singular moments and wider shared principles our contemporary mediascape has been forever altered by our illicit 'unconscious R&D' (Gibson, 1999). We are now left with a digital retail system that has rendered our media commodities into services, altering our relationship with them. We have media that self-regulates and surveys, and media that is marketing and marketing that is media. We still have illicit systems of media distribution, grand networks of information transfer that, thanks to a decade of sustained judicial testing, has become more decentralised and robust than Napster ever hinted at. As the capacity to create and distribute media has diffused to the population, we have cultivated an ideological challenge to long-held conceptions of IP and rights to culture alongside a resurgence of the public domain. The digital culture industry is neither an all-out reformation of the media concentration that many had hoped for, nor a dystopic algorithmically powered enclosure of all cultural engagement. It is a median between the two, a balance of two forces perpetuating the cultural sphere and keeping each other in check. The precedent demonstrated in this work suggests that it is this friction that will continue to drive change in our digital culture industry.

Change

The chapters of this book tell a tale of the progression of the illicit marketplace, but in doing so also tell the tale of the conflict over media dissemination, and the wider changes occurring around those particular social assemblages. The point of these narratives was to be intricate, and in doing so they enriched our understanding of how the conflict drove change. Though in broad terms it can be said that the statements presented in this conclusion can be supported by the preceding work, its simplification is also an injustice to the intricacy of how these changes came about. There is more value in the description that lays out the complexity and contingency of every assemblage, than there could ever be in a singular simplified conclusion. As much as the histories have revealed substantive changes in an aspect of social life, they are also able to illuminate more abstract insights regarding the process of change. The charting of the history of digital distribution was a charting of the mechanisms that brought about those changes. As much as it was a history of how digital distribution came to be, it was a history of how change has occurred. It should be obvious by the density of the histories that have been presented, that great emphasis has been placed on small details – the wording of legal statements, the operation of network architecture and the interactions between individuals; the morass of elements that make up social reality. Rather than aiming to produce a macro statement of some new social epoch (Savage, 2009), the research has always veered towards the micro.

The process of charting a history was itself why the micro became perceived as being so valuable. Though in the beginning I had perceived the history of digital distribution to be procedural movements from one state to another, as the histories were written it became increasingly obvious that the details within them were the drivers of that movement. Instead of beginning with a grand statement about how social change unfolds, I sought to describe it, and in doing so inadvertently revealed the larger process of social change. Perhaps what is more important is that micro descriptive histories can reveal the complexity of social change: the messy inelegance, the ungraspable mass. In Chapter 2, when discussing event biographies I stated that description can be as analytical as it is informative. If the reader was sceptical of that assertion before reading the histories I hope that they are now more able to understand my position. Though description is often invoked as a word that is in opposition to analysis, it is only through the detailed accounting of social change that we are able to see how it has occurred, and from that derive an analysis of the process.

By taking the time to describe social change we are afforded a window onto the process itself, rather than an approximation based on the larger consequences of the process. It is an approach that, rather than beginning with the 'ends', seeks to take the time to consider the 'means'. A collection of small details can, through an awareness of their relations, connections and arrangement, form a much larger picture of a social element and of a social process. In doing so we are provided a much richer understanding of the element and are able to derive conclusions supported by the granular details; conclusions which can support much grander understandings about process. A granular approach can reveal the untidiness of social change and can undermine assumptions of 'progress' and the singular directed timeline. The 'unintended consequence' was a repeated theme throughout the histories and on some occasions these moments were the lynchpins around which major shifts in digital distribution and wider society occurred. Broadly, it is arguable that all the actions of the actors within the histories had consequences that they never intended; however, it is interesting to chart some of the more poignant unintended consequences that played key roles in the narratives.

Frankel's decentralised design was inspired in reaction to both Napster's fate, and his own expression of the hacker ethic, believing it better to have no mechanisms of control over the network, keeping it safe from censorship and unable to be exploited for profit. However, the robust and ideologically influenced design achieved Frankel's aspirations, but was also re-appropriated for purposes that Frankel would not have approved of. The same type of design allowed Zennström and Friis to retain its resilience and avoid legal responsibility, but also allowed them to exploit the movement of information through the licensing of their FastTrack system. When their system ended up in court, Frankel's design protected them as the apparent inability to regulate the networks placed it under the protection of the Betamax precedent. However, this loss also led to the refocusing of the RIAA's attention on individual downloaders rather than the (P2P) providers. Furthermore, the revelation of the weakness in the law led to the development of 'inducement' in US copyright law to work around the disassociation of responsibility that decentralised network architecture had produced. Individuals wishing to distribute information were now under more surveillance, and at greater risk of lawsuits. Furthermore, the Inducement Act meant that any system that transmitted information could be closed down based on the more flexible concept of 'intention'. Frankel's original design, far from empowering individuals to distribute information freely, had made systems like his more vulnerable and subjected their users to increased scrutiny and personal risk.

In another example the design of the BitTorrent system expressed Cohen's values of neutrality towards data transmission by both greatly facilitating data transfer but making no efforts to obscure that transfer. This neutrality meant that it was released freely on the internet and allowed it to be re-appropriated by both sides of the digital distribution conflict. The Pirate Bay made BitTorrent the bane of the media industries whilst various programming communities reworked and added to the protocol. This work developed an illicit BitTorrent strain that became incredibly robust through the addition of complementary elements such as peer-exchange DHT, and other facilities to prevent identification by law enforcement. Similarly, BitTorrent was also diverted down another path, appropriated into a variety of successful legitimate ventures as an underlying robust data-transfer system. BitTorrent became the pirate's protocol of choice as well as a great back-end for online corporate operations and Cohen had little interest in either. Together these occurrences contributed to the development of the conditions for the formation of the Pirate Party, and their eventual effect on international and European politics. These unintended consequences provide an argument against straight technological determinism and instead favour Hutchby's (2001) application of 'affordances'. Though technologies were designed with certain intended outcomes and values in mind, once out in society they were reformed and redefined through use. The technological foundations of those network designs still played a role in their trajectory, but social structures and human agency also directed them in an unintended way. The technologies had affordances, unseen by their designers, but revealed through their use and appropriation. Under the spectrum of possible outcomes afforded by the technical design, it was the small contingent moments where social factors, constrained by technological realities, defined the technology's effect, and recursively redefined the technology.

As discussed earlier in this chapter, much of the development towards decentralisation and both the legal and technical design of the distribution networks were derived from legal action against the operators of the systems. Development on both sides was driven by the conflicts between the incumbent and the disruptive. The conflicts were also part of the dissemination and re-appropriation of these technologies. Some transformations from illicit to formal were in some respects violent top-down re-appropriations borne of court cases or hostile corporate takeovers – actions taken to halt the operation of these illicit systems whilst also appropriating the spoils. Others were more fluid, gradual processes where technology and brands were adopted and reutilised for new ventures. The role of conflict as a driver also applies from a much wider perspective; the histories can be seen as the charting of a conflict between two spheres. Based on the micro description we can extrapolate a macro narrative of incumbent media industries and an established paradigm, bumping up against the disruption of information technology and a hacker ethic.

This macro narrative can then be understood under the terms of the structuralist framework of change invoked in Chapter 2. The widening capacity of computer systems to digitise previously object-instantiated media meant that the informational sphere became the rupture in the balance maintained by the structures of society. We can see the various illicit ventures as attempts at disruption and the proceeding court actions by the incumbent industries as the structures seeking to resume stability. Structuration theory assumes persistence and stability, maintained by cultural schemas, modes of power and the distribution of resources. However, the disruption of the informational sphere can be conceived as a result of an alteration of these stabilising mechanisms. Resources of production and distribution disseminated outside the media industries through the proliferation of computing technology and technical programming skill. With this proliferation, the ability to convert media industry products into data moved them into the domain of the informational sphere, and placed them under its remit. This sphere brought with it new cultural schemas, new understandings of rights and ownership based upon the subcultural heritage derived from multiple sources but bound together by a shared involvement with information technology. This disparate but joined community had their own cultural schemas regarding what was valued and what was not, which were indirectly applied to media products as they were worked with by these groups. The structures of incumbent industry and the law attempted to quell this disruption through their modes of power, their ability to denote what cultural schemas were acceptable. The incumbents were seeking to ensure the retention of the cultural schemas that defined IP, schemas upon which their industry was reliant. However, the cultural schemas of the informational sphere began to propagate through the digital replication of their outputs, their software and networks, and began to formalise in political movements. What resulted was a conflict that sought stabilisation yet in the process of regaining stability, the structure was altered. The formal sphere of media production and distribution changed, appropriating elements of the disruptor to further entrench themselves. To retrieve a previously invoked quote; events are 'sequences of occurrences that result in transformations of structures' (Sewell, 1996: 843). The current state of digital distribution and the associated ideological shift is the structural transformation that has resulted from the sequence of events presented here.

This of course is simply a framework of conceptualising a broader process of change – a macro story built on many micro ones. Structuration recognises that the process of change is a reflexive one, the agents impacting upon the structures and the structures impacting upon the agents, each both influencing and reacting to the other. However, ultimately it could be considered that the concept of social stability is unfounded beyond a certain level of detail and granularity. It is a mirage derived from simplification of narratives and broad macro statements. When attempts are made to look at the micro, what becomes apparent is that there is a constant milieu of conflicts, actions, reactions and small stabilisations. Change is always occurring; stability is a fallacy. Under this focus it is possible to merge a perspective that assumes stability and one that assumes instability. A view that takes instability would be actor-network theory (Latour, 2005; Law, 1992) which instead argues that the real oddity in society is that we can stabilise an arrangement of actors, objects and texts long enough to denote them as a 'thing' (e.g. the arrangement of individual elements that makes up what we term 'parliament'). In the case of this work the two perspectives can be applied. The language and model of structuration theory is a useful utility to explain the process of social change, but it should not define the final explanation, which is one much more akin to 'instability'; an always conflicting, always changing conception of reality that actor-network theory brings. In a sense we can conceive of the operation of structuration theory as striving for the ideal type. The structures always seek to regain stability, yet stability is always just out of reach as new disruptions step forward and bring new challenges. Of course, as a set of histories they are empirical data, and so arguably can be interpreted through other frameworks of social change as well. However, the process of generating this empirical data was informed by an ontology based on these two theories of social change. These theories supported the conceptual tool of the 'event biography', which was key to structuring the research. Actor-network theory and structuration theory guided and drove the method and the work, and so are ingrained throughout the book, from the style of presentation through to the focus on detail and singular, contingent events.

What then is this history about? It is about many things. As a documentation of a small element of social history it, like any other element of social history, touches upon and is derived from so many different topics. Substantively it has been about the history of the digital distribution of media, and the role that illicit piracy networks have played in that development. It has also been about the role that the capacities of digital media have had in that development: how the nuts and bolts of magnetic storage, code, and the more often-cited properties of digital media, have influenced the development of the digital distribution market. Importantly, as much as it has been about technology it has been about people, and their actions, and how those actions, whether perceived to be great or insignificant, have contributed to the alterations in the way people engage with culture through media. It has been about the social structures in society, of law and normative conventions that have shaped and constrained the decisions those individuals have made and shaped the technologies as they have developed. It has also been about how an industry has changed in response to those decisions and how others changed in response to that. It has been about very human elements, about ideals and ideology, values and causes and how their conflicts have led to significant real change. It has been about obsession, creativity, idealism, compulsion, greed, fear and arrogance. It has been about disruption in one element of the social world, and how its impact has reached far beyond it. It has been about the process of change, about the value of the insignificant, and the dynamism of the unintended. It has been about why a description can be more valuable than an analysis and about why details matter. It has specifically been about the realities behind digital media, the biographies of events, and about the value that can be derived from a hacker's market.

Notes

4 GNUtella: Decentralising the Masses

1. Pronounced 'nu'tella', a play on the GNU free-software project and *Nutella*, a favourite chocolate spread.
2. www.reaper.fm
3. 'Crawlers', 'bots' or 'spiders' are automated software agents that wander the internet collecting information to add to their search engine database.
4. Mosaic, later renamed to Netscape Navigator, is often credited as producing the internet boom of the 1990s. It became one of the first popular multimedia web browsers and boasted features such as having pictures embedded in the page rather than as a separate downloads and bookmarks. Many browsers emulated Netscape's design, including Microsoft's Internet Explorer, which still cites Mosaic in its 'About' section of the application. Netscape set the standard for the free business model, giving away its browser to make its money from services. Netscape eventually became Mozilla, which is better known today as Firefox (Moody, 2007).

5 FastTrack: The Business of Piracy

1. The Motion Picture Association of America (MPAA) is a similar trade interest group to the RIAA but represents the interests of the US film industry.
2. http://blog.tmcnet.com/blog/tom-keating/skype/skype-in-legal-fight-with-joltid-over-p2p-technology.asp, last accessed 23 June 2010.
3. The authority and validity of the comment is of course questionable and, though alone it neither confirms nor rebukes Streamcast's suspicions, it is worth including as an addition to the other pieces of evidence.

6 BitTorrent: Revolution in the Network

1. Roth reports from his interview with Cohen that Cohen both learned to read and code in tandem. The first words he learned to read being 'goto', 'run' and 'print' on the family's Timex Sinclair computer (Roth, 2005).
2. http://finance.groups.yahoo.com/group/decentralization/message/3160, last accessed 28 June 2010.
3. This was not piracy. Linux, being an open and free (in most iterations) operating system, meant that programs were also often free and so BitTorrent was used to legitimately share the work that Linux users had made with the community.

4. CodeCon 2002 Conference programme available from the Internet Archive's Wayback Machine at: http://web.archive.org/web/2011061319 1807/http://www.codecon.org/2002/program.html, last accessed 25 November 2012.
5. http://www.valvesoftware.com/awards.html
6. Today the games on Steam's service can be the size of three or four DVDs.
7. A list of these complete with current capacity use can be seen at http://www.steampowered.com/status/content_servers.html, last accessed 28 April 2010.
8. Most sites moderate to remove Torrent files that direct to sexually abhorrent content such as child pornography or imagery of sexual assault, and files that may be dangerous to their users systems such as viruses or trojan programs masquerading as something else.
9. Demos in this context refer to pieces of programming that produce audio and visual arrangements to show off programming and creative skill.
10. After its use one site member added a stylised giant ape to the Pirate Bay front-page logo.
11. A comprehensive history of 'the Scene' can be found at http://www.defacto2.net/defacto2/counterculture, last accessed 25 November 2012.
12. An English translation of the speech can be found at http://piratbyran-in-eng.blogspot.com/2006/06/speech-by-fredrik-neij-pirate-bay-here.html, last accessed 25 May 2010.
13. Magnet links work by utilising the DHT hash tags rather than storing the full Torrent file. When a magnet link is clicked the site passes on the identifying hash tag to the user's BitTorrent client, which uses the information to query a DHT database and find one individual in the swarm. Once in the swarm the original Torrent can be downloaded from one of the peers and the process can continue as normal.
14. At the time of writing Svartholm is still missing.

7   Hacking the Market

1. In 2011 Morris took the CEO position at Sony Music Entertainment.
2. This statement from Al Smith is according to Gerry Kearby's recollection and so the quote is attributed to Kearby.
3. 'Phreak' was a slang term for the hackers that lurked on the phone networks – an amalgamation of 'phone' and 'freak'.
4. Phone phreaking did not stop; it is still prevalent today, more so due to the explosion of mobile phones and the more manipulatable nature of digital phone networks.
5. The survey was carried out across 684 software developers from 287 F/OSS projects.
6. A conflation of the private enterprise and the collective action models of organisation. See Von Hippel and Von Krogh (2003) for further elaboration.

8   New Media Gatekeepers

1. Now just Apple Inc.
2. A licensing agreement, typical to software, which presents the rights and responsibilities of both licensor and licensee.
3. The American Law Institute withdrew from the project and the UCC2B became UCITA (Uniform Computer Information Transactions Act). Only passed in two states, UCITA was considered a failure, especially as many more states passed UCITA bomb-shelter statutes, protecting their citizens against the enforcement of any UCITA licence (thanks to Professor Samuelson for this explanation of UCC2B's eventual trajectory).
4. http://www.steampowered.com
5. Console games are still predominantly sold boxed via retail outlets. Digital download outlets, though operational on all three major home consoles (Sony PlayStation, Microsoft Xbox and Nintendo Wii) primarily sell small games, leaving the major properties to be boxed and shipped. Due to the proprietary control over the console ecosystems, other vendors are unable to attempt their own full digital outlet, comparable to those on the relatively open PC platform.
6. Valve's best-known product, *Half-Life 2*, has received numerous 'Game of the Year' and 'Game of the Decade' awards from various publications and industry groups.

Bibliography

A&M Records v Napster (2000); *A&M v Napster* Ruling: Full Text. United States District Court Northern District of California, available at: http://news.cnet.com/News/Pages/Special/Napster/napster_patel.html, last accessed 7 October 2009.

A&M Records v Napster (2001) United States Ninth Circuit Court of Appeals Summary. *Harvard Cyber Law Journal*, available at: http://cyber.law.harvard.edu/~wseltzer/summary.html, last accessed 7 October 2009.

Abbott, A. (2009) The Future of Knowing. SPEECH: 'Brunch with Books': University of Chicago, available at: http://home.uchicago.edu/~aabbott/Papers/futurek.pdf, last accessed 18 October 2010.

Adorno, T. and Horkheimer, M. (1997) *Dialectic of Enlightenment*, London: Verso.

Alleyne, B. (2011) Challenging Code: A Sociological Reading of the KDE Free Software Project. *Sociology* 45: 496–511.

Amazon EU S.a.r.l. (2011a) Amazon MP3 Music Service: Terms of Use. Amazon.co.uk: Amazon MP3 Downloads, available at: http://www.amazon.co.uk/gp/help/customer/display.html/ref=hp_left_sib?ie=UTF8& nodeId=200285010, last accessed 21 April 2011.

Amazon EU S.a.r.l. (2011b) Amazon.co.uk Kindle License Agreement and Terms of Use. Amazon.co.uk: Warranties & Notices, available at: http://www.amazon.co.uk/gp/help/customer/display.html?nodeId=200501450, last accessed 21 April 2011.

Anderson, N. (2009) Reservella: The Shadowy Company Behind the Pirate Bay. Ars Technica: Law & Disorder, available at: http://arstechnica.com/tech-policy/news/2009/10/who-owns-the-pirate-bay-part-ii.ars, last accessed 12 May 2011.

Anderson, N. (2010a) Air Force May Suffer Collateral Damage from PS3 Firmware Update. Ars Technica: Opposable Thumbs, available at: http://arstechnica.com/gaming/news/2010/05/how-removing-ps3-linux-hurts-the-air-force.ars, last accessed 7 April 2011.

Anderson, N. (2010b) No, You Don't Own it: Court Upholds EULAs, Threatens Digital Resale. Ars Technica: Law & Disorder, available at: http://arstechnica.com/tech-policy/news/2010/09/the-end-of-used-major-ruling-upholds-tough-software-licenses.ars, last accessed 21 April 2011.

Anderson, N. (2010c) Pirate Party Hosting Pirate Bay in Pro-P2P Political Gesture. Ars Technica: Law & Disorder, available at: http://arstechnica.com/tech-policy/news/2010/05/pirate-party-hosting-pirate-bay-in-pro-p2p-political-gesture.ars, last accessed 17 May 2011.

Anderson, N. (2011) How One Man Tracked Down Anonymous – And Paid a Heavy Price. Ars Technica: Law & Disorder, available at: http://

arstechnica.com/tech-policy/news/2011/02/how-one-security-firm-tracked-anonymousand-paid-a-heavy-price.ars, last accessed 14 June 2011.
Ansari, A, Essegaier, S. and Kohli, R. (2000) Internet Recommendation Systems. *Journal of Marketing Research* XXXVII: 363–375.
Apple Inc. (2003) Apple Launches the iTunes Music Store. Press Release, available at: http://www.apple.com/pr/library/2003/apr/28musicstore.html, last accessed 29 April 2010.
Apple Inc. (2005) Apple Announces iTunes 6 with 2,000 Music Videos, Pixar Short Films & Hit TV Shows. Press Release, available at: http://www.apple.com/pr/library/2005/oct/12itunes.html, last accessed 29 April 2010.
Apple Inc. (2009) Changes Coming to the iTunes Store. Press Release, available at: http://www.apple.com/pr/library/2009/01/06itunes.html, last accessed 29 April 2010.
Apple Inc. (2011) Terms and Conditions. Apple.com/Legal, available at: http://www.apple.com/legal/itunes/us/terms.html, last accessed 7 January 2011.
Axon, S. (2010) Hitler 'Downfall' Parodies Removed from YouTube. Mashable, available at: http://mashable.com/2010/04/20/dmca-hitler/, last accessed 7 April 2011.
Babenhauserheide, A. (2004) GnuFU: Gnutella for Users. Available at: http://www1.draketo.de/inhalt/krude-ideen/gnufu-en.pdf, last accessed 12 October 2009.
Bagdikian, B. (1983) *The Media Monopoly*, Boston: Beacon Press.
Bagdikian, B. (2004) *The New Media Monopoly*, Boston: Beacon Press.
Barnes, C. (2000) Napster CEO Fights for Life of Music Firm. CNET News: Newsmakers, available at: http://news.cnet.com/2008-1082-243765.html, last accessed 7 October 2009.
Barnett, E. (2009) Sir Martin Sorrell: Rupert Murdoch's Pay Wall Plan Is Right. Telegraph.co.uk, available at: http://www.telegraph.co.uk/technology/news/6255272/Sir-Martin-Sorrell-Rupert-Murdochs-pay-wall-plan-is-right.html, last accessed 7 October 2009.
BBC News (2008) Spore at Top of the Piracy Charts. BBC News (online), available at: http://news.bbc.co.uk/1/hi/technology/7772962.stm, last accessed 6 July 2012.
BBC News (2011) Scottish Election: Pirate Party UK Profile. BBC News: Scotland Politics, available at: http://www.bbc.co.uk/news/uk-scotland-scotland-politics-12997090, last accessed 17 May 2011.
BBC Press Office (2007) Anthony Rose Appointed BBC Head of Digital Media Technology. BBC Press Office, available at: http://www.bbc.co.uk/pressoffice/pressreleases/stories/2007/09_september/17/rose.shtml, last accessed 19 April 2010.
Beer, D. (2009) Power Through the Algorithm? Participatory Web Cultures and the Technological Unconscious. *New Media & Society* 11: 985–1002.
Benholm, S. (2010) 'Det kommer bli väldigt svårt att röra The Pirate Bay nu' (Translation: 'It Will Be Very Difficult to Move the Pirate Bay Now') SVT.se, available at: http://svt.se/2.27170/1.2005911/det_kommer_bli_valdigt_svart_att_rora_the_pirate_bay_nu, last accessed 18 July 2011.

Benkler, Y. and Nissenbaum, H. (2006) Commons-based Peer Production and Virtue. *The Journal of Political Philosophy* 14: 394–419.

Berfield, S. (2008) Do I Look Like a CEO? *Business Week*, 23 October, available at: http://www.thefreelibrary.com/'DO I LOOK LIKE A CEO?'-a01611680164, last accessed 24 November 2012.

Berry, D. M. (2011) *The Philosophy of Software: Code and Mediation in the Digital Age*, Basingstoke: Palgrave Macmillan.

Berry, D. M. and Moss, G. (eds) (2008) *Libre Culture*, Canada: Pygmalion Books.

Bijker, W., Hughes, T. and Pinch, T. (1987) *The Social Construction of Technological Systems: New Directions in the Sociology and History of Technology*, Cambridge, MA: MIT Press.

BMG. (2000) Bertelsmann and Napster Form Strategic Alliance; Will Establish Industry Accepted Community for File Sharing. PR Newswire Europe, 31 October 2000, available at: http://www.thefreelibrary.com/Bertelsmann+and+Napster+Form+Strategic+Alliance%3B+Will+Establish...-a066570307, last accessed 24 November 2012.

Bolter, J. D. (1991) *Writing Space: The Computer, Hypertext, and the History of Writing*, Hillsdale, NJ: Lawrence Erlbaum Associates.

Borland, J. (2000a) MP3.com Loses Legal Battle to RIAA. CNET News: Media, available at: http://news.cnet.com/MP3.com-loses-legal-battle-to-RIAA/2100-1023_3-239861.html?tag=mncol, last accessed 6 October 2009.

Borland, J. (2000b) MP3.com Recasts as Music 'Infrastructure' Company. CNET News: Media, available at: http://news.cnet.com/MP3.com-recasts-as-music-infrastructure-company/2100-1023_3-242187.html?tag=mncol, last accessed 6 October 2009.

Borland, J. (2000c) Napster-like Technology Takes Web Search to New Level. CNET News: Media, available at: http://news.cnet.com/Napster-like-technology-takes-Web-search-to-new-level/2100-1023_3-241223.html?tag=mncol, last accessed 14 January 2010.

Borland, J. (2001a) Musicians Sue MP3.com. CNET News: Media, available at: http://news.cnet.com/Musicians-sue-MP3.com/2110-1023_3-257241.html?tag=mncol, last accessed 6 October 2009.

Borland, J. (2001b) Suit Hits Popular Post-Napster Network. CNET News: Media, available at: http://news.cnet.com/2100-1023-273855.html, last accessed 16 February 2010.

Borland, J. (2001c) Sun Aims at Peer-to-Peer Search with Acquisition. ZDNet News: Internet, available at: http://news.zdnet.co.uk/internet/0,1000000097,2084865,00.htm, last accessed 25 January 2010.

Borland, J. (2002a) The Brains Behind Kazaa. CNET News: Newsmaker, available at: http://news.cnet.com/The-brains-behind-Kazaa/2008-1082_3-890072.html?tag=mncol, last accessed 18 October 2010.

Borland, J. (2002b) Kazaa Steps Out of the Shadows. CNET News: Media, available at: http://news.cnet.com/Kazaa-steps-out-of-the-shadows/2100-1023_3-890197.html?tag=mncol, last accessed 24 February 2010.

Borland, J. (2002c) Kazaa, Morpheus Legal Case Collapsing. CNET News: Media, available at: http://news.cnet.com/Kazaa,-Morpheus-legal-case-collapsing/2100-1023_3-920557.html?tag=mncol, last accessed 24 February 2010.

Borland, J. (2002d) Morpheus' Downfall: Bills Weren't Paid. CNET News: Media, available at: http://news.cnet.com/Morpheus-downfall-Bills-werent-paid/2100-1023_3-851330.html?tag=mncol, last accessed 24 February 2010.

Borland, J. (2002e) Napster Buyout Blocked; Fire Sale Likely. CNET News: Music, available at: http://news.cnet.com/Napster-buyout-blocked-fire-sale-likely/2100-1027_3-956382.html, last accessed 6 October 2009.

Borland, J. (2002f) Napster CEO Quits as Sale Rejected. CNET News: Media, available at: http://news.cnet.com/Napster-CEO-quits-as-sale-rejected/2100-1023_3-913555.html, last accessed 6 October 2009.

Borland, J. (2002g) Record Labels Mull Suits Against File-traders. CNET News: Media, available at: http://news.cnet.com/Record-labels-mull-suits-against-file-traders/2100-1023_3-941547.html?tag=mncol, last accessed 11 April 2010.

Borland, J. (2002h) RIAA, File-swappers Ask for Trial's End, available at: http://news.cnet.com/RIAA,-file-swappers-ask-for-trials-end/2100-1027_3-957227.html?tag=mncol, last accessed 24 February 2010.

Borland, J. (2003) Judge: File-swapping Tools Are Legal. CNET News: Music, available at: http://news.cnet.com/Judge-File-swapping-tools-are-legal/2100-1027_3-998363.html?tag=mncol, last accessed 24 February 2010.

Borland, J. (2006) BitTorrent to Crack Down on Use of Name. CNET News: Web Software, available at: http://news.cnet.com/BitTorrent-to-crack-down-on-use-of-name/2100-1032_3-6035800.html?tag=mncol, last accessed 29 April 2010.

Borland, J. and Hu, J. (2001) MP3.com Buy: The Taming of a Generation. CNET News: Media, available at: http://news.cnet.com/MP3.com-buy-the-taming-of-a-generation/2100-1023_3-257993.html?tag=mncol, last accessed 6 October 2009.

Boyle, J. (2009) *The Public Domain: Enclosing the Commons of the Mind*, London: Yale University Press.

Bradshaw, T. and Palmer, M. (2010) Skype Founders Raise $165m for New Fund. FT.com: Technology, available at: http://www.ft.com/cms/s/2/f04786d2-3512-11df-9cfb-00144feabdc0.html, last accessed 20 April 2010.

Briet, S. (1951) Qu'est-ce que la documentation, Paris (English translation available at http://ella.slis.indiana.edu/~roday/briet.htm).

Buckland, M. (1991) Information as Thing. *Journal of the American Society for Information Science* 42: 351–360.

Buckland, M. (1997) What Is a 'Document'? *Journal of the American Society for Information Science* 48: 804–809.

Buckland, M. (1998) What Is a 'Digital Document'? ischool.berkley.edu, available at: http://people.ischool.berkeley.edu/~buckland/digdoc.html, last accessed 20 February 2012.

Bulkley, K. (2006) Preparing Themselves for a Torrent of Users. *The Guardian* (Technology Section), 19 October 2006, p. 5, London.

Burgess, R. G. (1984) *In the Field: An Introduction to Field Research*, London: Allen and Unwin.

Burke, A. and Montgomery, C. (2002) You Say You Want a Revolution? A Case Study of MP3.com. *International Journal of Entrepreneurship Education* 1: 107–132.

Byfield, B. (2009) Interview with Pirate Party Leader: 'These Are Crucial Freedoms'. Datamation: IT Management, available at: http://itmanagement.earthweb.com/osrc/article.php/12068_3825206_1/Interview-with-Pirate-Party-Leader-These-are-Crucial-Freedoms.htm, last accessed 12 May 2011.

Chan, K. (2007) Virtual Island for a Virtual World. *The Globe and Mail*, 18 January 2007 (International News), p. A13, London.

Chibber, K. (2009) The Man Who Saved the BBC. *Wired* (online), available at: http://www.wired.co.uk/wired-magazine/archive/2009/04/features/the-man-who-saved-the-bbc.aspx?page=all, last accessed 19 April 2010.

Chirot, D. (1984) Social and Historical Landscape of Marc Bloch. In: Skocpol, T. (ed.) *Vision and Method in Historical Sociology*, Cambridge: Cambridge University Press.

Christensen, C. M. (2006) *The Innovator's Dilemma*, New York: Collins Business Essentials.

Christian, B. (2012) The A/B Test: Inside the Technology That's Changing the Rules of Business. *Wired* (online), available at: http://www.wired.com/business/2012/04/ff_abtesting/, last accessed 5 July 2012.

Cisneros, O. (2000) States: Labels Fixed CD Prices. *Wired* (online): Politics: Law, available at: http://www.wired.com/politics/law/news/2000/08/38103, last accessed 9 March 2011.

Clark, A. (2009) Ebay Decides to Disconnect Skype with Share Floatation. *The Guardian* (Financial Section), 15 April 2009, p. 23, Final Edition, London

Clark, M. (2000) Music Giants Join the Revolution. *The Guardian* (Technology Section), 2 November 2000, available at: http://www.guardian.co.uk/technology/2000/nov/02/news.onlinesupplement, last accessed 24 November.

Coleman, E. G. (2011) Anonymous: From the Lulz to Collective Action. The New Everyday: A Media Commons Project, available at: http://mediacommons.futureofthebook.org/tne/pieces/anonymous-lulz-collective-action, last accessed 19 July 2011.

Coleman, E. G. and Golub, A. (2008) Hacker Practice: Moral Genres and the Cultural Articulation of Liberalism. *Anthropological Theory* 8: 255–277.

Copyright.gov (1998) The Digital Millennium Copyright Act of 1998. US Copyright Office, available at: http://www.copyright.gov/legislation/dmca.pdf, last accessed 8 October 2009.

David, M. (2010) *Peer to Peer and the Music Industry: The Criminalization of Sharing*, London: Sage.

Davidson, A. (2005) Skype Chief Takes His Place as Tech Hero from Zero. *The Times* (online): Business: Telecoms, available at: http://business.timesonline.co.uk/tol/business/industry_sectors/telecoms/article597043.ece, last accessed 18 April 2010.

Deare, S. (2005) Australian Court Rules Against Kazaa. CNET News: Corporate & Legal, available at: http://news.cnet.com/Australian-court-rules-against-Kazaa/2100-1030_3-5849480.html?tag=mncol, last accessed 29 March 2010.

Delio, M. (2002) Quiet, Sad Death of Net Pioneer. *Wired*: Culture: Lifestyle, available at: http://wired-vig.wired.com/culture/lifestyle/news/2002/07/53704?currentPage=all, last accessed 25 January 2010.

Deutsch, C. (2002) Suit Settled Over Pricing of Recordings at Big Chains. *The New York Times*, 1 October 2002, New York.

Doctorow, C. (2008) *Content: Selected Essays on Technology, Creativity, Copyright, and the Future of the Future*, San Francisco: Tachyon Publications.

Doctorow, C. (2010) DRM-free Kindle Books: Are They Any Free-er? BoingBoing.net, available at: http://boingboing.net/2010/01/21/drm-free-kindle-book.html, last accessed 7 January 2011.

Dougherty, M. and Schneider, S. M. (2011) Web Historiography and the Emergence of New Archival Forms. In: Park, D. W., Jankowski, N. W. and Jones, S. (eds) *The Long History of New Media*, New York: Peter Lang Publishing.

Easley, R. (2005) Ethical Issues in the Music Industry Response to Innovation and Piracy. *Journal of Business Ethics* 62: 163–168.

Easley, R., Michel, J. and Devaraj, S. (2003) The MP3 Open Standard and the Music Industry's Response to Internet Piracy. Communications of the ACM 46.

The Economist. (2012) History Flushed: The Digital Age Promised Vast Libraries, but They Remain Incomplete. *The Economist* (online), available at: http://www.economist.com/node/21553410, last accessed 6 July 2012.

Ekman, I. (2005) In Sweden, Paradise for the Movie Pirates. *The International Herald Tribune* (Finance Section), 16 May 2005, p. 9, Stockholm.

Enigmax. (2009a) 50% of Charges Against Pirate Bay Dropped. TorrentFreak, available at: http://torrentfreak.com/50-of-charges-against-pirate-bay-dropped-090217/, last accessed 24 May 2010.

Enigmax. (2009b) Chased from Sweden, Pirate Bay Sails to Ukraine. TorrentFreak, available at: http://torrentfreak.com/chased-from-sweden-pirate-bay-sails-to-ukraine-091002/, last accessed 18 July 2011.

Enigmax. (2009c) Day 3 – The Pirate Bay's 'King Kong' Defence. TorrentFreak, available at: http://torrentfreak.com/g-defense-090218/, last accessed 24 May 2010.

Enigmax. (2009d) GGF: Pirate Bay Purchase Will Happen August 27. TorrentFreak, available at: http://torrentfreak.com/ggf-pirate-bay-purchase-will-happen-august-27-090730/, last accessed 12 May 2011.

Enigmax. (2009e) Napster's $10 Million Bid for the Pirate Bay Rejected. TorrentFreak, available at: http://torrentfreak.com/napsters-10-million-bid-for-the-pirate-bay-rejected-090731/, last accessed 12 May 2011.

Enigmax. (2009f) New Pirate Bay Host Got Hollywood Threats in 20 Minutes. TorrentFreak, available at: http://torrentfreak.com/new-pirate-bay-host-got-hollywood-threats-in-20-minutes-090916/, last accessed 18 July 2011.

Enigmax. (2009g) News from the Pirate Bay Press Conference. TorrentFreak, available at: http://torrentfreak.com/news-from-the-pirate-bay-press-conference-090215/, last accessed 24 May 2010.

Enigmax. (2009h) No Pirate Bay Deal, Says Key GGF Technology Partner. TorrentFreak, available at: http://torrentfreak.com/no-pirate-bay-deal-says-key-ggf-technology-partner-090828/, last accessed 12 May 2011.

Enigmax. (2009i) OpenBitTorrent Tracker Muscles in On the Old Pirate Bay. TorrentFreak, available at: http://torrentfreak.com/openbittorrent-tracker-muscles-in-on-the-old-pirate-bay-090705/, last accessed 18 July 2011.

Enigmax. (2009j) Pirate Bay Buyer Has Car and Motorcycle Repossessed. TorrentFreak, available at: http://torrentfreak.com/pirate-bay-buyer-has-car-and-motorcycle-repossessed-090829/, last accessed 12 May 2011.

Enigmax. (2009k) The Pirate Bay Demand Webcast of Trial. TorrentFreak, available at: http://torrentfreak.com/the-pirate-bay-demand-webcast-of-trial-090207/, last accessed 24 May 2010.

Enigmax. (2009l) The Pirate Bay Sold to Software Company, Goes Legal. TorrentFreak, available at: http://torrentfreak.com/the-pirate-bay-sold-to-software-company-goes-legal-090630/, last accessed 12 May 2011.

Enigmax. (2009m) The Pirate Bay Taken Offline by Swedish Authorities. TorrentFreak, available at: http://torrentfreak.com/the-pirate-bay-taken-offline-by-swedish-authorities-090824/, last accessed 18 July 2011.

Enigmax. (2009n) Pirate Bay Trial Audio Will Be Streamed Online. TorrentFreak, available at: http://torrentfreak.com/pirate-bay-trial-audio-will-be-streamed-online-090211/, last accessed 24 May 2010.

Enigmax. (2009o) Pirate Bay Trial Day 9: BitTorrent Is Not Evil. TorrentFreak, available at: http://torrentfreak.com/pirate-bay-trial-day-9-bittorrent-is-not-evil-090226/, last accessed 17 May 2011.

Enigmax. (2009p) Suspicions of Insider Trading Surround Pirate Bay Buyers. TorrentFreak, available at: http://torrentfreak.com/suspicions-of-insider-trading-surround-pirate-bay-buyers-090701/, last accessed 12 May 2011.

Enigmax. (2010a) The Pirate Bay/CyberBunker/MPA Injunction in Full. TorrentFreak, available at: http://torrentfreak.com/the-pirate-bay-cyberbunker mpa-injunction-in-full-100516/, last accessed 17 May 2011.

Enigmax. (2010b) Pirate Bay Supreme Court Appeal 'Should Consider ISP Liability'. TorrentFreak, available at: http://torrentfreak.com/pirate-bay-supreme-court-appeal-should-consider-isp-liability-101221/, last accessed 13 May 2011.

Enigmax. (2011) Pirate Bay Founder 'Disappears', But Not with Malice. TorrentFreak, available at: http://torrentfreak.com/pirate-bay-founder-disappears-but-not-110308/, last accessed 13 May 2011.

Eriksson, N. (2009) Här fraktas hans mc bort. Aftonbladet, available at: http://www.aftonbladet.se/nyheter/article5710948.ab, last accessed 12 May 2011.

Ernesto. (2006a) BitTorrent Inc Buys uTorrent. TorrentFreak, available at: http://torrentfreak.com/bittorrent-inc-buys-%C2%B5torrent/, last accessed 4 May 2010.

Ernesto. (2006b) Bram Cohen Interview. TorrentFreak, available at: http://torrentfreak.com/bram-cohen-interview/, last accessed 28 April 2010.

Ernesto. (2006c) The Pirate Bay Back Home. TorrentFreak, available at: http://torrentfreak.com/the-piratebay-back-home/, last accessed 10 May 2010.

Ernesto. (2007a) Pirate Bay Politics for Dummies. TorrentFreak, available at: http://torrentfreak.com/pirate-bay-politics-for-dummies/, last accessed 12 May 2010.

Ernesto. (2007b) The Pirate Bay Wants to Buy Sealand. TorrentFreak, available at: http://torrentfreak.com/the-pirate-bay-to-buy-sealand/, last accessed 10 May 2010.

Ernesto. (2009a) Anakata Explains in Court How 'The Scene' Works. TorrentFreak, available at: http://torrentfreak.com/anakata-explains-in-court-how-the-scene-works-090220/, last accessed 25 May 2010.

Ernesto. (2009b) Biased Pirate Bay Judge Judged by More Biased Judges. TorrentFreak, available at: http://torrentfreak.com/biased-pirate-bay-judge-judged-by-more-biased-judges-090520/, last accessed 12 May 2011.

Ernesto. (2009c) BREIN Disconnects the Pirate Bay, for Now. TorrentFreak, available at: http://torrentfreak.com/brein-disconnects-the-pirate-bay-for-now-091005/, last accessed 18 July 2011.

Ernesto. (2009d) Download a Copy of the Pirate Bay Before It's Gone. TorrentFreak, available at: http://torrentfreak.com/download-a-copy-of-the-pirate-bay-before-its-gone-090816/, last accessed 12 May 2011.

Ernesto. (2009e) Pirate Bay Closer to a Retrial, Demands New Investigation. TorrentFreak, available at: http://torrentfreak.com/pirate-bay-getting-closer-to-a-retrial-090511/, last accessed 12 May 2011.

Ernesto. (2009f) The Pirate Bay Relocates to a Nuclear Bunker. TorrentFreak, available at: http://torrentfreak.com/the-pirate-bay-relocates-to-a-nuclear-bunker-091006/, last accessed 18 July 2011.

Ernesto. (2009g) Pirate Bay Sale Dead in the Water. TorrentFreak, available at: http://torrentfreak.com/pirate-bay-sale-dead-in-the-water-090728/, last accessed 12 May 2011.

Ernesto. (2009h) The Pirate Bay Trial – First Day in Court. TorrentFreak, available at: http://torrentfreak.com/the-pirate-bay-trial-first-day-in-court/, last accessed 24 May 2010.

Ernesto. (2009i) Pirate Bay Witness' Wife Overwhelmed with Flowers. TorrentFreak, available at: http://torrentfreak.com/pirate-bay-witness-wife-overwhelmed-with-flowers-090227/, last accessed 17 May 2011.

Ernesto. (2009j) The Pirate Bay's Founders Sail On. TorrentFreak, available at: http://torrentfreak.com/the-pirate-bays-founders-sail-on-090705/, last accessed 18 July 2011.

Ernesto. (2010a) Facebook Uses BitTorrent, and They Love It. TorrentFreak, available at: http://torrentfreak.com/facebook-uses-bittorrent-and-they-love-it-100625/, last accessed 28 June 2010.

Ernesto. (2010b) The Final Day of the Pirate Bay Appeal. TorrentFreak, available at: http://torrentfreak.com/the-pirate-bay-appeal-verdict-101126/, last accessed 13 May 2011.

Ernesto. (2010c) The Pirate Bay Appeal Verdict: Guilty Again. TorrentFreak, available at: http://torrentfreak.com/the-pirate-bay-appeal-verdict-101126/, last accessed 13 May 2011.

Ewing, A. (2006) US Threatened Sweden with Sanctions Over Piracy. TheLocal.se, available at: http://www.thelocal.se/4128/20060621/, last accessed 10 May 2010.

Falcone, J. P. (2007) Apple TV: Handicapping the Competition. CNET News: Crave, available at: http://news.cnet.com/8301-17938_105-9698010-1.html?tag=mncol, last accessed 29 April 2010.

Falkvinge, R. (2011) Why the Name 'Pirate Party'? Falkvinge on InfoPolicy, available at: http://falkvinge.net/2011/02/20/why-the-name-pirate-party/, last accessed 12 May 2011.

Featherstone, M. (2000) Archiving Cultures. *British Journal of Sociology* 51: 161–184.

Feenberg, A. (1999) *Questioning Technology*, New York: Routledge.

Fisher, K. (2009) Why Amazon Went Big Brother on Some Kindle E-books. Ars Technica: Law & Disorder, available at: http://arstechnica.com/tech-policy/news/2009/07/amazon-sold-pirated-books-raided-some-kindles.ars, last accessed 7 January 2011.

Forrest, B. (2005) Two Wild and Crazy Moguls ... *Vanity Fair*. No. 541, available at: http://brettforrest.com/wp-content/uploads/VF%20Skype.pdf, last accessed 24 November 2012.

France, L. R. (2009) In Digital Age, Can Movie Piracy Be Stopped? CNN.com, available at: http://edition.cnn.com/2009/TECH/05/01/wolverine.movie.piracy.index.html?iref=mpstoryview, last accessed 6 July 2012.

Friedman, B. (1997) *Human Values and the Design of Computer Technology*, Cambridge: Cambridge University Press.

Friedman, B. and Nissenbaum, H. (1997) Bias in Computer Systems. In: Friedman, B. (ed.) *Human Values and the Design of Computer Technology*. Cambridge, NY: Cambridge University Press.

Frissen, V. (1995) Gender Is Calling: Some Reflections on Past, Present and Future Uses of the Telephone. In: Grint, K. and Gill, R. (eds) *The Gender–Technology Relation*. London: Taylor and Francis.

Fuller, M. (2008) *Software Studies: A Lexicon*, London: MIT Press.

Gane, N. and Beer, D. (2008) *New Media: The Key Concepts*, Oxford: Berg.

Gibson, O. (2003) Court Rejects Case Against Kazaa. *The Guardian* (online): Media Guardian, available at: http://www.guardian.co.uk/media/2003/dec/19/digitalmedia.netmusic, last accessed 18 April 2010.

Gibson, W. (1999) *All Tomorrow's Parties*, London: Penguin.

Giddens, A. (1981) *A Contemporary Critique of Historical Materialism. Volume 1: Power, Property and the State*, London: Macmillan.

Gitelman, L. and Pingree, G. B. (2004) *New Media: 1740–1915*, Cambridge, MA: MIT Press.

Github (2010) lg/murder. Github: Social Coding, available at: http://github.com/lg/murder, last accessed 4 May 2010.

Glasner, J. (1999) MP3 Squabble Settles Amicably. *Wired* (online): Tech Biz: Media, available at: http://www.wired.com/techbiz/media/news/1999/06/19983, last accessed 6 October 2009.

Glusman, L. J. (1995) It's My Copy, Right?: Music Industry Power to Control Growing Resale Markets in Used Digital Audio Recordings. *Wisconsin Law Review* 1995(3): 709–1475.

Gonzalez, I. G. (2000) Recording Industry Association of America, Inc. v Diamond Multimedia Systems, Inc. *Berkley Technology Law Journal* 15: 67–83.

Grandwell, T. (2006) *Swedish Official Denies Government Acted on US Pressure in Crackdown on File-sharing*. Stockholm, Sweden: The Associated Press (Business News), 21 July 2006.

Greenfeld, K. T., Taylor, C. and Thigpen, D. E. (2000) Meet the Napster. *Time*, available at: http://www.time.com/time/magazine/article/0,9171,998068, 00.html, last accessed 7 October 2009.

Grint, K. and Woolgar, S. (1997) *The Machine at Work*, Cambridge: Polity.

Gross, G. (2004) Tech Groups Fight Copyright Infringement Bill. InfoWorld: Security Central, available at: http://www.infoworld.com/d/security-central/tech-groups-fight-copyright-infringement-bill-671, last accessed 23 June 2010.

Hampshire, E. and Johnson, V. (2009) The Digital World and the Future of Historical Research. *Twentieth Century British History* 20: 396–414.

Hansell, S. (2000) Media Megadeal: The Overview; America Online Agrees to Buy Time Warner for $165 Billion; Media Deal Is Richest Merger. *The New York Times*, 11 January 2000, Late Edition.

Hansen, E. (2001a) Free MP3.com Technology Takes Cue from Open-source Movement. CNET News: Media, available at: http://news.cnet.com/Free-MP3.com-technology-takes-cue-from-open-source-movement/2100-1023_3-251014.html?tag=mncol, last accessed 6 October 2009.

Hansen, E. (2001b) MP3.com Signs with Online Retailer CD Baby. CNET News: Media, available at: http://news.cnet.com/MP3.com-signs-with-online-retailer-CD-Baby/2110-1023_3-277059.html?tag=mncol, last accessed 6 October 2009.

Harmon, A. (2000) Free Music Software May Have Rattled AOL. *The New York Times*, available at: http://www.nytimes.com/2000/03/20/business/technology-free-music-software-may-have-rattled-aol.html, last accessed 13 October 2009.

Harrison, A. (2006) The Pirate Bay: Here to Stay? *Wired* (online), available at: http://www.wired.com/science/discoveries/news/2006/03/70358, last accessed 6 May 2010.

Hartley, M. (2009) Thank You, Napster. *The Globe and Mail*: Download Decade, available at: http://www.theglobeandmail.com/news/technology/download-decade/thank-you-napster/article1014979/, last accessed 7 October 2009.

Healey, J. (2007) Trapping File-sharers? *Los Angeles Times* (online), available at: http://opinion.latimes.com/bitplayer/2007/09/trapping-file-s.html, last accessed 6 July 2012.

Healey, J. (2008) Morpheus Throws in the Towel. *Los Angeles Times*: Blogs: Bit Player, available at: http://opinion.latimes.com/bitplayer/2008/05/morpheus-throws.html, last accessed 11 April 2010.

Hemos. (2000) Open Source Napster: Gnutella. Slashdot, available at: http://tech.slashdot.org/story/00/03/14/0949234/Open-Source-Napster-Gnutella?art_pos=8, last accessed 13 October 2009.

Hertzfeld, A. (2005) *Revolution in the Valley: The Insanely Great Story of How the Mac Was Made*, Sebastopol, CA: O'Reilly Media.

Hesmondhalgh, D. (2007) *The Cultural Industries*, Second Edition, London: Sage Publications.

Himanen, P. (2001) *The Hacker Ethic, and the Spirit of the Information Age*, London: Vintage.

Hu, J. (1998) New Web Radio Technology Aims for Masses. CNET News: Media, available at: http://news.cnet.com/New-Web-radio-technology-aims-for-masses/2100-1023_3-219634.html?tag=mncol, last accessed 8 October 2009.

Hu, J. (2000a) MP3.com Settles Copyright Dispute with Warner, BMG. CNET News: Media, available at: http://news.cnet.com/MP3.com-settles-copyright-dispute-with-Warner%2C-BMG/2100-1023_3-241677.html?tag=mncol, last accessed 6 October 2009.

Hu, J. (2000b) MP3.com, Music Publishers Sound Out Licensing Deal. CNET News: Media, available at: http://news.cnet.com/MP3.com%2C-music-publishers-sound-out-licensing-deal/2100-1023_3-247218.html?tag=mncol, last accessed 6 October 2009.

Hu, J. (2001) No Shrink-wrap: MP3.com Sells Digital Albums. CNET News: Media, available at: http://news.cnet.com/No-shrink-wrap-MP3.com-sells-digital-albums/2100-1023_3-257376.html?tag=mncol, last accessed 7 October 2009.

Hu, J. (2004) Controversial WinAmp Creator Resigns from AOL. CNET News: Web Software, available at: http://news.cnet.com/Controversial-Winamp-creator-resigns-from-AOL/2100-1032_3-5147599.html?tag=mncol, last accessed 14 October 2009.

Hutchby, I. (2001) Technologies, Texts and Affordances. *Sociology* 35: 441–456.

IIS Fraunhofer. (2009) The Story of MP3. IIS Fraunhofer website, available at: http://www.iis.fraunhofer.de/EN/bf/amm/products/mp3/mp3history/mp3history01.jsp, last accessed 6 October 2009.

Introna, L. D. and Nissenbaum, H. (2000) Shaping the Web: Why the Politics of Search Engines Matters. *The Information Society*, 169–185, available from http://www.ingentaconnect.com/content/routledg/utis/2000/00000016/00000003/art00002.

Isaacson, W. (2011) *Steve Jobs*, New York: Simon & Schuster.

Jenkins, H. (2008) *Convergence Culture: Where Old and New Media Collide*, New York University Press.

Johnson, B. (2009) Skype's Future Is on the Line. *The Guardian* (Technology Section), 16 April 2009, London.

Johnson, S. (2010) *Where Good Ideas Come From: A Natural History of Innovation*, London: Allen Lane.

Jones, C. (2000) Open-Source 'Napster' Shut Down. *Wired*, available at: http://www.wired.com/science/discoveries/news/2000/03/34978, last accessed 13 October 2009.

Jones, M. A. (1999) MP3.com Sued by PlayMedia. ZDNet UK, available at: http://news.zdnet.co.uk/emergingtech/0,1000000183,2071967,00.htm, last accessed 8 October 2009.

Kan, G., Gnutella and GoneSilent.com. (2001) Gnutella. In: Oram, A. (ed.) *Peer-to-Peer: Harnessing the Benefits of a Disruptive Technology*, Sebastopol: O'Reilly & Associates.

Kane, M. (2002) Roxio Snapping Up Napster Assets. CNET News: Media, available at: http://news.cnet.com/2100-1023-965960.html, last accessed 6 October 2009.

Kaplan, C. S. (1999) In Court's View, MP3 Player Is Just a 'Space Shifter'. Harvard Cyber Law Journal, available at: http://cyber.law.harvard.edu/is99/RioSpaceShifter.htm, last accessed 6 October 2009.

Kary, T. (2001) Another Lawsuit for MP3.com. CNET News: Miscellaneous, available at: http://news.cnet.com/Another-lawsuit-for-MP3.com/2100-12_3-259952.html?tag=mncol, last accessed 7 October 2009.

Kazaa. (2002) SuperNodes. The Guide, available at: http://www.kazaa.com/us/help/faq/supernodes.htm, last accessed 14 January 2010.

Keen, A. (2008) *The Cult of the Amateur: How Blogs, Myspace, YouTube and the Rest of Today's User-generated Media Are Killing Our Culture and Economy*, London: Nicholas Brealey Publishing.

Kirwan, P. (2009) Guardian Struggles to Avoid the E-word. *Wired*, available at: http://www.wired.co.uk/news/archive/2009-10/02/guardian-struggles-to-avoid-the-e-word.aspx, last accessed 7 October 2009.

Kiss, J. (2009) Pirate Bay: Preparing for Another Week Humiliating the Man. *The Guardian* (online), available at: http://www.guardian.co.uk/media/pda/2009/feb/23/pirate-bay-file-sharing, last accessed 6 July 2012.

Kitchin, R. and Dodge, M. (2011) *Code/Space: Software and Everyday Life*, Cambridge, MA: MIT Press.

Kittler, F. (1999) *Gramophone, Film, Typewriter*, Stanford, CA: Stanford University Press.

Klinker, E. (2010) Twitter Using BitTorrent on the Backend. BitTorrent Blog, available at: http://blog.bittorrent.com/2010/02/09/twitter-using-bittorrent-on-the-backend/, last accessed 4 May 2010.

Knopper, S. (2009) *Appetite for Self-Destruction: The Spectacular Crash of the Record Industry in the Digital Age*, London: Simon & Schuster.

Kogut, B. and Metiu, A. (2001) Open-Source Software Development and Distributed Innovation. *Oxford Review of Economic Policy* 17: 248–264.

Konrad, R. (2000) MP3.com Chief Shrugs Off Hype Surrounding Lawsuit. CNET News: Media, available at: http://news.cnet.com/MP3.com-chief-shrugs-off-hype-surrounding-lawsuit/2100-1023_3-240401.html?tag=mncol, last accessed 7 October 2009.

Kuchera, B. (2010) It No Longer Does Everything: No More Linux on PlayStation 3. Ars Technica: Opposable Thumbs, available at: http://arstechnica.com/gaming/news/2010/03/it-no-longer-does-everything-no-more-linux-on-playstation-3.ars, last accessed 7 April 2011.

Kushner, D. (2004) The World's Most Dangerous Geek. *Rolling Stone* (online), available at: http://www.rollingstone.com/news/story/5938320/the_worlds_most_dangerous_geek, last accessed 6 October 2009.

Lacy, S. (2006) BitTorrent Goes Legit. Bloomberg Businessweek, available at: http://www.businessweek.com/technology/content/oct2006/tc20061023_551741.htm, last accessed 29 April 2010.

Lakhani, K. and Wolf, R. (2005) Why Hackers Do What They Do: Understanding Motivation and Effort in Free/Open Source Software Projects. In: Feller, J., Fitzgerald, B., Hissam, S., et al. (eds) *Perspectives on Free and Open Source Software*, Cambridge, MA: MIT Press.

LaMonica, M. (2004) Sun Shines of Jxta. ZDNet: CNET News, available at: http://news.zdnet.co.uk/software/0,1000000121,39144961,00.htm, last accessed 25 January 2010.

Langlois, C. V. and Seignobos, C. (1908) *Introduction to the Study of History*, London: Duckworth.

Lanxon, N. (2009) iPlayer Uncovered: What Powers the BBC's Epic Creation? CNET: Crave: Software, available at: http://crave.cnet.co.uk/software/0,39029471,49302215-1,00.htm, last accessed 19 April 2010.

Lash, S. and Lury, C. (2007) *Global Culture Industry: The Mediation of Things*, Cambridge: Polity.

Latour, B. (2005) *Reassembling the Social: An Introduction to Actor-Network Theory*, Oxford: Oxford University Press.

Law, J. (1992) Notes on the Theory of the Actor-Network: Ordering, Strategy, and Heterogeneity. *Systems Practice* 5(4): 379–393.

Lee, E. (2005) The Ethics of Innovation: p2p Software Developers and Designing Substantial Noninfringing Uses Under the Sony Doctrine. *Journal of Business Ethics* 62: 147–162.

Lessig, L. (2005) *Free Culture: The Nature and Future of Creativity*, New York: Penguin Books.

Lessig, L. (2008) *Remix: Making Art and Commerce Thrive in the Hybrid Economy*, London: Bloomsbury Academic.

Lettice, J. (2003) 'Don't Shoot the MP3.com Archive', Pleads Founder Robertson. The Register: Music and Media, available at: http://www.theregister.co.uk/2003/11/19/dont_shoot_the_mp3_com/, last accessed 6 October 2009.

Levinson, P. (1997) *Soft Edge: A Natural History and Future of the Information Revolution*, London: Routledge.

Levy, D. M. (1994) Fixed or Fluid? Document Stability and New Media. ECHT '94 Proceedings of the 1994 ACM European conference on Hypermedia technology, 24–31 September 1994, New York: Association for Computing Machinery.

Levy, D. M. (1999) The Universe Is Expanding: Reflections on the Social (and Cosmic) Significance of Documents in a Digital Age. *Bulletin of the American Society for Information Science* 25: 17–20.

Levy, D. M. (2000a) Where's Waldo? Reflections on Copies and Authenticity in a Digital Environment. In: Smith, A. (ed.) *Authenticity in a Digital Environment*, Washington, DC: Council on Library and Information Resources, available from http://www.clir.org/pubs/reports/pub92/pub92.pdf.

Levy, S. (2000b) The Man Can't Stop Our Music. *Newsweek US* (Science and Technology), 27 March 2000, p. 68.

Levy, S. (2001) *Hackers, Heroes of the Computer Revolution*, London: Penguin.
Levy, S. (2006) *The Perfect Thing*, Chatham: Random House.
Lipton Krigel, B. (1999a) AOL Buys Spinner, Nullsoft for $400 Million. CNET News: Media, available at: http://news.cnet.com/AOL-buys-Spinner%2C-Nullsoft-for-400-million/2100-1023_3-226540.html?tag=mncol, last accessed 8 October 2009.
Lipton Krigel, B. (1999b) MP3 Firms Clash Over Copyrighted Code. CNET News: Media, available at: http://news.cnet.com/2100-1023-223010.html, last accessed 8 October 2009.
Lipton Krigel, B. (1999c) MP3.com IPO Prices Over Top of Range. CNET News: Media, available at: http://news.cnet.com/MP3.com-IPO-prices-over-top-of-range/2100-1023_3-228739.html, last accessed 6 October 2009.
Lipton Krigel, B. (1999d) PlayMedia Settles Nullsoft Copyright Suit. CNET News: Media, available at: http://news.cnet.com/PlayMedia-settles-Nullsoft-copyright-suit/2100-1023_3-226609.html?tag=mncol, last accessed 8 October 2009.
Lipton Krigel, B. (1999e) Tom Petty Joins MP3 Bandwagon. CNET News: Media, available at: http://news.cnet.com/Tom-Petty-joins-MP3-bandwagon/2100-1023_3-222361.html, last accessed 6 October 2009.
The Local (2006) 'Pirate Party' Targets Swedish Election. TheLocal.se, available at: http://www.thelocal.se/article.php?ID=2791&date=20060103, last accessed 12 May 2011.
Lowensohn, J. (2010) Ubisoft's Controversial 'Always On' PC DRM Hacked. CNET News: Web Crawler, available at: http://news.cnet.com/8301-27076_3-20003120-248.html, last accessed 1 April 2011.
Luening, E. (2000) MP3 Chief: Company Will Prevail Despite Legal Storm. CNET News: Media, available at: http://news.cnet.com/MP3-chief-Company-will-prevail-despite-legal-storm/2100-1023_3-245605.html?tag=mncol, last accessed 6 October 2009.
Macavinta, C. (1998) Copyright Law Will Cost Net Radio. CNET News: Media, available at: http://news.cnet.com/2100-1023-217284.html&tag=mncol%3btxt, last accessed 8 October 2009.
Macavinta, C. (2000a) EMI Heads Toward Full Digital Distribution. CNET News: Media, available at: http://news.cnet.com/EMI-heads-toward-full-digital-distribution/2100-1023_3-237124.html?tag=mncol, last accessed 6 October 2009.
Macavinta, C. (2000b) Mp3.com's Move to Copy CDs Stirs Debate. CNET News: Media, available at: http://news.cnet.com/MP3.coms-move-to-copy-CDs-stirs-debate/2100-1023_3-236237.html?tag=mncol, last accessed 6 October 2009.
Mackenzie, A. (2006) *Cutting Code: Software and Sociality*, New York: Peter Lang.
Mackintosh, H. (2005) Talk Time: Niklas Zennström. *The Guardian* (online), available at: http://www.guardian.co.uk/technology/2005/jul/14/onlinesupplement.skype, last accessed 14 January 2010.
Maney, K. (2000) Techie's Napster-like Idea Blasted Off; Now He's Flying High. *USA Today* (22 November 2000), p. 3B. Final Edition, Burlingame, CA.

Mariano, G. (2001a) Indie Label Wins MP3.com Suit. CNET News: Media, available at: http://news.cnet.com/Indie-label-wins-MP3.com-suit/ 2110-1023_3-253672.html?tag=mncol, last accessed 6 October 2009.

Mariano, G. (2001b) MP3.com President Steps into Top Spot. CNET News: Media, available at: http://news.cnet.com/MP3.com-president-steps-into-top-spot/2100-1023_3-272423.html?tag=mncol, last accessed 6 October 2009.

Mariano, G. (2001c) MP3.com Splits into Two. CNET News: Media, available at: http://news.cnet.com/MP3.com-splits-into-two/2100-1023_3-274700.html?tag=mncol, last accessed 6 October 2009.

Markoff, J. (2005) *What the Dormouse Said: How the Sixties Counter-Culture Shaped the Personal Computer Industry*, London: Penguin Books.

McCandless, D. (1997) Warez Wars. *Wired* (online), available at: http:// www.wired.com/wired/archive/5.04/ff_warez_pr.html, last accessed 25 May 2010.

McCarthy, C. (2006) With Settlement, Kazaa Casts Off Its Pirate Garb. CNET News: Music, available at: http://news.cnet.com/With-settlement, -Kazaa-casts-off-its-pirate-garb/2100-1027_3-6099064.html?tag=mncol, last accessed 29 March 2010.

McChesney, R. W. (1993) *Telecommunications, Mass Media and Democracy*, New York and Oxford: Oxford University Press.

McChesney, R. W. (1999) *Rich Media, Poor Democracy*, Urbana and Chicago, IL: University of Illinois Press.

McChesney, R. W. (2004) *The Problem of the Media*, New York: Monthly Review Press.

McCourt, T. and Burkart, P. (2003) When Creators, Corporations and Consumers Collide: Napster and the Development of On-line Music Distribution. *Media Culture Society* 25: 333–350.

McCullagh, D. (2004) Senate Bill Would Ban P2P Networks. CNET News: Music, available at: http://news.cnet.com/Senate-bill-bans-P2P-networks/ 2100-1027_3-5244796.html, last accessed 23 June 2010.

Menn, J. (2003) *All the Rave: The Rise and Fall of Shawn Fanning's Napster*, New York: Crown Publishing Group.

Metro-Goldwyn-Mayer Studios Inc. et al. v Grokster Ltd et al. (2003) United States District Court: Central District of California, available at: http://w2.eff .org/IP/P2P/MGM_v_Grokster/030425_order_on_motions.pdf, last accessed 16 April 2010.

Meyers, M. (2005) Grokster Dies but Debate Lives On. CNET News: News Blog, available at: http://news.cnet.com/8301-10784_3-5938222-7.html? tag=mncol, last accessed 11 April 2010.

Microsoft. (2011) Microsoft to Acquire Skype. Microsoft News Center, available at: http://www.microsoft.com/presspass/press/2011/may11/ 05-10corpnewspr.mspx, last accessed 7 July 2011.

Miège, B. (1989) *The Capitalization of Cultural Production*, New York: International General.

Miles, S. (1999) Infighting Threatens to Kill Net Music Antipiracy Standard. CNET News: Personal Tech, available at: http://news.cnet.com/2100-1040-255669.html, last accessed 6 October 2009.

Mims, C. (2010) How iTunes Genius Really Works. MIT Technology Review, available at: http://www.technologyreview.com/blog/mimssbits/25267/, last accessed 10 January 2011.

Minar, N. and Hedlund, M. (2001) A Network of Peers: Peer-to-Peer Model Through the History of the Internet. In: Oram, A. (ed.) *Peer-to-Peer: Harnessing the Benefits of a Disruptive Technology*, Sebastopol: O'Reilly & Associates.

Mnookin, S. (2007) Universal's CEO Once Called iPod Users Thieves. Now He's Giving Songs Away. *Wired* (online): Entertainment: Music, available at: http://www.wired.com/entertainment/music/magazine/15-12/mf_morris?currentPage=all, last accessed 28 March 2011.

Moody, G. (2007) The Netscape Story: From Mosaic to Mozilla. Computer World UK: Open Enterprise, available at: http://blogs.computerworlduk.com/open-enterprise/2007/12/the-netscape-story-from-mosaic-to-mozilla/index.htm, last accessed 14 January 2010.

Mook, N. (2005) Justin Frankel Reveals Life After WinAmp. BetaNews, available at: http://www.betanews.com/article/Justin-Frankel-Reveals-Life-After-Winamp/1104776162, last accessed 14 October 2009.

Mossberg, W. (2002) PressPlay Outshines MusicNet as Legal Successor to Napster. *The Wall Street Journal: Personal Technology*, available at: http://online.wsj.com/article/SB101303856475786800.html, last accessed 17 April 2011.

Nadan, C. H. (2004) Software Licensing in the 21st Century: Are Software 'Licenses' Really Sales, and How Will the Software Industry Respond? *AIPLA Quarterly Journal* 32: 555–655.

Naughton, J. (2001) They Tried to Murder Napster – But Shot Themselves Instead. *The Guardian* (online), available at: http://www.guardian.co.uk/technology/2001/feb/18/business.theobserver, last accessed 6 October 2009.

Needleman, R. (2007) BitTorrent Entertainment Network Hands-on: 10 Pros and Cons. CNET News: Webware, available at: http://news.cnet.com/8301-17939_109-9691178-2.html?tag=mncol, last accessed 29 April 2010.

The New York Times (2002) Roxio Buys Napster Assets. nytimes.com, available at: http://www.nytimes.com/2002/11/28/business/roxio-buys-napster-assets.html, last accessed 6 October 2009.

Norton, Q. (2006) Secrets of The Pirate Bay. *Wired* (online), available at: http://www.wired.com/science/discoveries/news/2006/08/71543, last accessed 6 May 2010.

NPD. (2010a) Amazon Ties Walmart as Second-Ranked US Music Retailer, Behind Industry-Leader iTunes. NPD Market Research Press Release, available at: http://www.npd.com/press/releases/press_100526.html, last accessed 3 March 2011.

NPD. (2010b) PC Full-Game Digital Downloads Surpass Retail Unit Sales. NPD Market Research Press Release, available at: http://www.npd.com/press/releases/press_100920.html, last accessed 17 December 2010.

Olsen, S. (1999) MP3.com Strikes Deal with Buy.com. CNET News: e-business, available at: http://news.cnet.com/MP3.com-strikes-deal-with-Buy.com/2100-1017_3-234493.html?tag=mncol, last accessed 6 October 2009.

Orlowski, A. (2004) Vivendi Spinoff Takes MP3.com Archive Private. The Register: Music and Media, available at: http://www.theregister.co.uk/2004/01/12/vivendi_spinoff_takes_mp3_com/, last accessed 6 October 2009.

Otlet, P. (1934) *Traité de documentation*, Brussels: Editiones Mundaneum (1989, Liege: Centre de Lecture Publique de la Communauté Française).

Out-Law.com. (2007) Pirate Bay's Sovereign Ambitions Blasted. Out-Law.com: Law Blog of Law Firm Pinsent Masons, available at: http://www.out-law.com/page-7661, last accessed 10 May 2010.

Pariser, E. (2011) *The Filter Bubble: What the Internet Is Hiding from You*, New York: The Penguin Press.

Patel, K., Smith, B. C. and Rowe, L. A. (1993) Performance of a Software MPEG Video Decoder. Proceedings of the First ACM International Conference on Multimedia. Anaheim, California, US: ACM, 75–82, available from http://doi.acm.org/10.1145/166266.166274.

Pearce, J. (2004) Piracy Fighter Raid Offices of Kazaa, Others. CNET News: Music, available at: http://news.cnet.com/Piracy-fighters-raid-offices-of-Kazaa,-others/2100-1027_3-5154506.html?tag=mncol;txt, last accessed 29 March 2010.

Pemberton, J. A. (2000) Update: *RIAA v Diamond Multimedia Systems* – Napster and MP3.com. *The Richmond Journal of Law and Technology* 7: 6 (Fall 2000), available at: http://jolt.richmond.edu/v7i1/note3.html, last accessed 24 November 2012.

Pinch, T. and Bijker, W. (1984) The Social Construction of Facts and Artefacts: or How the Sociology of Science and the Sociology of Technology Might Benefit Each Other. *Social Studies of Science* 14: 399–441.

Platt, J. (1981) Evidence and Proof in Documentary Research 1: Some Specific Problems of Documentary Research. *Sociological Review* 29: 31–52.

Plummer, K. (2001) *Documents of Life 2: An Invitation to a Critical Humanism*, London: Sage Publications.

Poster, M. (1995) *The Second Media Age*, Cambridge: Polity Press.

Potts, J., Cunningham, S., Hartley, J., et al. (2008) Social Network Markets: A New Definition of the Creative Industries. *Journal of Cultural Economics* 32: 167–185.

Prior, L. (2003) *Using Documents in Social Research*, London: Sage Publications.

Reece, D. (2005) Niklas Zennström: Music Industry's Nemesis Is Busy Doing the Same to World Telecoms. *The Independent* (Business Section), 3 September 2005, p. 53, London.

Rehn, A. (2004) The Politics of Contraband: The Honor Economies of the Warez Scene. *Journal of Socio-Economics* 33: 359–374.

Reyman, J. (2010) *The Rhetoric of Intellectual Property: Copyright Law and the Regulation of Digital Culture*, New York: Routledge.

Roettgers, J. (2007) The Pirate Bay in Trouble Over Connections to Neo-Nazi. P2P Blog, available at: http://www.p2p-blog.com/item-290.html/index.php?memberid=1, last accessed 12 May 2010.

Roper, L. (2006) US Government Behind Pirate Bay Raid. TheLocal.se, available at: http://www.thelocal.se/3969/20060602/, last accessed 10 May 2010.

Roth, D. (2004) Skype: Catch Us If You Can. Danielroth.net online republication – originally published in *Fortune Magazine*, available at: http://www.danielroth.net/archive/2004/01/skype.html, last accessed 16 April 2010.

Roth, D. (2005) Torrential Reign. *Fortune Magazine* (online), available at: http://money.cnn.com/magazines/fortune/fortune_archive/2005/10/31/8359146/index.htm, last accessed 25 April 2010.

Rothenberg, J. (2000) Preserving Authentic Digital Information. In: Smith, A. (ed.) *Authenticity in a Digital Environment*, Washington, DC: Council on Library and Information Resources, available from http://www.clir.org/pubs/reports/pub92/pub92.pdf

Russell Perez, J. (2002) *Music Industry May Sue File-swappers*. Boston: *The Boston Herald* (Finance Section), 4 July 2002.

Russinovich, M. (2005a) More on Sony: Dangerous Decloaking Patch, EULAs and Phoning Home. Mark's Blog, available at: http://blogs.technet.com/b/markrussinovich/archive/2005/11/04/more-on-sony-dangerous-decloaking-patch-eulas-and-phoning-home.aspx, last accessed 17 December 2010.

Russinovich, M. (2005b) Sony, Rootkits and Digital Rights Management Gone Too Far. Mark's Blog, available at: http://blogs.technet.com/b/markrussinovich/archive/2005/10/31/sony-rootkits-and-digital-rights-management-gone-too-far.aspx, last accessed 17 December 2010.

Sacco, D. (2011) Valve: Ad Agencies Almost 'Worthless'. MCV, available at: http://www.mcvuk.com/news/43536/Valve-Ad-agencies-almost-worthless, last accessed 8 April 2011.

Samuelson, P. (1999) Does Information Really Have to Be Licensed? In: Machinery AfC (ed.) *Intellectual Property in the Age of Universal Access*, New York: ACM P.

Samuelson, P. (2003) DRM {and, or, vs.} the Law. *Communications of the ACM* 46(4): 41–45, available at: http://people.ischool.berkeley.edu/~pam/papers/acm_v46_p41.pdf, last accessed 24 November 2012.

Savage, M. (2009) Against Epochalism: An Analysis of Conceptions of Change in British Sociology. *Cultural Sociology* 3: 217–238.

Schiesel, S. (2004) File Sharing's New Face. *The New York Times*, Late Edition, New York, available.

Scott, J. (1990) *A Matter of Record: Documentary Sources in Social Research*, Cambridge: Polity Press.

Sewell, W. H. (1992) A Theory of Structure: Duality, Agency, and Transformation. *The American Journal of Sociology* 98: 1–29.

Sewell, W. H. (1996) Historical Events as Transformations of Structures: Inventing Revolution at the Bastille. *Theory and Society* 25: 841–881.

Shah, S. K. (2005) Motivation, Governance and the Viability of Hybrid Forms in Open Source Software Development. *Management Science* 52(7): 1000–14.

Skocpol, T. (1984) Sociology's Historical Imagination. In: Skocpol, T. (ed.) *Vision and Method in Historical Sociology*, Cambridge: Cambridge University Press.

Smaran (2006) The Pirate Bay, Piratbyran Take a Stance Against Net Censorship. TorrentFreak, available at: http://torrentfreak.com/the-pirate-bay-piratbyran-against-net-censorship/, last accessed 12 May 2010.

Smith, E. and Fowler, G. A. (2010) Amazon Can't Dent iTunes. *The Wall Street Journal* (online), available at: http://online.wsj.com/article/SB100 01424052748704073804576023913889536374.html?mod=rss_whats_news_technology, last accessed 17 December 2010.

Smith, E. and McBride, S. (2008) Web Piracy: The Enemy Within? *The Wall Street Journal* (online), available at: http://online.wsj.com/article/SB121781125541508813.html, last accessed 6 July 2012.

Spitz, D. and Hunter, S. (2005) Contested Codes: The Social Construction of Napster. *The Information Society* 21: 169–180.

Spring, T. (2002) Digital Music: Worth Buying Yet? PC World: Home Theater, available at: http://www.pcworld.com/article/80564/digital_music_worth_buying_yet.html, last accessed 25 March 2011.

Stelter, B. and Stone, B. (2009) Digital Pirates Winning Battle with Studios. *The New York Times* (online), available at: http://www.nytimes.com/2009/02/05/business/media/05piracy.htm?_r=1, last accessed 6 July 2012.

Sterling, B. (2002) *The Hacker Crackdown: Law and Disorder on the Electronic Frontier*, McLean, VA: Indypublish.

Sterne, J. (2006) The MP3 as Cultural Artifact. *New Media Society* 8: 825–842.

Sternfeld, J. (2010) Thinking Archivally: Search and Metadata as Building Blocks for a New Digital Historiography. Conference: Digital Humanities 2010. Kings College London: 7–10 July 2010, available at: http://dh2010.cch.kcl.ac.uk/academic-programme/abstracts/papers/html/ab-747.html.

Stone, B. (2007) Software Tool of Pirates Gets Work in Hollywood. *The New York Times* (online), available at: http://www.nytimes.com/2007/02/26/technology/26bit.html, last accessed 29 April 2010.

Stone, B. (2008) BitTorrent Sacks Half Its Staff. *The New York Times* (online), available at: http://bits.blogs.nytimes.com/2008/11/07/bittorrent-sacks-half-its-staff/, last accessed 29 April 2010.

Swartz, O. (2009a) The Pirate Bay Guilty; Jail for File-Sharing Foursome. *Wired* (online): Threat Level, available at: http://www.wired.com/threatlevel/2009/04/pirateverdict/, last accessed 12 May 2011.

Swartz, O. (2009b) Prosecution Baffled by Pirate Bay's Anarchic Structure. *Wired* (online): Threat Level, available at: http://blog.wired.com/27bstroke6/2009/02/neij.html, last accessed 4 March 2009.

Söderberg, J. (2008) *Hacking Capitalism: The Free and Open Source Software Movement*, New York and London: Routledge.

TF2 Team (2009a) The Final Countdown. Teamfortress.com, available at: http://www.teamfortress.com/post.php?id=3037, last accessed 8 April 2011.

TF2 Team (2009b) Important Financial Report. Teamfortress.com, available at: http://www.teamfortress.com/post.php?id=3036, last accessed 8 April 2011.

Thompson, C. (2005) The BitTorrent Effect. Wired (Online), available at: http://www.wired.com/wired/archive/13.01/bittorrent.html, last accessed 25 April 2010.

Thorpe, V. (2009) The End of the Age of Free. *The Guardian* (online), available at: http://www.guardian.co.uk/media/2009/may/10/music-news-murdoch-free-google, last accessed 6 October 2009.

The Times (2009) Swedish Pirates Fire a Warning Shot Over Internet Censorship. *The Times* (online), available at: http://www.timesonline.co.uk/tol/news/politics/elections/article6452298.ece, last accessed 12 May 2011.

Tito, G. (2010) Portal ARG Still Ongoing. The Escapist, available at: http://www.escapistmagazine.com/news/view/99105-Portal-ARG-Still-Ongoing, last accessed 8 April 2011.

Toffler, A. (1981) *The Third Wave*, London: Collins.

Torsson, P. and Fleischer, R. (2005) The Grey Commons – Strategic Considerations in the Copyfight. Speech Transcript from 22C3, Berlin, December 2005, available at: http://publication.nodel.org/The-Grey-Commons, last accessed 6 May 2010.

TPB. (2009) Worlds Most Reilliant Tracking. The Pirate Bay Blog, available at: http://thepiratebay.org/blog/175, last accessed 18 July 2011 (May be blocked by some ISPs).

Valve. (2010) Steam Realizes Extraordinary Growth in 2009. Valve News, available at: http://www.valvesoftware.com/news/?id=3390, last accessed 29 April 2010.

Valve Corp. (2010a) *Portal 2* Announced. Steampowered.com: News, available at: http://store.steampowered.com/news/3559/, last accessed 8 April 2011.

Valve Corp. (2010b) *Portal 2* Coming to Sony PlayStation 3. Valve Software: News, available at: http://www.valvesoftware.com/news/?id=3953, last accessed 10 January 2011.

Valve Corp. (2010c) Steam for Mac Launch Details Revealed. Valve Software: News, available at: http://www.valvesoftware.com/news/?id=3809, last accessed 10 January 2011.

Valve Corp. (2011a) *Half-Life 2* Episode 1: Gameplay Stats. Steampowered.com: Statistics, available at: http://www.steampowered.com/status/ep1/, last accessed 10 January 2011.

Valve Corp. (2011b) Steam® Subscriber Agreement. Steampowered.com, available at: http://store.steampowered.com/subscriber_agreement/, last accessed 7 January 2011.

Valve Corp. (2011c) *Team Fortress 2*: Gameplay Statistics. Steampowered.com: Statistics, available at: http://www.steampowered.com/status/tf2/tf2_stats.php, last accessed 10 January 2011.

Van Buskirk, E. (2006) Justin Frankel Rocks On. *Wired* (online): Online Rights, available at: http://www.wired.com/politics/onlinerights/commentary/listeningpost/2006/10/71876?currentPage=all, last accessed 8 October 2009.

Vernor v Autodesk (2010) United States Ninth Circuit Court of Appeals Summary. Available at: http://www.ca9.uscourts.gov/datastore/opinions/2010/09/10/09-35969.pdf, last accessed 21 April 2011.

Viborg, M. (2006) Operation Take Down. Mikael Viborg's Personal Blog: The Take Down of the Pirate Bay, available at: http://viborginternational.blogspot.com/2006/06/operation-take-down.html, last accessed 10 May 2010.

von Hippel, E. and von Krogh, G. (2003) Open Source Software and the 'Private-Collective' Innovation Model: Issues for Organization Science. *Organization Science* 14: 209–223.

von Lohmann, F. (2005) Now the Legalese Rootkit: Sony-BMG's EULA. EFF: Deeplinks Blog, available at: https://www.eff.org/deeplinks/2005/11/now-legalese-rootkit-sony-bmgs-eula, last accessed 17 December 2010.

von Lohmann, F. (2006) IAAL: What Peer-to-Peer Developers Need to Know About Copyright Law. EFF: White Paper, available at: http://w2.eff.org/IP/P2P/p2p_copyright_wp.php, last accessed 1 April 2010.

Walker, R. (2009) We're Practically (But Not Actually) GIVING the Game Away! Teamfortress.com, available at: http://www.teamfortress.com/post.php?id=3014, last accessed 8 April 2011.

Whitney, L. (2011) Anonymous Warns NATO Not to Challenge It. CNET News: Security, available at: http://news.cnet.com/8301-1009_3-20070283-83/anonymous-warns-nato-not-to-challenge-it/, last accessed 14 June 2011.

Williams, R. (2003) *Television: Technology and the Cultural Form*, London: Routledge.

Winston, E. I. (2006) Why Sell What You Can License? Contracting Around Statutory Protection of Intellectual Property. *George Mason Law Review* 14: 93–133.

Wisniowski, M. (2008) Justin Frankel on WinAmp and the Reaper. Digital Tools, available at: http://digitaltools.node3000.com/interview/170-justin-frankel-on-winamp-and-the-reaper, last accessed 8 October 2009.

YouTube (2011) Audio ID and Video ID. YouTube.com: Copyright Overview, available at: http://www.youtube.com/t/contentid, last accessed 7 April 2011.

Index

distribution platform
  hardware/software, 174–5
  marketing, 178–81, 191
  in the three part system, 169, 185
  and vendors, 168–9
  see also iTunes; Kindle; Steam;
    Three-part system of digital
    distribution
DMCA, 55, 65, 166
documentary analysis. *see* digital
  documentary analysis
documents. *see* digital documents
DRM
  as algorithmic enforcer, 92, 106,
    107, 165–6
  on CDs, 153
  circumvention of, 156–9, 166
  DRM-free, 176
  fairplay, 107, 155
  hardware based, 43–4, 53
  justifications for, 167–8
  Sony XCP, 156–9
  in the three part system, 169, 185
  see also distribution platform;
    licensing; three-part system of
    digital distribution

end user licence agreement. *see*
  EULA
EULA, 161, 166
  and CDs, 156–9
  see also licensing; software
event biography (concept), 200
  definition, 13–16
  event, 13
  ruptures, 14, 198
  see also digital documentary
    analysis; methodology;
    structuration (concept)

Fanning, John, 47–50, 62, 124
Fanning, Shawn, 44, 47, 49, 50, 58
FastTrack
  Bluemoon, 77–8
  as a business, 80–1, 82–4, 91–2,
    147

Grokster, 80, 85
Grokster v MGM, 85–9
  influence of Gnutella, 77–80
Kazaa, 7, 80
  licensing conflicts, 82–4
Morpheus, 80, 84
network design, 78–9
origin of, 76–8
popularity of, 80–1
Sharman Networks, 82–3, 89–90
Skype, 84–5
Supernodes, 78
on trial, 82–90
Filez, 41, 45
  see also MP3.com
first sale, 163–4, 172–3
Frankel, Justin, 6, 41
  ideological transmission, 75
  and Nullsoft, 64–70
  post-Gnutella projects, 70
  Sustainable Software, 65
  see also Gnutella; Nullsoft
Fraunhofer Institute, 39
  see also MP3
free and open source software. *see*
  open software
Friis, Janus. *see* FastTrack

Giddens, Anthony. *see* structuration
  (concept)
Gnutella
  AOL's disassociation from,
    69–70
  development of, 67–9
  legacy of, 75, 77–8, 80, 196
  Mayland, Bryan, 71
  network design, 67–9
  reverse-engineering of, 71
  see also Frankel, Justin; Kan, Gene;
    Nullsoft; Pepper, Tom
Google, 41
Grokster, 80, 124
  v MGM, 85–9
  see also FastTrack

GPSR Compliance
The European Union's (EU) General Product Safety Regulation (GPSR) is a set
of rules that requires consumer products to be safe and our obligations to
ensure this.

If you have any concerns about our products, you can contact us on

ProductSafety@springernature.com

In case Publisher is established outside the EU, the EU authorized
representative is:

Springer Nature Customer Service Center GmbH
Europaplatz 3
69115 Heidelberg, Germany